DEVELOPMENTAL LANGUAGE INTERVENTION

Psycholinguistic

Applications

DEVELOPMENTAL LANGUAGE INTERVENTION: Psycholinguistic Applications, edited by Kenneth F. Ruder, Ph.D., and Michael D. Smith, Ph.D., is the seventh volume in the **Language Intervention Series**—Richard L. Schiefelbusch, series editor. Other volumes in this series include:

Language Intervention Series
Volume VII

DEVELOPMENTAL LANGUAGE INTERVENTION
Psycholinguistic Applications

Edited by

Kenneth F. Ruder, Ph.D.
Bureau of Child Research
University of Kansas

and

Michael D. Smith, Ph.D.
Program in Communication Disorders
Western Carolina University

Series Editor
Richard L. Schiefelbusch

Technical Editor
Marilyn Fischer

University Park Press
Baltimore

UNIVERSITY PARK PRESS
International Publishers in Medicine and Human Services
300 North Charles Street
Baltimore, Maryland 21201

Typeset by Maryland Composition Company, Inc.
Design by S. Stoneham, Studio 1812, Baltimore.
Manufactured in the United States of America by
The Maple Press Company

Library of Congress Cataloging in Publication Data
Main entry under title:
Developmental language intervention.

(Language intervention series ; v. 7)
Includes index.
1. Speech disorders in children. 2. Children—
Language. 3. Language acquisition. 4. Psycholinguistics.
I. Ruder, Kenneth F. II. Smith, Michael D. III. Series.
RJ496.S7D48   1984   618.92'85506   83-23426
ISBN 0-8391-1632-2

contents

contributors

Robert E. Kretschmer, Ph.D.
Special Education
Teachers College
Columbia University
525 W. 120th
New York, New York 10027

Laurence B. Leonard, Ph.D.
Audiology and Speech Sciences
Heavilon Hall
Purdue University
West Lafayette, Indiana 47907

Thomas M. Longhurst, Ph.D.
Speech Pathology and Audiology
Box 8116
Idaho State University
Pocatello, Idaho 83209

John R. Muma, Ph.D.
Speech and Hearing Sciences
Texas Tech University
Lubbock, Texas 79413

Kenneth Roberts, Ph.D.
Human Development and
    Family Life
130 Haworth
University of Kansas
Lawrence, Kansas 66045

Kenneth F. Ruder, Ph.D.
Bureau of Child Research
223 Haworth
University of Kansas
Lawrence, Kansas 66045

Ronald Schaefer, Ph.D.
Linguistics and African
    Languages
University of Benin, PMB 1154
Benin City, Nigeria
West Africa

Richard L. Schiefelbusch, Ph.D.
Bureau of Child Research
223 Haworth
University of Kansas
Lawrence, Kansas 66045

Michael D. Smith, Ph.D.
Communication Disorders
Western Carolina University
Cullowhee, North Carolina 28723

Kathleen Stremel-Campbell, M.S.
Oregon State System of Higher
    Education
Teaching Research Division
Monmouth, Oregon 97361

Carol Lynn Waryas, Ph.D.
Speech and Hearing Institute
University of Texas Health Science
    Center
Houston, Texas 77004

Marcia Weber-Olsen, Ph.D.
Speech and Hearing Sciences
Texas Tech University
Lubbock, Texas 79413

foreword

Developmental psycholinguistics, as the term implies, is a field concerned with the acquisition of functional language. The complex set of language features that is acquired largely during the preschool years includes much of the grammar and the semantic relationships that characterize the child's cultural identity, rate of acquisition, and social effectiveness. The developmental status of the child is also judged by the acquired range of language knowledge and the skills of usage. The contexts and transactions that seem to aid the thriving child in acquiring a functional language during the brief acquisitional years have become increasingly vital to developmental psycholinguists. Much of the current research, consequently, is devoted to how normal language is acquired.

It can be implied from this, of course, that developmental psycholinguists, who provide most of the data base in child language, are interested primarily in the language of normal children. This is consistent with the broader discipline of child development, which provided for the analysis of normal states, normal processes, and normal acquisitional rates and ranges. Such analyses tell us what to expect and give us comparative bases for assessing and planning for normal children.

However, as the title of this book implies, its contributors are concerned with those children for whom intervention strategies are indicated. This book addresses these questions: What procedures will best aid the child whose language has lagged seriously behind his age peers? How can the child with serious cognitive, motoric, sensory, or social deficits be stimulated and perhaps formally instructed to acquire needed functional language?

These questions must be answered by professional specialists whose work overlaps with but extends beyond the developmental psycholinguists that have defined the parameters of language acquisition. We might call them *applied* developmental psycholinguists. It seems logical that there should be such a group of specialists. However, for the most part the "professional specialists" are speech-language pathologists, teachers, developmental psychologists, or other practitioners who assume responsibility for children with developmental disabilities. Obviously, their responsibility is to use whatever knowledge is available in fashioning intervention programs.

At this point, it is important to explain that the process of intervention may not be primarily *remedial* in nature. The child usually does not have an adequately functional language, and he or she has never had one. Furthermore, there is not some discrete skill to be identified and taught, but rather a complex functional language system to be achieved. Significantly, the clinical tradition of speech-language pathologists and other language intervention specialists has been related closely to a remedial orientation. Simply explained, the traditional practice has been to assess the child's problem and to base the remedial plan on a design for correcting the deficit. The more specific the assessed issue, the more certain and specific has been the remedial strategy. The remedial strategy has usually been designed to fit the child's current needs as perceived by the evaluation team.

Specialists recently have added a great deal to this strategy by looking closely at behavioral events and by designing remedial approachs to alter the behavioral deficits. The behavioral deficits are altered by means of teaching units or programmed steps that bring the learner to a desired level of performance. Presumably, the objectives sought are both teachable and functional so that the child acquires needed communicative skills. The behavioral specialist has confidence that he or she can determine the functions to be taught and thus can intervene to bring about an altered state of functional performance. As conceived by such behavior specialists, remedial logic is concerned with the contingencies that seem to control responding by both the child and his or her communicant. Consequently, the language program is designed to give the child language skills to deal with these contingencies. The child learns that language has the power to influence, control, or secure desired outcomes. This functional analysis must include the child's age-related status.

This explanation implies that there now exists a rather explicit field of applied behavioral science that is available to those who would want to apply a remedial logic. However, this book is not focused upon that tactical strategy. It is explained here to provide perspective for a developmental approach.

The developmental approach as explained by Ruder and Smith (1974) and Miller and Yoder (1974) is more concerned with the language system itself, the program of language structures, and semantic functions to be taught. They acknowledge the power of language, its systematic nature, and the importance of the sequences through which children normally go in acquiring it. They regard themselves as *applied* developmental psycholinguists and assume that needed language programs, as well as the tactics for teaching them, can be derived from a developmental logic.

Each logic is important. In many ways, these two logics already are accommodated largely to the other. Obviously, applied behavior analysis is a system for designing instructional environments, instructional tactics, and outcome measures. Developmental psycholinguistics is an explicative system that guides the interventionist in assessing language and in designing a functional plan. Each logic and each professional system has much to offer the other. The fact that each is still evolving and changing is clearly apparent throughout the book. For instance, each system, and perhaps both working together, must deal with the complex challenge of pragmatic functions and sociolinguistics described by Bates (1976) and Ervin-Tripp and Mitchell-Kernan (1977) respectively. It is apparent that neither developmental psycholinguistics nor applied behavior analysis has essentially dealt with the contextual issues so readily apparent in social discourse. The importance of this challenge is obvious from a range of recent research that is both developmentally and functionally oriented.

Obviously, developmental approaches will become more functionally oriented as needed research adds additional data to that perspective. As we understand better how normal children acquire language usage functions, we will likely be able to teach these same skills to impaired children. Implicit in the tactics of teaching will be a transaction system—essentially, a communicative training system. The environmental designs for such teaching have already been largely established but a great deal of additional research by developmental psycholinguists and their applied colleagues is needed before the approaches are fully developed.

The content of this book should move us toward that objective.

Richard L. Schiefelbusch, Ph.D.

REFERENCES

Bates, E. 1976. Language and Context: The Acquisition of Pragmatics. Academic Press, New York.

Ervin-Tripp, S., and Mitchell-Kernan, C. (eds.). 1977. Child Discourse. Academic Press, New York.

Miller, J., and Yoder, D. 1974. An ontogenetic language teaching strategy for retarded children. In: R. L. Schiefelbusch and L. L. Lloyd (eds.), Language Perspectives—Acquisition, Retardation and Intervention. University Park Press, Baltimore.

Ruder, K. F., and Smith, M. D. 1974. Issues in language training. In: R. L. Schiefelbusch and L. L. Lloyd (eds.), Language Perspectives—Acquisition, Retardation, and Intervention. University Park Press, Baltimore.

preface

The impetus for this book began in 1973 at the Chula Vista Conference, which resulted in the book *Language Perspectives—Acquisition, Retardation, and Intervention* (edited by R. L. Schiefelbusch and L. Lloyd). This book raised a number of issues concerning language intervention and the bases for language intervention that are still pertinent. The topic of this volume, *developmental language interventions,* was a central issue of that conference and provided the forum for an exchange between proponents of a developmental model for language training and those for a remedial logic model.

Subsequent publications, including books in the language intervention series edited by Richard L. Schiefelbusch (*The Bases for Language Intervention,* 1978 and *Strategies of Language Intervention,* 1978) continued to raise the issue of developmentally based versus nondevelopmentally based language training approaches. In 1976, a symposium on applied psycholinguistics was held in conjunction with the Louisville Interdisciplinary Conference on Language. The symposium focused on the merits of developmental psycholinguistics as the bases for language intervention programming. Many of the participants in that symposium are contributors to this volume, and the views expressed herein reflect in part their presentations and discussions.

The introductory chapter of this volume sets the tone for the book. It delineates the issues concerning remedial logic versus a developmental logic. It also identifies pseudo-issues that are perhaps germane to a particular research strategy or philosophical inclination but nothing of substance within the practical framework of how the intervention is actually implemented and executed. The remainder of the volume provides examples of how developmental psycholinguistic data are being used within current assessment and training approaches to language intervention. These examples should also provide the reader with contemporary views and perspectives regarding developmental language interventions. Although each of the chapter's content could be considered to be more "middle of the road" than some psycholinguistic and behaviorist positions of the past, each articulates the essential features of the developmental intervention debate and presents the respective biases of the psycholinguistic and behavioral points of view. By discussing these issues, a relevant research and data base will be accumulated that will eventually lead to our goal of providing more efficient language interventions. These chapters are a step in this direction. In this sense, it is hoped that the present volume will be a valuable adjunct to previous books in the series, particularly *Bases of Language Intervention* and *Strategies for Language Intervention.*

Finally, the editors would like to acknowledge the contributions of individuals who assisted in the preparation of this volume. First, we would like to thank Dr. Robert St. Clair, University of Louisville, who organized and made possible the symposium presentation and the Louisville Interdisciplinary Conference on Language out of which much of the content of this book grew. We also acknowledge the advice, encouragement and assistance of Richard L. Schiefelbusch; the technical assistance of Julia Saenz and Mary Beth Johnston, who did much of the typing; and the editorial work of Robert K. Hoyt and Marilyn Fischer. Finally, we would be remiss if we did not acknowledge

xiv   Preface

the support of grant HD-00870 from NICHD to the Bureau of Child Research, University of Kansas for the support it provided in the collection of much of the data cited in this volume.

K. F. R.
M. D. S.

dedicated to the memory of
William A. Bricker

Design Strategy
for a Coherent
Applied Psycholinguistics

Michael D. Smith

Communication Disorders
Western Carolina University
Cullowhee, North Carolina

Kenneth F. Ruder

Bureau of Child Research
University of Kansas
Lawrence, Kansas

Carol Lynn Waryas

Speech and Hearing Institute
University of Texas Health Science Center
Houston, Texas

contents

During the 1970s, many interventionists engaged in a debate over which is the most viable model for language intervention: a developmentally-based model or a nondevelopmentally-based model (Ruder and Smith, 1974; Staats, 1974; Miller and Yoder, 1974; Harris, 1975; Leonard, 1975; Bricker et al., 1976; Risley, 1977; Guess et al., 1978; Muma, 1978; Bloom and Lahey, 1978; McLean and Snyder-McLean, 1978; Ruder, 1978; Hegde et al., 1979).

The search for coherent applied psycholinguistics continues into the 1980s. Still at issue is the question of whether or not developmental distinctions based on patterns characteristic of language development will emerge as behavioral distinctions or outcomes of training (Hegde, 1980, 1981; Schiefelbusch, 1980; Baer, 1981; Hogg, 1981; Prelock and Panagos, 1981; Schiefelbusch and Bricker, 1981; Aram and Nation, 1982; Campbell and Stremel-Campbell, 1982; Johnston, 1983).

Significant headway in the pursuit of more adequate models for language intervention may be made by examining the implications that developmental perspectives have for language intervention. The four developmental perspectives have been addressed by Schiefelbusch (1972), Miller and Yoder, (1974), Ruder and Smith (1974), and Stremel and Waryas (1974), with in-depth elaborations by Bloom and Lahey (1978), Muma (1978), Waryas and Stremel-Campbell (1978), Cole and Cole (1981), and Miller et al., (1983). By extending the work of these interventionists, the attributes of a developmental model for language intervention may provide more flexible and adequate intervention programming. A controversy similar to that over the framework of language intervention currently surrounds efforts to link the development of cognitive behavior in its normal state with its counterpart among less-than-normal or disordered populations (Weisz and Yeates, 1981; Kamhi, 1981; Kamhi and Johnston, 1982; Zigler and Balla, 1983). The debate encompasses a number of issues, not the least of which is whether or not developmental distinctions based on patterns characteristic of cognitive development in the normal state have the potential to emerge as behavioral distinctions or outcomes of training.

A DEVELOPMENTAL PERSPECTIVE

Incorporating a developmental model of language behavior into intervention programming (Miller and Yoder, 1974; Ruder and Smith, 1974; Stremel and Waryas, 1974) forces a strict consideration of factors tied to order-of-acquisition and, in turn, to the complexity of those linguistic forms undergoing acquisition. When selecting training targets, a de-

3

tailed analysis of prerequisite behaviors must be undertaken to meet the demands imposed by complexity. For example, if training targets include grammatical English morphemes that mark the most basic plural and past-tense distinctions (e.g., the semantic distinctions of oneness versus more-than-oneness or numerousity for the plural morpheme and ongoing activity versus earlierness of an event of brief duration for the past-tense morpheme), the training of the developmentally prior and less complex plural morpheme would precede that of the past-tense morpheme. No matter the training procedures or settings, the primary goal here is to train the principle of affixation; that is, the method of combining a free morpheme, such as *rattle,* with a bound morpheme, singling either the singular distinction (*rattle-rattle + s*) or the present-past distinction (*rattle-rattle + d*). Initial training that focuses on the less complex plural morphology may facilitate subsequent training of the more complex past-tense morphology and in fact result in significant partial training of the more demanding form (see Smith, Ruder, and Stremel-Campbell, this volume).

Once linguistic forms have been singled out and targeted for training, if order-of-training is aligned with order-of-acquisition, the opportunities to internalize basic linguistic distinctions in combination with regularities of distribution are enhanced beyond those provided in contexts that are not as controlled. We are here echoing Bloom and Lahey's (1978) claim that an intervention program should provide the language-impaired individual with *more* (of what the nonimpaired requires) and, at the same time, be *selective* to ensure that competing linguistic forms and interference are kept to a minimum. As part of advocating selectivity, we endorse what Leonard (1975) called *shaping sequences,* which are principally those training sequences that adhere to order-of-acquisition. Leonard (1975) distinguished between two types of response hierarchies: normal developmental hierarchies and additive hierarchies. For both the English negative modal and progressive aspect (consisting of the combination *do + no* and the complex discontinuous *be . . . ing,* respectively), normal developmental sequences represent response hierarchies that conform to ordinal patterns of acquisition. By contrast, additive sequences represent hierarchies tied to the increasing length of a linguistic response or context.

Negative Modal

Developmental Hierarchy	Additive Hierarchy
1. *no* play	1. *don't*
2. X *no* play	2. *don't* play
3. X *don't* play	3. X *don't* play

Progressive Aspect

Developmental Hierarchy	Additive Hierarchy
1. X play	1. *is* (be)
2. X *play* + *ing*	2. *is* play + *ing*
3. X *is* (be) play + *ing*	3. X *is* play + *ing*

While assessing the potential of such hierarchies, Leonard (1975) found that training sequences conforming to developmental hierarchies best shape the acquisition and use of the designated targets over training sequences conforming solely to increases in length of response.

Whatever the counterarguments, some identifiable, systematic, and therefore testable order must be imposed upon attempts at intervention. The primary goal remains to facilitate the process of acquisition among individuals who have experienced longstanding failure in the spontaneous acquisition of language. The obvious question is: How do we go about programming intervention for persons who are without adequate functional language?

Aside from following the inexact guidelines of programming for *more* of what a normal course of development provides, we might also profit by analyzing the factors in the selection and ordering of component structures that directly contribute to the training of target linguistic behaviors. A developmental model of language intervention necessitates consideration of the structural relationships and semantically relevant functions which together constitute the ingredients or substance of behaviors that are the nucleus of remediation. The intent is to impart a notion of *system* that has the potential to yield a repertoire of linguistic behaviors that register degress of receptive and expressive control and which is itself capable of transcending any one set of target items.

The basis for selecting initial target items may vary with a reasonable base being found in Brown (1973) and subsequent adaptations by Tyack and Gottsleben (1974), Miller and Yoder (1974), Stremel and Waryas (1974), Bloom and Lahey (1978), Muma (1978), Prutting (1979), and others. Although descriptive analyses of the sort found in Brown (1973) and Muma (1978) reflect successive and dependent stages of development encompassing specific goals and accomplishments (e.g., the stage of basic semantic and relational functions to the stage of grammatical morphemes and the modulation of meaning to the stage of utterance modality), few stable criteria have been proposed for stagewise acquisition (Von Glaserfeld, 1982; Golinkoff, 1983). None may be called for, at least in the sense that language acquisition does not seem to move in a lock-step or prescriptive fashion (Bloom and Lahey, 1978; Mahoney and Weller, 1980). Linguistic behavior develops within, as well as across, stages, with the singular proviso being that at least partial acquisition (i.e., substantial awareness) must occur at a primary or prerequisite level before advancing to higher levels.

Contrary to what is strongly implied in Winitz's (1982) developmental perspective on language intervention and given our applied psycholinguistic orientation, the stages of acquisition do not constitute mastery or specific achievement; rather, successive waves of learning contribute to the revision or altering of prior incomplete learning. In reference to the example outlined above, it is not necessary for explicit training of the auxiliary *be* to await full acquisition of the progressive aspect *-ing*. A viable alternative is to provide for the partial acquisition of *-ing* (by setting an intermediate level of performance criterion on the training of *-ing*) and then move on to the explicit and full training of *be* as linked to *-ing*. This example can be extended by training yes/ no questions that incorporate expressions of the progressive aspect. The explicit training of what is the surface equivalent of the auxiliary *be* inversion (i.e., "*X is* play + *ing*" expressed as "*Is* X play + *ing*?") may not need to await full acquisition of the auxiliary, *be*, as linked to *-ing*. There is little reason to believe that the fractionally acquired progressive aspect *be . . . ing* will not facilitate the explicit and full training of yes/no questions incorporating the progressive aspect and, in turn, contribute to the full training of the progressive aspect, itself. In order to appreciate the logic applied here, it must be recalled that under both contexts (declarative: "*X is* play + *ing*" and interrogative: "*Is* X play + *ing*?"), the progressive aspect is marked by a discontinuous combination of linguistic forms, with the surface contrast consisting of the extent of separation between the auxiliary, *be*, and *-ing*. The cumulative effect of the combined exposure is to bring the progressive structure into greater relief at the surface, thus permitting an intensive and varied form of instruction.

Another extension of the initial example is found in training wh-questions incorporating expressions of the progressive aspect (e.g., review portions of Wilcox and Leonard, 1978). If there is flexibility in building upon the lessons of language acquisition (in its normal state), the training of a network of structures that partake of common linguistic expressions may be carried out in a fashion that does not stipulate full acquisition either within or across stages of language development. Such views subsume an adaptation of what Stokes and Baer (1977) referred to as "loose training," a method of training wherein the acquisition of a particular linguistic form is designed to occur across more than a single stimulus condition or linguistic context, thus serving to enhance its pattern of distribution and, of no less importance, its potential for generalization.

Based on what has been discussed thus far, a developmental model of language intervention has as its primary thrust a deep concern for the stimulus side of language. It addresses the issue of how to meticulously select and order targets and, in the process, rigorously design training programs that are consistent. At this juncture, reference to Muma's (1978) interpretation of how we in the past have approached the challenge of intervention is appropriate. According to Muma (1978), far too much of what has been done in intervention programming is arbitrary and authoritarian, reflecting a generally poor understanding of the nature and complexity of linguistic structure and its use. He went on to say that, as a result:

> Theories of intervention are practically nonexistent. The positions at present are little more than authoritarianism. Although highly structured intervention programs are available, the probability is high that they may be of little relevance to individual needs (p. 229).

An assessment of this sort reaffirms Perkins' (1977) statement that much of what has been done is tied to educated guessing and a modus operandi of trial and error. This cannot be completely ignored, nor can we skirt the more recent challenges embedded in pointed questions asked by Aram and Nation (1982):

> What . . . are speech-language pathologists using to treat . . . language disorders? Are the selections idiosyncratic? Are there principles that govern the choices that are made? Are the choices made based on strong theoretical foundations? Are the choices made on models of intervention (p. 225)?

In looking specifically at the stimulus side of language, an initial response to these questions is that developmental guidelines should be imposed on intervention designs. Very little has been done to test the affects of linguistic structure and function on intervention programming. Evidence of this point is found in Welch's (1981) review and analysis of research on language training, wherein it is asked if certain forms should be trained before others and, beyond that, whether it may be advantageous to follow developmental guidelines when designing intervention programs. The undeniable fact is that intervention, whether viewed linguistically or communicatively, *deals at a very significant level with the structure of language and the interdependence of form*. We at least for a time acknowledged this fact (Schiefelbush and Lloyd, 1974). However, through the latter portion of the 1970s and into the 1980s, we became rather fast-paced and capable of adjusting to major shifts in attention, ranging from exploring the links between semantics and cognition (Bowerman, 1978; Leonard, 1978; Rice, 1980,

1983) to the links between communicative function, process, and prag-matics—factors that are essentially outside-of-language as opposed to inside-of-language (Prutting, 1979, 1982; Bates et al., 1981). Most in-terventionists do now understand the importance of cognitively or prag-matically oriented pursuits. But, unfortunately, what has followed in the wake of such pursuits is the secondary status accorded structural phenomena and their inherent linguistic functions (Cromer, 1981; Keil, 1981; Slobin, 1981; Bruner, 1982; Wanner and Gleitman, 1982).

If we are to solve eventually the riddle of how to best train lan-guage, there must be a renewed focus on factors related to linguistic form and function per se as opposed to treating them like by-products of causal forces attributed to communicative function or use. Admit-tedly, this suggestion may have all the appearances of a literal step back in time. Yet, it is indeed possible that with the shifts in attention, we have denied ourselves ample time to accumulate a *critical mass* of information fundamental to those linguistic domains out of which come targets for intervention programming. In light of Bates et al.'s (1981) point that theory has outstripped data on issues both inside-of- and outside-of-language, concerted attempts to compile a comprehensive data base are warranted. As part of moving toward a coherent applied psycholinguistics, there is a need to generate testable hypotheses, with priority placed upon the manipulation of inside-of-language phenomena (Ruder and Smith, 1974; Ruder, 1978; Prelock and Panagos, 1981). If tests are well-structured and represent sensitive and prudent use of existing operant technology, a balance may be struck between those mapping operations that are developmentally relevant and those that are relevant strictly to intervention (i.e., emerge as outcomes of train-ing). There is a parallel between what is being promoted here and Bru-ner's (1982) treatment of language development in its normal state. It is a parallel of attempts to isolate what of language constitutes a *prob-lem space of its own* and attempts to better scaffold or sequence that which is specifically linguistic and thus facilitate language acquisition under intervention conditions.

A NEUTRALIZATION OF BASIC DIFFERENCES

A number of interventionists have interpreted the above as conforming to a *developmental logic* of intervention and have contrasted it to a *remedial logic* of intervention. Consider for a moment the contrast as explained by Guess et al. (1978):

> Developmental logic supposes that the best way or perhaps the only ef-fective way to teach language to a deficient child is in the sequence in

which normal children learn language. If language has a complex structure, such that parts of it depend for their function on other parts of it already being mastered, then the normal developmental sequence must represent at least one effective sequence of learning these interdependencies. Conceivably, there is no alternate sequence in which language can be learned, at least by children learning it at the usual stages of their development. This possibility is bolstered by the reported uniformity with which children acquire language.

Remedial logic, by contrast, supposes that children being taught language relatively late in their lives, because they have failed to acquire it adequately in their earlier experiences, no longer possess the same collection of abilities and deficits that normal children have when they begin to acquire language. . . . Remedial logic, then, will not ask in what order the retarded child needs to learn language but rather in what order the language taught most quickly will accomplish some improvement in the child's communication. . . . Thus, a program based on remedial logic will try to establish first the most useful elements of language that the child might need. What these are will depend on the child's environment (pp. 283–284).

The same basic distinction is underscored by Risley (1977); Siegel and Spradlin (1978); Switzky et al. (1979); and Baer (1981). At a first glance, the contrast between the two logics of intervention is an appealing one. As Siegel and Spradlin (1978) suggested, a developmental logic may be more appropriate when programming intervention for impaired individuals who are capable of functioning at relatively higher levels (e.g., the developmentally delayed or learning disabled) than those who are not so capable (e.g., the truly disordered or retarded) and for whom remedial logic may be more appropriate.

Each logic has as a critical ingredient a concern for order-of-training. The real strength of a developmental model is its capacity to isolate the interrelationships that exist among linguistic forms and functions and, thus, possibly to *expand* order-of-training options—along with the loftier goal of determining which options are best (Ruder and Smith, 1974). A first approximation of how order-of-training options might be isolated and subsequently measured is presented in Smith, Ruder, and Stremel-Campbell's (this volume) training study of past-tense morphology.

Unlike what is implied in Guess et al.'s (1978) interpretation of a developmental logic, there exist alternative sequences of training and acquisition. For instance, no less than a decade ago, Bloom (1970) called attention to individual differences in early language development. And where alternate courses to acquisition are concerned, Nelson (1973, 1981) suggested that the sequence in which a child acquires language may be tied to variables in both the linguistic environment and patterns of interaction. The point is that when speaking of a developmental logic, more than a single order is permitted to the internalization of target behaviors and the formation of linguistic rules.

And to the issue of linguistic rules, we might do well to reflect on Staats' (1974) point that confusion over what is meant by the claim that *Language is rule-governed behavior* must somehow be resolved in order to successfully design training programs that will facilitate the acquisition of functional language. The exchange concerning Courtright and Courtright (1981) and Connell et al. (1981) exemplifies the ongoing confusion generated by just such a claim, and it underscores the fact that we have yet to heed sufficiently to Staat's note of caution. Both parties to the exchange acknowledge the existence of rules (on logical and empirical grounds) and agreed that intervention programs have no choice but to focus directly on the training of rules (e.g., constraints governing auxiliary *be* placement, pluralization, past-tense formation, various noun-verb combinations, etc.), but none agreed on what constitutes a rule or the principles of rule training.

At least as an interim gesture, to reduce confusion over the claim that *language is a rule-governed behavior*, little is risked by considering the implications of Slobin's (1979) rather lenient proposal. Slobin (1979) chose to view things ontogenetically. A rule-of-language refers to the product of a constellation of observations involving the use of particular linguistic forms; over time, observations of these forms combine to reflect constraints on or regularities of distribution. Because the individual who has failed to acquire language in the expected way may not be capable of coping with the demands of a typical linguistic environment, one which, for the language-impaired person, is composed of scattered points of assistance, a more controlled and restricted linguistic environment might be introduced. The option preferred is to provide for more points of concentrated assistance by instituting controls for prerequisite behaviors and, in turn, singling out and highlighting the distribution of forms targeted for training. Whatever the outcomes of training are called (for example, the *rules* for those following a developmental orientation or the *response classes* for those following a behavioral orientation), our interpretations of the outcomes are likely to match, that is, resemble statements of surface distribution. In support of this point, a sizeable group of recent developmental studies (Braine, 1976; Karmilov-Smith, 1978; Maratsos and Chalkley, 1979; Maratsos et al., 1979; Ingram, 1980; Moerk, 1980; Nelson, 1981) encourage narrow interpretations that reflect surface phenomena in contrast to broad interpretations that too much reflect underlying structure.

Of renewed interest is Brown's (1973) observation on the dynamics of some critical early acquisitions, especially those that blur the distinction between a spontaneously acquired rule-of-language and an operant-conditioned response class. Brown (1973) attempted to explain the acquisition of various grammatical morphemes:

> The learning of the intricate network of rules governing the fourteen grammatical morphemes is more like habit formation and operant conditioning than anyone has supposed. . . . The variable character of the grammatical morpheme suggests a kind of rule learning that proceeds on a rather molecular level and gradually rather than abruptly. In certain respects, then, it is like operant conditioning or habit acquisition, and yet there is no doubt that what is learned is a set of rules, since the responses generalize in just the ways that the rules describe (p. 388).

Brown's (1973) assessment might be compared to Derwing's (1973) more general stance. According to Derwing (1973), psycholinguists are far better off when:

> . . . we are talking about a notion of linguistic rules which can be directly elicited from surface structures, hence one which does not put unreasonable demands upon the language learner. All that is required to learn rules of this sort are general capacities which human beings possess: power to discriminate, to generalize and, most important, to extract regularity from the environment (p. 310).

TOWARD AN APPLIED PSYCHOLINGUISTICS

Proposals that recognize the significance of a rule-of-language in conjunction with the significance of alternate courses of acquisition yield the impression that the developmental and remedial logics share common ground. The twist, however, is that the current state of the art is such that too few temperate readings are encouraged. Whatever their merits, arguments that the two logics are more alike than not are fraught with ambiguities. For example, Switzky et al. (1979) prefaced their general review of what a developmental model implicates for remediation programming by stating that:

> Normative development sequences cannot provide educational program contents in a direct fashion as educational objectives. Educators are now deemphasizing "normal development" and are taking a remedial approach to strengthen specific skills regardless of hypothesized "developmental sequences and readiness" (p. 168).

Certainly more optimism was expressed by Hogg (1981), who offered the opinion that developmental ". . . frameworks are of heuristic value in giving direction to intervention activities."

Where might we go from here? Numerous questions remain to be resolved in the pursuit of a coherent applied psycholinguistics. As was made clear by Ruder and Smith (1974) and repeatedly emphasized in this chapter, the major problem regarding the use of a developmental model is to determine the order-of-training options that are the most appropriate for intervention. This is an empirical issue, and by increasing order-of-training options, the two logics are brought closer together.

Whether we remain part of one logic of intervention or another, our goal as applied psycholinguists is to structure and simplify the language-learning environment. We also need to provide exposure that fosters the development of an integrated linguistic system, no matter how minimal it might seem when compared to the system of the non-impaired. In short, we do not want to run the risk of becoming interventionists who simplify or oversimplify until only a set of independent utterance routines follow our attempts at remediation. Most important, as we move closer to agreement on issues involving order-of-training options, the more likely it is that we shall provide training environments that are conducive to the development of functional and enduring language.

We might now attempt to merge the various facets of language intervention that are emphasized in Schiefelbusch and Bricker's (1981) more global analysis of the intervention process with those in the less global analysis provided above. The purpose is simply to forge an alliance with interventionists who lean toward outside-of-language phenomena with those who hold to the inside-of-language phenomena. Assuming that we agree with Stokes and Baer's (1977) claim that behavior change triggered by intervention does not itself ensure generalization (inside- or outside-of-language) of what was explicitly trained, the need for a coherent and flexible design strategy becomes obvious. Appropriate targets for training fall within the domain of pragmatics, as do issues associated with the selection of appropriate training settings and training methodologies. On the other hand, the more precise issues of how target items reflect a system of linguistic behavior and, hence, issues relevant to order-of-training fall outside the domain of pragmatics. Extending the observation of Stokes and Baer (1977), the point here is that if generalization outside-of-language (i.e., across settings) is obtained, it does not necessarily follow that generalization inside-of-language (i.e., across similar or related linguistic behaviors) will be obtained. Our primary goal is to design a system of linguistic behavior that has the potential to generate behavior beyond that directly trained. It is incumbent upon us to struggle again and again with questions that focus on the substance of linguistic systems per se. For those individuals with whom we engage in the process of intervention, the more efficient they are in the inside-the-language game (on a trial-by-trial, session-by-session, day-by-day, etc. basis), the more efficient they will become in the outside-of-language game. The heart of the matter is language itself and ultimately the *shaping sequences* we derive as part of intervention programming.

CONCLUSION

That applied psycholinguistics is an emerging discipline in its own right is not at issue here. Look at the ever-increasing literature being embraced by researchers and practitioners alike as *applied psycholinguistics research*. Indeed, if the development of a field of study is considered legitimatized by the emergence of a literature so homogeneous that it warrants a journal to report research findings, then the field of applied psycholinguistics came into its own with the publication of the *Journal of Applied Psycholinguistics* in 1980. On November 2, 1982, the International Society of Applied Psycholinguistics was founded. Its purpose was to stimulate and promote teaching and research in applied psycholinguistics, to strengthen the contacts and exchange opportunities in the field (Slama-Cazacu et al., 1982).

Developmental Language Intervention is divided into two principal sections totaling eight different chapters. The first section focuses on the degree to which contemporary approaches to language assessment reflect developmental factors. Considerable discussion revolves around the manner in which procedures of language assessment do or do not reflect a sensitivity to developmental psycholinguistic data. The second section focuses on what are considered to be critical substantive and methodological issues as they impact on the enterprise of language intervention.

This first chapter serves as the introductory chapter to this volume on language intervention. However, it is free-standing in a number of ways and for a number of reasons. Consider that the content herein has pleaded the case for the return to the stimulus side of language. As emphasized a few moments ago, no matter how interventionists elect to view the enterprise of language intervention (linguistically or communicatively), the heart of the matter is the structure of language, itself. In the spirit of Slobin's (1979, 1981) rendition of developmental psycholinguistics, we agree that much of our own intervention literature has skirted too far afield from the investigation of those linguistic properties that constitute the underpinnings of language as an object of acquisition. Extending Slobin's (1981) descriptive phrasing, we seem to be practicing a *psychology without language or the equivalent of language without grammar*. What is called for is surely not a return to the days of autonomous syntax or transformational grammar, but very simply a return to a deep concern for the painstaking study of the linguistic and generative properties of language (Wanner and Gleitman,

1982) and how such properties can best be programmed into our language intervention designs (Wilbur, 1983). As the contents of this volume well attest, such pursuits do not rule out the concurrent study of cognitive or pragmatic factors and how they might impinge on language as an object of acquisition. All we actually need to do is to tune in more sensitively to how the substance of language itself can best be embedded into our attempts at language intervention. To continue to transform and view language as a phenomenon with little internal structure of its own is to risk missing the mark through the decade of the 1980s.

REFERENCES

Aram, D.M., and Nation, J.E. 1982. Child Language Disorders. C.V. Mosby, St. Louis.

Baer, D. 1981. The nature of intervention research. In: R.L. Schiefelbusch and D. Bricker (eds.), Early Language: Acquisition and Intervention. University Park Press, Baltimore.

Bates, E., Beeghly-Smith, M., Bretherton, I., and McNew, S. 1981. Social bases of language development: A reassessment. In: H. Reese and L. Lipsitt (eds.), Advances in Child Development and Behavior. Academic Press, New York.

Bloom, L. 1970. Language Development: Form and Function in Emerging Grammars. MIT Press, Cambridge, MA.

Bloom, L., and Lahey, M. 1978. Language Development and Language Disorders. John Wiley and Sons, New York.

Bowerman, M. 1978. Semantic and syntactic development. In: R.L. Schiefelbusch (ed.), Bases of Language Intervention. University Park Press, Baltimore.

Braine, M. 1976. Children's First Word Combinations, SRCD Monograph 40: 1 (No. 164). University of Chicago Press, Chicago, IL.

Bricker, D., Ruder, K., and Vincent-Smith, L. 1976. An intervention strategy for language deficient children. In: N. Haring and R.L. Schiefelbusch (eds.), Teaching Special Children. McGraw-Hill, New York.

Brown, R. 1973. A First Language. Harvard University Press, Cambridge, MA.

Bruner, J. 1982. The formats of language acquisition. Am. J. Semiot. 1:1–17.

Campbell, R., and Stremel-Campbell, K. 1982. Programming "loose training" as a strategy to facilitate language generalization. J. of Appl. Behav. Anal. 15:295–301.

Cole, M., and Cole, J. 1981. Effective Intervention with the Language Impaired Child. Aspen Systems, Rockville, MD.

Connell, P., Gardner-Gletky, D., Dejewski, J., and Park-Reinick, L. 1981. Response to Courtright and Courtright. J. Speech Hear. Disord. 46:146–148.

Courtright, J., and Courtright, I. 1981. Some comments on validity, tautology, and methodology: A reply to Connell et al. J. Speech Hear. Disord. 46:148–150.

Cromer, R. 1981. Reconceptualizing language acquisition and cognitive development. In: R.L. Schiefelbusch and D. Bricker (eds), Early Language: Acquisition and Intervention. University Park Press, Baltimore.

Derwing, B. 1973. Transformational Grammar as a Theory of Language Acquisition. Cambridge University Press, Cambridge, MA.

Golinkoff, R. M. (ed.). 1983. The Transition from Prelinguistic to Linguistic Communication. Lawrence Erlbaum Assoc. Hillsdale, NJ.

Golinkoff, R. M., and Gordon, L. 1983. In the beginning was the word: A history of the study of language acquisition. In: R.M. Golinkoff (ed.), The Transition from Prelinguistic to Linguistic Communication. Lawrence Erlbaum Assoc. Hillsdale, NJ.

Guess, D., Sailor, W., and Baer, D. 1974. To teach language to retarded children. In: R.L. Schiefelbusch and L.L. Lloyd (eds.), Language Perspectives—Acquisition, Retardation, and Intervention. University Park Press, Baltimore.

Guess, D., Sailor, W., and Baer, D. 1978. Children with limited language. In: R.L. Schiefelbusch (ed.), Language Intervention Strategies. University Park Press, Baltimore.

Harris, S. 1975. Teaching language to nonverbal children. Psychol. Bull. 82:565–580.

Hegde, M. 1980. Issues in the study and explanation of language behavior. J. Psycholing. Res. 9:1–22.

Hegde, M. 1981. An experimental-clinical analysis of grammatical and behavioral distinctions. J. Speech Hear. Res. 23:864–876.

Hegde, M., Noll, M., and Pecora, R. 1979. A study of some factors affecting generalization of language. J. Speech Hear. Disord. 44:301–320.

Hogg, J. 1981. Strategies and evaluation of early intervention. In: R.L. Schiefelbusch and D. Bricker (eds.), Early Language: Acquisition and Intervention. University Park Press, Baltimore.

Ingram, D. 1980. Early patterns of grammatical development. Paper presented at the Conference on Language Behavior in Infancy and Early Childhood, October, Santa Barbara, CA.

Johnston, J. 1983. What is language intervention? The role of theory. In: J. Miller, D. Yoder, and R.L. Schiefelbusch (eds.), Contemporary Issues in Language Intervention (ASHA Reports 12). American Speech-Language-Hearing Assoc., Rockville, MD.

Kamhi, A. 1981. Developmental versus difference theories of mental retardation: A new look. Amer. J. Ment. Defic. 86:1–7.

Kamhi, A., and Johnston, J. 1982. Towards an understanding of retarded children's linguistic deficiencies. J. Speech Hear. Res. 15:435–446.

Karmilov-Smith, A. 1978. The interplay between syntax, semantics, and phonology and language acquisition processes. In: R. Campbell and P. Smith (eds.), Recent Advances in the Psychology of Language. Plenum Press, New York.

Keil, F. 1981. Constraints on knowledge and cognitive development. Psychol. Rev. 88:197–227.

Leonard, L. 1978. Cognitive factors in early linguistic development. In: R.L. Schiefelbusch (ed.), Bases of Language Intervention. University Park Press, Baltimore.

Leonard, L. 1975. Modeling as a clinical procedure in language training. Lang. Speech Hear. Serv. Schools. 6:72–85.

Mahoney, G., and Weller, E.L. 1980. An ecological approach to language intervention. In: D. Bricker (ed.), Language Intervention with Children. Jossey-Bass Publishers, San Francisco.

Maratsos, M., and Chalkley, M. 1979. The internal language of children's syntax. In: K.E. Nelson (ed.), Children's Language (II). Gardner Press, New York.

Maratsos, M., Kuczaj, S., Fox, D., and Chalkley, M. 1979. Some empirical studies in the acquisition of transformational relations. In: W. Collins (ed.), Children's Language and Communication. Lawrence Erlbaum Associates, Hillsdale, NJ.

McLean, J., and Snyder-McLean, L. 1978. A transactional approach to early language training. Charles E. Merrill, Columbus, OH.

Miller, J., and Yoder, D. 1974. An ontogenetic language teaching strategy for retarded children. In: R.L. Schiefelbusch and L.L. Lloyd (eds.), Language Perspectives—Acquisition, Retardation, and Intervention. University Park Press, Baltimore.

Miller, J., Yoder, D., and Schiefelbusch, R.L. (eds.). 1983. Contemporary Issues in Language Intervention (ASHA Reports 12). American Speech-Language-Hearing Assoc., Rockville, MD.

Moerk, E. 1980. Relationships between parental input frequencies and language acquisition. J. Child Lang. 7:105–119.

Muma, J. 1978. Language Handbook. Prentice-Hall, Englewood Cliffs, NJ.

Nelson, K. 1981. Individual differences in language development: Implications for language and development. Dev. Psychol. 17:170–187.

Nelson, K. 1973. Structure and Strategy in Learning to Talk. SRCD Monograph 38:1–2 (No. 149) University of Chicago Press, Chicago, IL.

Perkins, W. 1977. Speech Pathology: An Applied Behavioral Science. C.V. Mosby, St. Louis.

Prelock, P., and Panagos, J. 1981. The middle ground in evaluating language programs. J. Speech Hear. Disord. 46:436–438.

Prutting, C. 1982. Pragmatics as social competence. J. Speech Hear. Disord. 47:123–134.

Prutting, C. 1979. Process: The action of moving forward progressively from one point to another on the way to completion. J. Speech Hear. Disord. 44:3–26.

Rice, M. 1980. Cognition to Language: Categories, Word Meanings, and Training. University Park Press, Baltimore.

Rice, M. 1983. Contemporary accounts of the cognition/language relationship: Implications for speech-language clinicians. J. Speech Hear. Disord. 48:347–360.

Risley, T. 1977. The development and maintenance of language: An operant model. In: B. Etzel, J. LeBlanc, and D. Baer (eds.), New Developments in Behavioral Research. Lawrence Erlbaum Associates, Hillsdale, NJ.

Ruder, K.F. 1978. Planning and programming for language intervention. In: R.L. Schiefelbusch (ed.), Bases of Language Intervention. University Park Press, Baltimore.

Ruder, K.F., and Smith, M.D. 1974. Issues in language training. In: R.L. Schiefelbusch and L.L. Lloyd (eds.), Language Perspectives—Acquisition, Retardation, and Intervention. University Park Press, Baltimore.

Schiefelbusch, R.L. 1972. Language of the Mentally Retarded. University Park Press, Baltimore.

Schiefelbusch, R.L., and Lloyd, L.L. (eds.). 1974. Language Perspectives—Acquisition, Retardation, and Intervention. University Park Press, Baltimore.

Schiefelbusch, R.L., and Bricker, D. 1981. Early Language: Acquisition and Intervention. University Park Press, Baltimore.

Schiefelbusch, R.L. 1980. Synthesis of trends in language intervention. In: D. Bricker (ed.), Language Intervention with Children. Jossey-Bass Publishers, San Francisco.

Siegel, G., and Spradlin, J. 1978. Programming for communication and language therapy. In: R.L. Schiefelbusch (ed.)., Language Intervention Strategies. University Park Press, Baltimore.

Slama-Cazacu, T., Dechert, H., and Raupach, M. (eds.). 1982. Psycholinguistics Newsletter: Vol. 2. AILA Commission on Psycholinguistics, Kassel, West Germany.

Slobin, D. 1979. Psycholinguistics. Scott, Foresman and Company, Glenview, IL.

Slobin, D. 1981. Psychology without linguistics—language without grammar. Cognition 10:275–280.

Staats, A. 1974. Behaviorism and cognitive theory in the study of language: A neopsycholinguistics. In: R.L. Schiefelbusch and Lloyd, L.L. (eds.), Language Perspectives—Acquisition, Retardation, and Intervention. University Park Press, Baltimore.

Stokes, T., and Baer, D. 1977. An implicit technology of generalization. J. Appl. Behav. Anal. 10:349–367.

Stremel, K., and Waryas, C. 1974. A behavioral psycholinguistic approach to language training. In: L. McReynolds (ed.), Developing Systematic Procedures for Training Children's Language, Monograph #18. American Speech-Language-Hearing Assoc., Rockville, MD.

Switzky, H., Rotatori, A., Miller, T., and Freagon, S. 1979. The developmental model and its implications for assessment and instruction for the severely/profoundly handicapped. Ment. Retard. 17:167–170.

Tyack, D., and Gottsleben, R. 1974. Language Sampling, Analyses and Training. Consulting Psychologists Press, Palo Alto, CA.

Von Glaserfeld, E. 1982. On the concepts of period, phase, stage, and level. Human Dev. 15:152–160.

Wanner, E., and Gleitman, L. R. 1982. Language Acquisition: The State of the Art. Cambridge University Press, Cambridge, MA.

Waryas, C., and Stremel-Campbell, K. 1978. Grammatical training for the language delayed child. In: R.L. Schiefelbusch (ed.), Language Intervention Strategies. University Park Press, Baltimore.

Weisz, J., and Yeates, K.O. 1981. Cognitive development in retarded and nonretarded persons: Piagetian tests of the similar structure hypothesis. Psychol. Bull. 90:153–178.

Welch, S.J. 1981. Teaching generative grammar to mentally retarded children: A review and analysis of a decade of research. Ment. Retard. 19:277–284.

Wilbur, R. 1983. Where do we go from here? (A discussion of Part III—Deciding how to carry out language intervention). In: J. Miller, D. Yoder, and R.L. Schiefelbusch (eds.), Contemporary Issues in Language Intervention (ASHA Reports 12). American Speech-Language-Hearing Assoc., Rockville, MD.

Wilcox, M.J., and Leonard, L. 1978. Experimental acquisition of wh-questions in language disordered children. J. Speech Hear. Res. 21:220–240.

Winitz, H. 1982. Use and abuse of the developmental approach. In: H. Winitz (ed.), Treating Language Disorders: By Clinicians for Clinicians. University Park Press, Baltimore.

Zigler, E., and Balla, D. 1983. Mental Retardation: The Developmental-Difference Controversy. Lawrence Erlbaum Associates, Hillsdale, NJ.

Section

I

Developmental Approaches to Language Assessment

In this section, Longhurst (Chapter 2) and Muma (Chapter 3) discuss and evaluate language assessment procedures within the perspective of developmental psycholinguistics.

In Chapter 2, Longhurst critically reviews and evaluates some of the more traditional approaches to language assessment. The consensus of this review is that most if not all of these formal tests provide only a fragment of the child's communicative competence and that, ultimately, a picture of the child's communication abilities and disabilities is more useful in planning remediation than is an attempt to assemble fragments of behavior to produce a composite facsimile.

Longhurst's discussion of communication assessment is valuable to understanding the chapters that follow it. Longhurst focuses on assessment as being closely tied to comprehensive intervention procedures. He presents a critical review of some of the major clinical assessment tools used for speech and language evaluation. The purposes and scope of each test are summarized, and data on its clinical utility are presented. The final section of this chapter emphasizes major points made by Muma in Chapter 3—that a major purpose of assessment is to gather data upon which intervention may be based.

In Chapter 3, Muma focuses on the need for assessment models that take into account the recent data and approaches to the study of normal language acquisition. He describes a comprehensive assessment procedure that focuses on descriptive evaluation of a child's cognitive, linguistic, and communicative systems. Muma maintains that such a comprehensive descriptive approach is ultimately more productive in a comparable amount of time than normative procedures and is unequivocally more useful for planning an intervention strategy than formal tests of syntax and communication ability.

chapter 2

The Scope of
Normative
Language Assessment

Thomas M. Longhurst

Speech Pathology and Audiology
Idaho State University
Pocatello, Idaho

contents

Language is an integral part of the growth and development of a normal or handicapped child. Language is frequently the most important single factor used to assess a child's growth and development. As Kretschmer and Kretschmer (1978) noted: "Language evaluation is a necessary component in educational planning" (p. 143). It is vital to the researcher, clinician, and educator to establish an accurate representation of a child's language.

This chapter reviews the standardized or normative approach to language assessment. A recognized language assessment authority has recently written:

> A standardized test is one that has been given to large numbers of children from various populations, has demonstrated reliability (internal and/or test-retest), is valid as determined by external or face-validity criteria, and has normative data that provide either scale-score, age equivalent, or numerical score comparisons for individual children tested (Miller, 1978, p. 291).

Three principal domains of language are reviewed. They involve the production and comprehension processes for: 1) forming words (morphology); 2) forming sentences (syntax); and 3) word meanings and relations (lexical semantics). These levels of language are intimately related, and they are separated here only for the purpose of discussion. Table 1 illustrates how the various assessment procedures to be discussed below may be classified in accordance with these principal domains of language structure. Phonological assessment and procedures designed to assess the pragmatic level have been excluded because of limitations of the scope of this chapter.

With only a few exceptions, the tests and procedures discussed in this chapter are commercially available and have been frequently used. This is not to suggest that formal or standardized tests are the only, or even the primary, means of language assessment. However, these tests are valuable resources for students of language assessment. They help to focus and sharpen our observational skills. They are particularly valuable in structured screening programs and in diagnostic evaluations, where the primary purpose is to decide if the child does or does not have a significant problem as compared to age peers. They can also provide a guide to further assessment. Additionally, they occupy an important place in research, where standard measures are often required. Nonetheless, the more informal assessment methods developed by experienced clinicians and teachers often prove to be invaluable adjuncts when prescribing specific intervention programming and monitoring language progress (Miller, 1981; Muma, this volume). Ultimately, as Siegel (1975) so keenly observed, the best assessment instrument is:

Table 1. Language assessment paradigm

	Production		Comprehension	
Forming words (morphology)	Berry-Talbot			
	ITPA:	Grammatic Closure		
	TOLD:	Grammatic Completion		
	Language sampling			
Forming words (syntax)	MLU		TACL	(STACL)
	DSA		ACLC	
	LSAT		NSST:	Receptive
	MILE		TOLD:	Grammatic Understanding
	SPLT			
	NSST:	Expressive		
	CELF:	Producing Model Sentences	CELF:	Processing Word and Sentence Structure
	OLSIDI	(OLSIST)		
	CELI			
	ELI			
	DTLA:	Auditory Attention Span for Related Syllables		
Words and word relationships (lexical semantics)	MPLI:	Expressive Vocabulary	PPVT-R	
			TOLD:	Picture Vocabulary
	EOWPVT		MSCA:	Word Knowledge
	WORD:	Synonyms	TOLD:	Oral Vocabulary
	WORD:	Antonyms	WISC-R:	Vocabulary
			WISC-R:	Similarities
	MSCA:	Opposite Analogies	DTLA:	Social Adjustment
			DTLA:	Likenesses Differences
	MSCA:	Word Knowledge	VCS	
	ITPA:	Auditory Association	BTBC	
	DTLA:	Verbal Opposite	TOKEN:	Part V
			CELF:	Processing Linguistic Commands
			CELF:	Processing Relationships and Ambiguities
			CELF:	Processing Word Classes
			WORD:	Association, Semantic Absurdities, Definitions, and Multiple Definitions

Refer to running text for test abbreviations.

. . . a clinician who has some knowledge of research and theory in language, some experience in describing and dealing with important communication behaviors, and some reservoir of confidence in his or her own abilities to observe behavior, develop hypotheses, and change ideas and approaches when necessary (p. 213).

TEST STANDARDIZATION

Before discussing specific test procedures, there are several aspects of test standardization that warrant attention, primarily because they are often overlooked by the student of language assessment. They are: 1) test scores and norms; 2) reliability; and 3) validity.

Test Scores and Norms

Raw test scores have very little meaning unless they are interpreted further. Also, to compute a percentage of correct items adds little information unless these scores are somehow compared with other children's scores on the same measure. When scores for larger groups of children are available, it is possible to develop an arithmetic average or mean for a given measure. The middle score of ranked scores is the median, usually referred to as the norm. Norms take on meaning when the score of the child being tested is compared to them; however, the relevance or appropriateness of norms is being increasingly questioned (Muma, this volume).

One popular method of interpreting scores is to compute a percentile score. The 50th percentile conforms to the median for a particular sample. Thus, a child whose score falls at the 81st percentile performed better than 80% of the children in the comparison sample. Sometimes, percentile ranks that divide the scores into blocks of 10, 20, or sometimes 25 are used; hence, a child may be reported to score in the upper quartile.

The use of age scores is a popular procedure in many language assessment procedures. Usually, the number of items passed or some measure of language at a particular age level in a normative sample is compared with the child's test performance. This method of interpretation usually produces a statement such as, "His score conforms to the mean for three-year-olds." This is a deceptively simple practice. It assumes that the behavior of all three-year-olds is relatively invariant and that a single test score adequately describes an individual child's behavior. However, this is certainly not the case.

Whereas some types of normative data can be useful in interpreting test scores, there are many precautions or limitations that require discussion. If different methods were used to collect the normative data than are used by the examiner, it may be inappropriate to compare scores. The specific characteristics of the child examined and those in the normative sample should be similar. It may be just as inappropriate to compare scores of white middle-class children from rural Kansas with white middle-class children from New York City as it is to compare white middle-class children with Chicano children. Examiners are being encouraged to develop normative data that conform with their own geographic or cultrual populations. Normative scores are often reported along with some form of variability, such as standard deviations. Often, there are large differences among the language test scores of young children; that is, young children's language is inherently variable. Because of this, the fact that the test child's score falls at a specific age line may not be particularly meaningful unless the score deviates significantly from the norm.

Reliability

Any language assessment procedure should produce similar results from one time to the next and for different examiners. Test-retest reliability or temporal reliability is a measure of a test's ability to produce similar results after some critical period of time. When there are many sequentially arranged items on a test, the author may report split-half correlations. Usually, odd-numbered items are compared with even-numbered items. Because adjacent items should test the same skill, there should be a high correlation. Likewise, when tests contain alternate forms, these forms should produce high correlations. Interexaminer reliability is a measure of how comparable the scores of two or more examiners administering the same test are under similar conditions. To ensure consistency from examiner to examiner, a test should have good interexaminer reliability.

Validity

A language assessment procedure is valid if it measures what it purports to measure. This is a difficult judgment to make when dealing with something as encompassing and amorphous as language. The usual procedure for determining validity of a particular test is to administer it as well as other similar tests to the same children. The scores on the tests are then compared to see how well they are correlated. Most authors of popular language tests, however, do not report validity statistics for their tests.

Many of the authors of language tests attempt to establish validity of their test by comparing teachers' ratings with test scores. This method is considered to be a relatively weak form of computing validity. Another popular form of reporting validity is to show that increasingly higher scores on a test are correlated with increasing chronological age. This also is a weak form of validity because so many other characteristics increase with chronological age, and chronological age is increasingly questioned as a good predictor of language development. Consequently, the validity of any standardized test might be open to question.

MORPHOLOGICAL AND SYNTACTIC ASSESSMENT

Evidence suggests that the acquisition of language skill follows a relatively set sequence (Brown, 1973). This knowledge has made it possible to construct tests that assess the child's morphological and syntactic structures at various stages of development. The greatest proliferation of tests and procedures in recent years has been in these areas. However, there is a major shift away from total reliance on standardized tests of the form or structure of language production to nonstandardized or informal procedures that assess form and structure and the use or function of language (Leonard et al., 1978; Muma, 1978; Prutting, 1979; Danwitz, 1981; Hubbell, 1981; Miller, 1981; Swisher and Aten, 1981). Although not technically within the scope of this chapter, several of these less formal or nonstandardized procedures are discussed because it is essentially impossible to conduct assessment of morphological and syntactic production without using these approaches.

MORPHOLOGICAL TESTING

The smallest meaningful linguistic unit is a *morpheme*, and the study of the rules that govern word formation is called *morphology*. Uninflected words, or root words, are free morphemes (to be discussed later in this chapter). Bound morphemes, or inflections, take the form of prefixes, suffixes, and infixes. Most of the concern in children's language has been directed to the use of suffixes. English suffixes are used, for example, to mark number (boys), case (boy's), tense (played), aspect (playing), comparative (bigger), and superlative (biggest). Children learning language often manifest problems in the morphological area.

Morphological testing examines the expressive ability to produce morphological inflection in speech and comprehend these inflections in the speech of others. The usual method for testing productive inflection is through the process of rule extension in a sentence completion, or *cloze* technique. In this procedure, the root word is orally presented to the child in an introductory sentence. Then the child is required to fill in the blank or cloze another related incomplete sentence by adding to the root word the appropriate inflection. Sometimes, the examiner may produce an inflected word target or a sentence that contains the target and ask the child to imitate it. In comprehension testing, the examiner usually presents a word or sentence that includes the inflection and the child is asked to point to a picture. Imitation and comprehension tests that include morphology are reviewed later.

Nonimitative Tests

In nonimitative tests of morphology, the test stimuli may consist of actual words, like in the Grammatic Closure Subtest of the Illinois Test of Psycholinguistic Abilities (ITPA), (Kirk et al., 1968) or the Grammatic Completion Subtest of the Test of Language Development (TOLD) (Newcomer and Hammill, 1977). Nonsense words were used in Berko's (1958) original procedure. Dever's (1968) modification of Berko's procedures and the commercially available Exploratory Test of Grammar (Berry and Talbot, 1966) also make use of nonsense items. The supposed advantage in using nonsense stimuli is that the child's response will not be biased by previous exposure to vocabulary items. Informally, as an alternative, it is possible to use concrete objects as stimuli to assist responding. It has been demonstrated that in testing educable mentally retarded (EMR) children, higher scores are obtained when real as opposed to nonsense items were used (Dever and Gardner, 1967). Dever (1968) found that a Berko-type test (for example, the Berry-Talbot) does not predict the occurrence of errors in the free speech of EMR children. There are formal scoring procedures for the ITPA and TOLD, but the Berry-Talbot test, Berko's test, and Dever's modifications are only scored informally.

Grammatic Closure (ITPA)   This subtest of the ITPA contains 35 items following the usual production cloze procedure. Pictures representing real objects are presented to the child along with stimulus sentences. Normative data for this subtest are reported for 962 Midwestern, suburban children ranging from 2–2 to 10–4. Test-retest reliability and internal reliability coefficients range from 0.60 to 0.74. The test-retest reliability of 0.46 and slightly higher at the younger ages is, at best, questionable. Considerable caution is suggested when using this test with children below 4 years of age.

Grammatic Completion (TOLD)   In this subtest of the TOLD, the child is required to cloze or complete a sentence using the appropriate inflected word. A stimulus sentence is given orally by the examiner without pictures or objects present. To produce a correct answer, the child must interpret the sentence and recall it as well as produce the correctly inflected word. The task requirements seem to be more difficult than under the ITPA. This subtest is made up of 30 items, with most of the frequently occurring inflections in children represented.

The TOLD was standardized on 1,014 children, ranging from 4–0 to 8–11 years of age. The sample was specifically chosen to represent the demographic characteristics of the 1970 census rather than a specific geographic area. The test-retest correlation coefficient was 0.96, although the analysis was made with only 21 subjects and a 5-day interval. This subtest of the TOLD was compared with the Grammatic Closure Subtest of the ITPA to establish concurrent validity coefficients of 0.79 to 0.89.

Exploratory Test of Grammar   This test, commonly known as the Berry-Talbot, is the commercially available version of Berko's (1958) original research test stimuli. The stimuli pictures mythical animals, attributes, and actions that should not be familiar to the child. Thus, although the test tends to assure that the child's responses should not be simply imitative responses, it is impossible to include the irregular forms of English morphology. This test was designed to be part of a battery of morphological and syntactic tests for administration to children from about 5 to 8 years of age. The other tests of the battery apparently have yet to be developed. The test of morphology was never standardized, so there are no normative data nor reliability or validity information reported. The authors, however, suggest that of the 27 test items, 5-year-olds should get the first five correct; 6-year-olds, the first 14; 7-year-olds, the first 20; and 8-year-olds should get all 27 correct.

SYNTACTIC PRODUCTION TESTING

Basically, there are three approaches to testing syntactic production: 1) spontaneous language sampling; 2) structured elicitation; and 3) elicited imitation. Much of the literature on the assessment of production deals with the analysis of spontaneous or elicited language samples (Longhurst, 1974; Barrie-Blackley et al., 1978). In the following sections, spontaneous language sampling procedures are represented here by:

1. Brown's (1973) mean length of utterance (MLU)
2. Lee's (1966) Developmental Sentence Types (DST)
3. Lee and Canter's (1971) Developmental Sentence Scoring (DSS)
4. Lee's (1974) Developmental Sentence Analysis (DSA)
5. Tyack and Gottsleben's (1974) Language Sampling, Analysis, and Training (LSAT)

Structured elicitation procedures are represented by:

1. Werner and Kresheck's (1978) Structured Photographic Language Test (SPLT)
2. Goldsworthy's (1982) Multilevel Informal Language Inventory (MILI)

Elicitation imitation procedures are represented by:

1. Carrow's (1974) Elicited Language Inventory (CELI)
2. Zachman et al.'s (1977) Oral Language Sentence Imitation Screening Test (OLSIST) and Oral Language Sentence Imitation Diagnostic Inventory (OLSIDI)
3. Newcomer and Hamill's (1977) Sentence Imitation Subtest of the TOLD
4. Semel and Wiig's (1980a) Producing Model Sentences Subtest of the Clinical Evaluation of Language Function (CELF)
5. Auditory Attention Span for Related Syllables Subtest of the Detroit Tests of Learning Aptitude (DTLA)
6. Expressive Subtest of the Northwestern Syntax Screening Test (NSST)
7. MacDonald's (1978a) Environmental Language Inventory (ELI) Although not strictly an imitation test. Lee's (1971) NSST is also relevant here.

Spontaneous Language Sampling

MLU   Brown (1973) described rules for determining mean length of utterance in morphemes (MLU-M). This stands as probably the best index of utterance length in that it is positively correlated with language development (Miller and Chapman, 1981), especially for children below a chronological age of about 4. An "upper bound" is usually also reported that consists of the longest utterance in a sample of 100 utterances. There is very little normative data for MLU-M, and caution should be used in comparing this measurement with traditional norms (Johnson et al., 1963) because MLU-M will be inherently greater than the more traditional MLU in words, especially for children above age 3. MLU-M does not tell much about the form of a child's syntactic development, but it does have meaning when placed within the context of Brown's (1973) five stages of development.

DST   Lee (1966) applied findings obtained in several developmental psycholinguistic studies of normal language acquisition to develop a procedure for diagnosing delayed language development. Lee's purpose was to investigate the observation that the "language delayed" child was not just slower in syntactic development but was also proceeding in a bizarre manner. A speech sample was collected and analyzed from a "normally developing" and a "clinic" child. Based on the comparison of the two children, Lee concluded that her DST method of classifying sentences showed marked differences in her two samples. Her analysis demonstrated not only slower development in the "clinic" child but also failure in the production of certain types of syntactic structures. Lee (1974) provided a somewhat updated version of DST, designed to analyze the speech of children speaking mostly in fragments or pre-sentences.

DSS   Lee and Canter (1971) developed a clinical procedure, called developmental sentence scoring (DSS). This was intended to estimate the status and progress of children currently undergoing language training in a clinic. Lee and Canter predicted that by analyzing a child's spontaneous, tape-recorded speech sample, a clinician could estimate if the child had generalized rules sufficiently to use them in verbal performance. The DSS procedure gave weighted scores to a developmental order of eight different morphological or syntactic constructions. Lee and Canter's objectives were: 1) to provide guidelines for planning lessons; and to estimate the status and rate of progress in children treated in a speech clinic. Lee (1974) updated the DSS procedure by reweighting some of the structures. The DSS procedure was standardized on a sample of 160 middle-class children, ranging in age from 3–0 to 6–11. When consistency among the eight components of the procedure was measured, a correlation of 0.71 resulted. The split-half correlation was 0.73, which indicates a good internal consistency.

DSA   Often in clinical application, both DST and DSS can be applied to the same child. The value of these procedures, over and above the value of the counts and scores that are derived, is that they require the examiner to collect samples of the child's behavior, put it on paper, and try to make sense of it. Beyond the scores, percentiles, and computed language ages is the internal grammatical analysis of the language sample. Lee (1974) made a number of concrete suggestions for facilitating this process and determining where to begin in intervention.

LSAT   The basic purpose of LSAT is to isolate and describe the morphological and syntactic rules the child has under control. Tyack and Gottsleben (1974) designed a number of specially constructed data forms to facilitate this process. The analysis includes computation of a word-morpheme index or mean and assignment of the sample to a linguistic level on the basis of this mean. Next, the child's constructions are sorted into categories that serve as a baseline for training. These categories are then used to determine training sequences.

Structured Elicitation

SPLT   Test (Werner and Kresheck, 1978), which is designed to measure the 4–0 to 8–11-year-old child's generation of morphological and syntactic structures, uses highly structured visual and auditory stimuli to elicit a language sample. The visual stimuli consist of color snapshots of children, adults, and animals in everyday situations. The use of very specific introductory statements, instructions, and prompts are suggested by the authors. Many of the structures tested are the same as those tested in Lee's (1974) DSS procedure, with the addition of items designed to elicit three cases of wh-questions. The child's responses are scored against adult standards; a percentage of correct responses is computed and compared with normative data. Next, an analysis is made of the child's responses. A "languagegram" is completed for children that score below the second standard deviation. This procedure allows the examiner to obtain a picture of the child's correct and incorrect responses and to compare these responses to the ones produced by similarly aged children. The test-retest reliability coefficient reported was 0.95, which suggests highly consistent results. Mean percentage of correct performance increases over age in the normative data. The authors reported that of 25 children diagnosed as language delayed by the SPLT, all were similarly diagnosed by the DSS procedure. The advantages of a structured elicitation procedure are that it can be completed in less time and it specifically elicits structures that may not appear in the usual spontaneous sample.

MILI   This procedure (Goldsworthy, 1982) was designed to measure the 4- to 12-year-old child's level of functioning in the production of selected critical semantic relations and syntactic constructions. The procedure is "leveled" in the sense that the tasks are developmentally ordered, the observations moved from general to specific, and the Probes section uses three levels to elicit target behaviors: Evoked Spontaneous, Elicited and Receptive. The language production observation proceeds from the child's description of one of two survey scenes; to the child's paraphrasing of two stories; to target probe procedures designed to elicit specific syntactic constructions and semantic relations in a relatively structured way. The procedure also includes receptive tasks. Using information from a recording form, the examiner can prepare a syntax profile and a semantic relations profile, which is generally composed with literature-derived normative data. The authors provide a discussion of the content validity and field-testing of the MILI, but because it is designed as an informal procedure, no standardization and norms are provided. This somewhat structured yet informal procedure holds considerable promise.

Elicited Imitation

Imitation of sentences has been used in varying degrees as a source of information about child language development (Menyuk, 1964, 1969; Lenneberg, 1967; McNeill, 1970; Slobin and Welsh, 1971; Bloom et al., 1974; Snow, 1981). There is still considerable controversy about the extent to which imitation involves linguistic processing (Fraser et al., 1963; Slobin and Welsh, 1971; ; Kuczaj and Maratsos, 1975; Hood and Lightbown, 1978; Fraser, 1981; Miller, 1981). Ervin (1964) and McNeill (1970) suggested that the grammar of a child's spontaneous speech is not noticeably different from the grammar of his or her imitations. There is also evidence that elicited imitations may be quite different (Menyk, 1964, Kuczaj and Maratsos, 1975; McDade et al., 1982). It is probably inappropriate to assume at this time that if a child correctly imitates a particular grammatical structure, that that structure should appear appropriately in his spontaneous speech, and vice versa. The elicited imitation approach does, however, offer a relatively quick method of observing a large number and variety of grammatical structures (Miller, 1981).

CELI   This test was designed to provide a standardized method of obtaining production data on a child's grammatical system. The child is asked to imitate 52 model utterances that contain a wide variety of grammatical features in several different types of sentences. The child's imitations are tape-recorded, transcribed onto a special scoring form, and then analyzed for error patterns. The CELI was standardized on 475 3–0- to 7–11-year-old children. The test-retest reliability coefficient was 0.98, with an interexaminer reliability coefficient of 0.99. Carrow reported that concurrent validity with the DSS procedures was 0.79, although Sinclair et al. (1977) found that these two procedures are not highly related. Percentile scores and stanine scores can be computed for the CELI. Although there are controversies about the elicited imitation approach, the CELI still represents one of the best constructed and standardized tests available in the 1980s.

OLSIST and OLSIDI   According to Zachman et al. (1977), the purpose of the OLSIST is twofold: 1) to assess whether a child's expressive language skills are within normal limits; and 2) to assess whether further testing is needed. Because there are presently no norms for the test, it really cannot accomplish the first purpose. It does, however, screen a representative sample of the most important syntactic and morphological structures included in Brown's (1973) three highest stages (Stages III, IV, and V). At each of these three stages as represented in the OLSIST, there are 20 sentences to be imitated by the child. The major strength of this approach lies in the OLSIDI, which contains individual sentence imitation tests, consisting of 10 sentences each. Depending on the structures missed in the OLSIST, the appropriate subtests in the OLSIDI can be administered collectively as a "deep" test. The testing procedure and score forms make it relatively easy to analyze the child's errors in imitation. However, the interpretation of the results is somewhat difficult because there are no norms or reports of test reliability. The authors do describe, although in a rather sketchy fashion, a study comparing their approach with spontaneous language sampling, suggesting a rather close approximation between the two.

Sentence Imitation Subtest (TOLD)   This subtest of the TOLD is similar in approach to the previously described imitation tests. It contains 30 model sentences, ranging in length from 5 to 12 words. The standardization of the TOLD has been described previously, and it is to be commended. The test-retest reliability coefficient for this subtest is 0.98, with a concurrent validity coefficient with the Detroit Tests of Learning Aptitude-Related Syllables (Baker and Leland, 1967) ranging between 0.77 to 0.89 for varying chronological ages.

Producing Model Sentences Subtest (CELF)   This subtest of the CELF (Semel and Wiig, 1980a) is designed to test productive control of syntactic and morphological structures through imitation of 23 grammatical and seven ungrammatical sentences. The length of the sentences ranges from five to 17 words. The deviation from other imitation tests to include ungrammatical sentences was prompted by the works of Newcombe and Marshall (1967) and Wiig and Reach (1975), which suggested that such an inclusion would help to differentially diagnose right from left hemisphere-damaged children and adults. The test-retest reliability coefficient for this subtest is 0.86 with a concurrent validity correlation coefficient of 0.67 when compared with the Verbal Expression Subtest of the ITPA. Additionally, normative data are reported for children from grades K through 12.

Auditory Attention Span for Related Syllables Subtest (DTLA)   This subtest of the DTLA (Baker and Leland, 1967) is designed to evaluate productive imitation of 42 model sentences. As its name suggests, attention span and memory limitations most assuredly affect the results of this test. The length of sentences is systematically controlled, ranging from five to 22 words. Although the normative data for the DTLA are somewhat dated (1958), they do represent some of the most substantial data available (especially for adolescents). The DTLA was standardized on 150 subjects at each age level from 3 to 19 years. Test-retest reliability was 0.96. However, no specific validity information is reported by the authors.

Expressive Subtest (NSST)   The NSST (Lee, 1971) is designed to screen, in an equivalent manner, expression (production) and reception (comprehension) of selected syntactic and morphological structures. The expressive portion, containing 20 items, is not an imitation test in the same sense as the imitation tests previously reviewed. In this test, the child is presented with a plate and two related sentences orally (for example, "The boy pulls the girl" and "The girl pulls the boy"). The examiner then asks, "What is this one?" and "What is that one?" while pointing to each of the pictures. The child is required to grammatically produce identical repetitions of the examiner's sentences. Imitation skill is involved but is also compounded with memory and other factors. The NSST was standardized on 242 children, ranging in age from 3–0 to 7–11 years. Reliability and validity data are not reported by the author. Ratusnik and Koenigsknecht (1975) administered the test to mentally retarded and severely expressively delayed children. Their results showed reliability coefficients for the two groups on the Expressive Subtest of 0.81 and 0.78, respectively. Prutting et al. (1975) found that the NSST accurately predicted children who were found to have severe language problems but that the NSST results did not correlate well with spontaneous language sample results. Several authors (Larson and Summers, 1976; Arndt, 1977; Byrne, 1977) questioned the normative data for the NSST. Lee (1977) wrote a reply to Arndt (1977) and Byrne (1977). Klee and Ratusnik (1980) reported on a shortened version of the NSST (11 test items receptively and 11 items expressively) that can be administered in 10 minutes.

Environmental Language Inventory (ELI)   The ELI (MacDonald, 1978a), in many ways, actually combines and builds upon the three major approaches to morphology and syntax production testing: spontaneous language sampling, structured elicitation, and elicited imitation. The emphasis of the ELI is on eight semantic-grammatical rule categories. It is designed to sample the child's early semantic-grammatical rules and utterance length in three modes: free-play, conversation, and imitation. Basically, the cued conversation (structured elicitation) and imitation modes are used in conjunction with free-play (spontaneous language sampling) in order to get a more representative picture of the child's productive abilities. Rather than insisting that the examiner apply the ELI exactly as constructed, MacDonald suggested that the clinician might want to modify and extend the ELI to fit specific needs. MacDonald (1978a) reviewed several studies that used the ELI with various populations and addressed the question of reliability and validity. The test has not been formally standardized, nor are normative data reported. However, there seems to be considerable evidence that the ELI is clinically very useful. The ELI should become increasingly popular, especially when routinely coupled with the Parent Administered Communication Inventory (OLIVER) (MacDonald 1978b), the Environmental Prelanguage Battery (EPB) (Horstmeier and MacDonald, 1978a), and the Ready, Set, Go (Horstmeier and MacDonald 1978b) intervention programs.

LEXICAL PRODUCTION TESTING

Children may be thought of as having two overlapping, intimately related vocabularies: 1) a productive vocabulary, or the words they use in their speech; and 2) a comprehension vocabulary, or the spoken words they can understand. Almost all of the words in the productive vocabulary should be in the child's comprehension vocabulary, but all of the words in the comprehension vocabulary need not be in the productive vocabulary. Most of the attention in the assessment of vocabulary has focused on comprehension vocabulary. The procedures for assessing productive vocabulary, until recently, have been very simplified or surface tests and are less structured and ambiguous. Many of the so-called "basic concept" tests are simply vocabulary tests designed to assess a specific set of lexical terms.

There are three approaches to measuring production of words and word relationships: 1) oral language samples, from which various vocabulary measurements can be made; 2) naming pictures—the child can be asked to name pictures that are pointed to by the examiner; and 3) antonymy, synonymy, or reciprocity—the child is asked to supply a word that expresses antonymy, synonymy, or reciprocity of a given stimulus word.

Oral Language Samples

The number of different words (NDW) used in a 50-response sample indicates a child's productive vocabulary. Templin (1957) found that NDW increased as age increased. NDW is sometimes difficult to interpret because it could be measuring a child's tendency to talk rather than the size of his or her vocabulary. Care should be taken to only compare NDW computed from similarly sized samples.

The type token ratio (TTR) is the ratio of the number of different words in a sample to the total number of words. It is a measure of word redundancy in speech. A minimum sample of 300 words is recommended for reliability purposes. As long as sample size is sufficiently large, TTRs for various word classes, such as nouns and verbs, can also be computed. The Carroll (1964) type token ratio (CTTR) consists of the number of different words in a sample, divided by the square root of twice the number of words in the sample. This measure is supposedly independent of sample size. Although there is little reliable normative data for TTR, it is a useful research tool and could be used over time to effectively measure increased productive vocabulary size in language training.

Naming Pictures

There has been very little development of formal tests of a child's ability to name pictures. This is probably because: 1) it is difficult to develop a set of standard pictures that will reliably elicit the same verbal response from children; and 2) only easily pictureable words can be reliably elicited (primarily nouns).

Expressive Vocabulary Subtest: Michigan Picture Language Inventory (*MPLI*) Wolski (1962) developed a test designed to elicit names of 25 test items pictured on a test plate matched against two foil items. Normative data for the MPLI are available for 180 children, comprised of 30 boys and 30 girls in each of three age groups (4, 5, and 6 years). Odd-even reliability correlation coefficients ranged between 0.53 and 0.83. The authors reported that scores increased with successive ages: however, this is a relatively weak form of establishing validity.

Expressive-One-Word Picture Vocabulary Test (*EOWPVT*) Gardner (1979) designed a test to elicit one-word responses to 110 line drawings. The stimuli depict general concepts, groupings (plurals), abstract concepts, and descriptive concepts. The words are arranged in ascending order by predetermined chronological age and difficulty levels. Mental age, IQ, percentile, and stamina can be computed from the child's raw score. Normative data are available for children for age levels 2–0 to 11–11. Split-half reliability coefficients ranged from 0.89 to 0.96, with a median of 0.94. Validity was determined through comparison with the PPVT (0.70) and the Columbia Mental Maturity Scale (0.39). It is considerably more difficult to require a child to label a picture than to point to a picture in response to the examiner saying a name (the usual vocabulary comprehension task).

Antonymy, Synonymy, and Reciprocity

There are essentially two approaches to testing expressive vocabulary through antonymy, synonymy, and reciprocity: 1) word association; and 2) incomplete verbal analogies. In the word association method, one member of a related word pair (antonyms or synomyms) is presented, and the child is required to produce the other member (for example, "cold-*hot*"). Sometimes, the examiner gives a list of words, one of which does not belong. In the analogies approach, the examiner usually says a complete sentence to introduce the topic, followed by an incomplete sentence (for example, "The sun is hot. Ice is _____."). The child is required to supply the appropriate word to complete the analogy.

Verbal Opposites Subtest (*DTLA*) The DTLA (Baker and Leland, 1967) represents the word association approach. In this subtest, 96 items are sequenced according to relative frequency and reading level along a concrete-abstract continuum. Standardization for the DTLA has been described above. The test-retest reliability correlation coefficient was reported to be 0.96.

Synonyms and Antonyms Subtests (*The WORD Test*) In these subtests (Jorgensen et al., 1981), the child is required to provide either the synonym or antonym to a list of words that is presented auditorily in statements such as "Tell me another word for enormous" or "What is the opposite of innocent?'' Normative data are provided for children from 7–0 to 11–11 years of age. Split-half correlations for the two subtests, Synonyms and Antonyms, were 0.87 and 0.84, respectively. Internal consistence of these subtests are reported to be quite good, although predictive and concurrent validity have not been established.

Auditory Association Subtest (ITPA)   This subtest of verbal analogies consists of 42 items, arranged sequentially according to a statistically determined progressive level of difficulty. General standardization has been previously described. Normative data for this subtest are available for the age range 2–4 to 10–11. Test-retest reliability correlation coefficients ranged from 0.83 to 0.90. Split-half correlation coefficients ranged from 0.74 to 0.85.

Opposite Analogies: McCarthy Scales of Children's Abilities (MSCA) This subtest (McCarthy, 1970) contains nine analogies, eight adjectives, and one preposition, each of which is presented in a similar fashion to the Auditory Association Subtest of the ITPA. The MSCA was standardized on 1,032 children, ranging in age from 2–6 to 8–6 years. Test-retest correlation coefficients ranged between 0.82 and 0.89 for the various ages. Validity correlations with the WPPSI Verbal Scale and Stanford-Binet IQ were 0.51 and 0.66, respectively.

SYNTACTIC COMPREHENSION TESTING

Most of the formal comprehension tests attempt to assess the processing of morphological and syntactic features by children. These comprehension tests are often used as predictors of later productive language development. This is reasonable because developmental psycholinguists believe that, generally speaking, passive control, or comprehension, precedes active control, or production, of the same linguistic features (McNeill, 1966; Brown, 1973; Ruder et al., 1974).

A test designed to probe comprehension skills should: 1) require minimal or no productive language from the child; and 2) accurately reflect the child's specific comprehension strengths and weaknesses. This second requirement of an effective comprehension test is probably the most difficult to ensure. If a child misses an item, it is virtually impossible to know whether the child lacks the knowledge to respond correctly, or whether he or she was distracted by a poorly constructed stimulus item. If, on the other hand, the child passes an item, the examiner may be fairly certain that the child has correctly comprehended it.

Several tests purport to accurately test syntax and morphological comprehension skills, and yet they each vary greatly in terms of structures tested, presentation format, scoring, and interpretation. The discerning examiner should evaluate each of these areas before using a test as a diagnostic tool. Many of the excellent reviews of these tests, included in Darley (1979), should prove to be helpful.

The following description of a master's thesis project, directed by this author (Emery, 1975), compares three major comprehension tests. The Grammatic Understanding Subtest of the TOLD, the Processing Word and Sentence Structure Subtest of the CELF, and the Assessment of Children's Language Comprehension (ACLC) by Foster et al. (1972) are also discussed. The ACLC represents an interesting and somewhat different approach to testing comprehension of morphological and syntactic constructions.

Three Comprehension Tests

Emery (1975) conducted a study to evaluate and compare three well-known comprehension tests by administering them to eight preschool children. The tests compared were the Carrow's (1973) Test of Auditory Comprehension of Language (TACL), the Miller-Yoder Test of Grammatical Comprehension (MY) (Miller and Yoder, 1975), and the NSST (Lee, 1971). The results of Emery's comparison study are included in the following test descriptions and reviews.

TACL   Carrow (1973) stated that the two functions of the TACL are: 1) to measure the auditory comprehension of structure; and in turn, 2) to allow the examiner to determine areas of linguistic difficulty. The test consists of a set of 101 plates, each containing from one to three line drawings representing vocabulary items, grammatical categories, and morphological and syntactic structures. A correct response consists of the child correctly pointing to a line drawing depicting a word, phrase, or sentence. The examiner presents each item in a specific manner; tag phrases such as "show me" are not used unless specifically indicated. Each correct response counts as 1 point, and the total score is the total number of items passed. The raw score is divided into subscores for broad category scores. Percentile scores and language ages can be derived for comparison, with norms ranging from 3–0 to 6–11 years of age. The test was standardized on 200 children. A test-retest reliability coefficient of 0.94 was reported, although this was for an earlier experimental version. Validity has been assessed by applying the test to clinical groups for the experimental version (Weiner, 1972; Bartel et al., 1971; Marquardt and Saxman, 1972; and Davis (1977) for the 1973 version. The Screening Test of Auditory Comprehension of Language (STACL) (Carrow, 1973), which contains 25 items from the TACL, is also available. The STACL was standardized on 418 children. The test-retest reliability for the STACL was 0.60.

MY   The MY test, designed to measure a child's grammatical comprehension, consists of 42 sentence pairs to be identified by a pointing response upon the presentation of stimulus sentences. There are 42 plates, each of which contains four line drawings, two foils, and two pictures identifiable from test sentences. Responses are recorded on a data sheet, and then they are transferred to a Comprehension Test Results Form to indicate the categories missed. No raw score is obtained, and thus, no percentile score or language age may be derived. The MY has not been standardized.

Receptive Subtest NSST   The NSST by Lee (1971) was intended to test a child's comprehension of grammatical features as well as production and to compare the two. For this reason, the NSST consists of 40 sentence pairs, with 20 to be identified receptively and 20 to be repeated expressively. Because the Expressive Subtest has already been reviewed and, for the purposes of Emery's comparison, the expressive portion of the test was not appropriate, discussion will be limited here to the Receptive Subtest. It consists of 20 plates, each containing four pictures (two foils and two pictures identifiable from test sentences). A correct response consists of the child pointing to the appropriate picture, one at a time, as the examiner repeats the two sentences. Each of the test pairs yield perfect scores of 2, scores of 1 if one sentence is missed, and 0 if both are missed. Norms range from 3.0 to 7.11 years of age and are expressed on charts from which a child's percentile score may be determined.

Comparison of Linguistic Structure in the Three Comprehension Tests

Item Comparison   Table 2 compares the linguistic features across the three comprehension tests according to test item. This table includes the collection of linguistic features found in the MY, the TACL, and the NSST and indicates which tests probed each feature. The following observations are evident in examining this chart:

1. The MY does not test any constructions using impersonal pronouns.
2. The NSST does not test the use of adjectives.
3. The TACL does not include a probe for object pronouns.

Although all three tests include items that are not included in the other two, the TACL proves to be the most carefully constructed. For example, it includes a lexicon of core words to ensure that a child does not fail an item because of a lack of prerequisite vocabulary.

Chi-Square Analysis   A summary of a chi-square analysis, comparing the proportions of correct responses on the three tests by linguistic feature, is presented in Table 3. The chi-square analysis revealed that there were significant differences in the proportion of correct answers among 20 of the 26 linguistic features common to all three tests.

Table 2.   Linguistic features across three comprehension tests according to test question

Linguistic feature	MY	TACL	NSST
Prepositions			
under	3, 4	45	1
on	3, 4	44	3
in	5, 6	46	3
beside	5, 6		
behind			1
between		48	
at the side of		47	
in front of		49	
Nouns			
Singular	24, 25	69	6
Plural	24, 25	66, 67, 68	6
Tense			
Past	31, 32	74	8
Present progressive	30, 31	64, 72, 73	12
Future	30, 32	76	12
Present perfect progressive		77	
Present perfect		75	
Noun/verb inflections			
is	28, 29	70	5
are	28, 29	71	5
Noun/verb agreement			
Singular	26, 27	91, 92	6, 15
Plural	26, 27		6, 15
Pronouns			
he	18, 20	60	2
she	19, 20	61	2
they	18, 19	59	
we		65	
her	15, 16		10
them	15, 17		
him	16, 17		
his		63	
their			10
Active reversibles			
Subject/Object	1, 2	78, 79	9
Passive reversibles			
Subject/Object	39, 40	80, 81	18
Affirmative/negative			
is	13, 14	85	4
is not	13, 14	86, 87, 98	4
has/doesn't have	9, 10		
can/can't	11, 12		
neither/nor		88	
no + *noun*		94	

Table 2. *(Continued)*

Linguistic feature	MY	TACL	NSST
Possessive	7, 8		11
Modification			
object	33, 34	96	
subject	35, 36	97	
obj./subj.	37, 38		
Indirect object		95	20
Reflexives	41, 42		7
Impersonal and interrogative			
Pronouns		82	13, 16
who		84	13
what			16
where		83	
when			19
this		42	19
that		43	
these			
Question reversal			14, 17
Lexicon		1–10	
nouns		29, 1–10, 30	
color	36, 37, 34	11–13	
quality		14–20	
quantity		21–28	
adverbs		39–41	
Derivational suffix		50–58	

Theoretically, if the child possesses control of a certain linguistic feature, he or she should be able to correctly answer any of the equivalent test items. However, these results indicate that children may not correctly answer comparable items from these tests. In fact, out of the 26 common linguistic features, only six showed similar results. Thus, it is difficult to determine whether or not a child truly possesses a linguistic feature and, hence, whether or not a specific test is valid.

Analysis of Variance Comparing Language Ages and Percentiles The language age in months and percentiles for the TACL and the NSST are presented in Table 4. Analyses of variance were used to compare the language age means and the percentile means for the TACL and the NSST. The MY was not included in these statistical analyses because the test does not provide language age or percentile scores. The results indicated significant differences between the TACL and the NSST on language age and on percentile scores. These results again bring into question the validity of such tests.

Table 3. Chi-square analysis of the proportion of correct responses on the three tests by linguistic feature

Linguistic feature	χ^2	df	Linguistic feature	χ^2	df
under	3.097	3	are	50.42^a	3
on	3.097	3	Singular noun/verb	14.654^a	5
in	3.097	3	agreement		
Singular noun	75.35^a	3	Plural noun/verb	67.098^a	3
Plural noun	2.534	5	agreement		
Past	169.26^a	3	she	29.936^a	3
Present progressive	25.39^a	5	he	44.462^a	3
future	324.89^a	3	they	4.210	2
is	185.55^a	3	Subject/object active	3.998^a	4
subject/object	33.992^a	4	reversible		
passive			Object modifier	1.947	2
negative/affirmative	7.227^a	3	Subject modifier	6.634^a	2
is			Indirect object	48.369^a	1
negative/affirmative	6.316^a	5	Reflexive	8.817^a	2
is not			who	7.360^a	2
Possessive	4.44^a	2	what	64.309^a	1

^{a} Significant at the 0.05 level.

Other Comprehension Tests

Grammatic Understanding Subtest (*TOLD*)   In this subtest of the TOLD (Newcomer and Hammill, 1977), a child is required to listen to 25 spoken sentences and choose one of three pictures that represents the meaning of the individual sentences. The standardization of the TOLD has been covered previously; however, the authors reported that the test-retest correlation coefficient for this subtest was 0.87.

Table 4. Subject scores and means for language age and percentile scores on the TACL and NSST

Child	Language age (in months)		Percentile	
	TACL	NSST	TACL	NSST
A	71	75	95	92
B	77	36	93	8
C	64	63	79	75
D	82	76	99	90
E	64	36	68	10
F	73	49	78	30
G	78	72	97	77
H	39	43	57	51
Mean	68.50^a	56.25^a	83.25^b	54.13^b

^{a} Significantly different at the 0.10 level.
^{b} Significantly different at the 0.05 level.

Concurrent validity coefficients for comparison with the Receptive Subtest of the NSST were 0.33 at age 8 and 0.67 at age 6.

Processing Word and Sentence Structure Subtest   This subtest of the CELF (Semel and Wiig, 1980a) contains 26 items; each item consists of a sentence associated with one of four pictures on a plate. The test-retest reliability correlation coefficient was reported to be 0.96, with a concurrent validity correlation coefficient of 0.53 when compared with the Receptive Subtest of the NSST.

Assessment of Children's Language Comprehension (ACLC)   The ACLC (Foster et al., 1972) was designed to assess the child's receptive ability to process, recall, and intepret 50 lexical items and 30 multiword utterances, 10 at each of three levels of increasing length. Each orally presented stimulus item is associated with one picture on a plate containing three to five choices. The plates are systematically designed so that the child's choice of the foil items can be used to interpret his receptive disability. Some clinicians and teachers view the ACLC as more a test of auditory perception and memory than a test of grammatical ability (Longhurst, 1979). The ACLC was standardized on 365 nursery and kindergarten children from 3–0 to 6–5 years of age. The authors did not report any measures of reliability or validity.

LEXICAL COMPREHENSION TESTING

Generally, there are four approaches to assessing the comprehension of words and relationships among words in children:

1. *Pointing to pictures*   Evaluate the child's comprehension vocabulary by having him or her point to a picture in an array in response to a word presented orally by the examiner (this is the traditional and most frequent approach).
2. *Word definition*   Have the child define the word.
3. *Similarities/differences*   Ask the child to describe either similarities or differences between words presented orally in pairs or larger groups (in some ways, similar to defining a word).
4. *Command completion*   Have the child demonstrate his or her comprehension of word meaning (usually prepositions or relational terms) by successfully following commands that involve pointing to pictures or objects or manipulating objects.

Although these four approaches share certain similarities, they seem to assess somewhat different skills. Relative comprehension vocabulary scores for different tasks may well be useful to the examiner.

Pointing to Pictures

In this approach, the child is usually shown a plate with 3 to 5 pictures and asked to point to the picture that corresponds to the word presented orally by the examiner. Usually, the items are arranged sequentially, from easy to difficult based on the frequency of occurrence and degree of abstraction required. The most popular test in this area is the *Peabody Picture Vocabulary Test-Revised* (*PPVT-R*) (Dunn and Dunn, 1981). On each of two forms of the PPVT-R (L and M), there are 175 items, which have been sequenced statistically. The PPVT-R has been highly standardized and can yield many useful scores. Extreme caution must be exercised in test administration because fatigue, distractibility, and inattention can adversely affect the results. The Picture Vocabulary Subtest of the TOLD (Newcomer and Hammill, 1977) is similar in design to the PPVT-R but contains only 25 items. The Full-Range Picture Vocabulary Test (FRPVT) (Ammons and Ammons, 1948) is in some ways even more comprehensive than the PPVT-R, but because of its length, complex administration format, and date of standardization statistics, it is seldom used.

Word Definition

Generally, defining words that are presented orally is viewed as more involved and difficult than just pointing to pictures. Usually, the words to be defined are arranged sequentially from the relatively concrete to the abstract. The child's definition is usually scored by the examiner on the basis of specific criteria. The tests in this area are: 1) the Oral Vocabulary Subtest of the TOLD; 2) the Vocabulary Subtest of the Wechsler Intelligence Scale for Children-Revised (WISC-R) (Wechsler, 1974); 3) the Social Adjustment Subtest of DTLA; 4) the Word Knowledge Subtest of the McCarthy Scales of Children's Abilities (MSCA); and 5) the Definitions and Multiple Definitions Subtests of The WORD Test.

Similarities/Differences

This method of assessing comprehension of words and word relationships requires the child to describe the similarities and/or differences between two to four words presented orally by the examiner. The child's responses are scored by applying specific criteria, such as descriptions of shape, color, function, hierarchical relationships, or classification/categorization. The tests that use this approach are: 1) the Processing Word Classes Subtest of the CELF; 2) the Likenesses and Differences Subtest of the DTLA; 3) the Similarities Subtest of the WISC-R; and 4) the Associations Subtest of The WORD Test.

Command Completion

Most of the so-called "basic concept" tests utilize the command completion approach to testing comprehension of words and word relationships. These tests are designed to standardized many of the informal observation procedures traditionally used by teachers and clinicians to see if children understand basic relational concepts. For example, the teacher might ask the child to: "Put the block *in* the can." If the child successfully follows the command, he or she is said to comprehend the preposition "in." The test stimuli may be pictures to which the child must point on command or tokens or objects the child must manipulate following specific commands.

The two tests that involve manipulation of objects are the Token Test for Children (DiSimoni, 1978) and the Vocabulary Comprehension Scale (VCS) (Bangs, 1975). The Token Test, designed originally for use with adult aphasics, has been revised for use with children (DiSimoni, 1978). The child manipulates tokens of different color, shape, and size in specific ways while following the directions of the examiner. In the VCS, the child is commanded to manipulate toys and objects in specific ways to demonstrate that he or she comprehends 85 words, including pronouns and relational terms denoting position, size, quality, and quantity.

The Boehm Test of Basic Concepts (Boehm, 1970) is the most popular of the tests that require a pointing response. The child marks or points to 50 picture sets, following commands that include words involving concepts of quantity, number, space, time, and combinations of these concepts. The concepts are particularly appropriate for children in kindergarten and first grade. An excellent profile form helps to summarize whole class problems and focus on the problems of an individual child.

Two subtests of the CELF, Processing Linguistic Concepts and Processing Relationships and Ambiguities, also are useful in assessing children's comprehension of words and word relationships. In the Processing Linguistic Concepts Subtest of the CELF, the child is given oral directions of various word lengths that are controlled for vocabulary. He or she then points to the appropriate picture in an array that is made up of pictures of lines of three colors. The emphasis is on linguistic concepts such as "all . . . except" and "neither . . . nor." The Processing Relationships and Ambiguities Subtest of the CELF emphasizes comparative, passive, spatial, temporal-sequential, familial, and analogous relationships as well as comprehension of idioms, metaphors, and proverbs. In this subtest, the examiner may produce a statement and then ask questions to which the child responds either yes or no. The Semantic Absurdities Subtest of The WORD Test tests the child's abilities to explain or correct sentences that are semantically absurd because of incorrectly used vocabulary words. Such procedures obviously emphasize more abstract knowledge than does pointing to pictures that represent single concrete words, like in the PPVT-R.

GLOBAL LANGUAGE TESTS

Global language tests, by definition, test most of the levels of language processing in both the production and comprehension modes. Such tests give an overall picture of a child's language problem. More specific tests or procedures can then be used to emphasize areas of deficiency that are revealed on the global test. The following discussion briefly presents these tests in three design areas: 1) screening tests; 2) informant-interview tests; and 3) direct administration tests. Three global language tests that are particularly appropriate for children are then compared and evaluated.

Screening Tests

Screening tests are designed to provide a very brief observation of a child's abilities and disabilities, usually for the purpose of singling out children who may have a problem and need further assessment. The Picture Articulation and Language Screening Test (PALST) (Rodgers, 1976) and the Riley Articulation and Language Test (RALT) (Riley, 1971) are designed to be administered in 2 to 5 minutes. The Fluharty Preschool Speech and Language Screening Test (Fluharty, 1978) is designed to be administered to 2- to 6-year-old children in about 6 minutes. The Stephens Oral Language Screening Test (SOLST) (Stephens, 1977) is also a relatively quick test, designed to be administered to children about 4-7 years old. The Communication Screen (Striffler and Willig, 1981) can also be administered in about 5 minutes to children 2–10 to 5–9 years old. The Merrill Language Screening Test (MLST) (Mumm et al., 1980) was designed to be administered to classroom groups, small groups, or to individual children in the first grade (CA64–85 months) in about 5 to 7 minutes. The Bankson (1977) Language Screening Test is considerably more extensive; however, it is too long (30 minutes) to be used as a practical screening test.

Semel and Wiig (1980a) authored an elementary level (grades K-5) screening and an advanced level (grades 5–12) screening test. Both tests contain processing and production items, which require about 15 minutes to administer. The substance of each test is appropriate for school-age populations, and the tests are well-standardized.

The Screening Test of Adolescent Language (STAL) (Prather et al., 1980) is another test that can be administered to older children and adolescents in about 7 minutes. The STAL includes 23 items, divided into four subtests: 1) Vocabulary; 2) Auditory Memory Span; 3) Language Processing; and 4) Proverb Explanation.

Informant-Interview Tests

Informant-interview tests are designed to be administered primarily to parents of children who are too young or impaired to be directly tested. The Verbal Language Development Scale (VLDS) (Mecham, 1971) is an extension of the communication portion of the Vineland Social Maturity Scale. The VLDS is administered to the child's mother or another reliable informant. Although the age range cited is from one month to 15 years, the test is most useful for providing rough language-age equivalents for children below 5 years of age. Bzoch and League's (1971) Receptive-Expressive Emergent Language Scale (REEL) is a similar test in that it is administered to a reliable informant. It consists of a series of questions focusing on expressive and receptive language acquisition from birth to 36 months. It yields a receptive quotient, an expressive quotient, and a composite or combined quotient. The REEL is especially useful in guiding the choice of questions in a parent case history interview. Because the age range is from 0–36 months, the test can often be administered to the parents of older handicapped preschool children, given that these children may be 2 to 3 years delayed. The Communicative Evaluation Chart (CEC) (Anderson et al., 1964) may also be administered to an informed adult. The CEC is divided into nine age levels, ranging from 3 months to 5 years. The CEC is useful for making a quick survey of the child's language functioning to determine if it is below normal limits. The Oliver: Parent Administered Communication Inventory by MacDonald (1978b) is also relevant in this area of tests.

Direct Administration Global Tests

There are a considerable number of global language tests that directly assess the language abilities of children and adolescents. These tests include the Hannah-Gardner Language Screening Test (Hannah and Gardner, 1974), the Houston Test for Language Development, Part II (Crabtree, 1963), the Utah Test of Language Development (Mecham et al., 1967), the Preschool Language Scale (Zimmerman et al., 1969), the Reynell Developmental Language Scale (Reynell, 1969), the Michigan Picture Language Inventory (Wolski, 1962), the Sequenced Inventory of Communication Development (Hedrick et al., 1976), the Test of Early Language Development (Hammill, 1980), and the Test of Adolescent Language (Hammill et al., 1980).

Comparison of Three Global Tests

King (1975) compared three of these global tests by administering each of them to eight 3- , 4- , and 5-year-old children. The tests evaluated were the Hannah-Gardner Language Screening Test, the Houston Test for Language Development, Part II, and the Utah Test of Language Development. A comparison of the common test items is presented in Table 5.

The mean language ages (in months) for the eight children on the Utah, Houston, and Hannah-Gardner tests were 53.50, 52.89, and 45.25, respectively, and within these means, a significant difference was found (p < 0.10). Application of a least significant difference procedure at the 0.10 level revealed that the means for the Utah and Houston Tests were not significantly different, but the means for these two tests were significantly different from the mean on the Hannah-Gardner. Thus, the Hannah-Gardner produced a significantly lower language age than the other two tests.

Because of the well-organized presentation of test items and the use of few extraneous stimulus materials beyond crayons and paper, the Utah proved to be the easiest of the three tests to administer. Response requirements are well-defined; hence, few subjective judgments are required of the examiner. The entire test may be scored during test presentation, and the language-age equivalent is easily com-

Table 5.   Comparison of the common test items on the Hannah-Gardner, Utah, and Houston tests

Hannah-Gardner	Utah	Houston
Copying geometric shapes	Copying geometric shapes	Imitating geometric shapes
Counting—receptive	Counting—receptive Graphic object counting	Counting—expressive Serial and object counting
Colors—receptive	Colors—receptive and expressive	Colors—expressive
Auditory memory— receptive and expressive Two sets of single syllable words and two commands	Auditory memory— expressive Digits and sentences	Auditory memory— expressive Repetition of one word (three syllables) to 14 words (15 syllables)
Prepositions—receptive		Prepositions—receptive
	Vocabulary—receptive and expressive Objects	Vocabulary—expressive Objects, action, and attributes
	Body parts—receptive	Body parts—receptive

puted following completion of the test. This test provides the examiner with the most complete language age in years and months. The Utah was, however, found to be the least effective in maintaining children's attention during administration. The Utah does not provide any interpretation of test results or a summary of the child's performance. This makes it difficult for the examiner to determine the areas in which further assessment or training should be concentrated.

The Houston was found to provide the most comprehensive review of the child's test performance and the greatest amount of information on relative strengths and weaknesses. The Houston also calls for the elicitation of a sample of the child's oral language. Although this provides valuable information, the examiner is required to score these sections following the test session. The response guidelines, however, are well-presented and provide for consistent scoring between children. The language age obtained from the raw score is expressed in yearly age levels.

The Hannah-Gardner was found to be the most effective of the three tests in maintaining attention. Test questions are adequately arranged, but more detailed response guidelines are needed to facilitate objective, consistent scoring. The stimulus materials require more extensive manipulation by the examiner than those included in the Utah and Houston. All responses are scored by the examiner following presentation of each stimulus item, and percentile scores are computed at the completion of the test.

CONCLUSION

As can be seen, there are an increasing number of standardized tests available with which the language specialist can examine the language skills of children and adolescents. More research that critically compares tests within language level and modality groups is desperately needed. Recent developments such as the work of MacDonald (1978a,b) and his colleagues for preschool children and that of Semel and Wiig (1980a,b) for school-age children and adolescents have facilitated the task of language assessment considerably. It is interesting to note that such major developments are closely tied to comprehensive intervention procedures. This reinforces our recognition that language assessment should not be separated from language intervention. Language assessment is an ongoing process that must be intimately interwoven with language intervention. Often, various nonstandardized and informal, methods, based on or linked to the standardized tests reviewed in this chapter, will facilitate the process of ongoing assessment.

To be knowledgeable about language assessment is a never-ending task as new tests and procedures are developed each year. As our technology increases with each passing year, we thus become better equipped to deal with the handicapped children and adolescents who require our assistance.

REFERENCES

Ammons, R.B., and Ammons, H.S. 1948. Full-Range Picture Vocabulary Test. Psychological Test Specialists, Missoula, MT.

Anderson, R., Miles, M., and Metheny, P. 1964. Communication Evaluation Chart. Golden Colorado Business Forms, Inc., Golden, CO.

Arndt, W.B. 1977. A psychometric evaluation of the Northwestern Syntax Screening Test. J. Speech Hear. Disord. 42:316–319.

Baker, H., and Leland, B. 1967. Detroit Tests of Learning Aptitude. Test Division of Bobbs-Merrill, Indianapolis.

Bangs, T.E. 1975. Vocabulary Comprehension Scale. Learning Concepts, Austin, TX.

Bankson, N. 1977. The Bankson Language Screening Test. University Park Press, Baltimore.

Barrie-Blackley, S., Musselwhite, C.R., and Rogister, S.H. 1978. Clinical Oral Language Sampling. Interstate Printers, Danville, IL.

Bartel, N.R., Bryen, D., and Keehn, S. 1971. Language comprehension in the moderately retarded child. Except. Child. 39:375–382.

Berko, J. 1958. The child's learning of English morphology. Word 14:150–177.

Berry, M.F., and Talbot, R. 1966. Exploratory Test of Grammar. Berry Publications, Rockford, IL.

Bloom, L., Hood, L., and Lightbown, P. 1974. Imitation in language development: If, when, and why? Cog. Psychol. 6:380–420.

Boehm, A.E. 1970. Boehm Test of Basic Concepts. Psychological Corp. New York.

Brown, R. 1973. A First Language: The Early Stages. Harvard University Press, Cambridge.

Byrne, M.C. 1977. A clinician looks at the Northwestern Syntax Screening Test. J. Speech Hear. Disord. 42:320–322.

Bzoch, K.R., and League, R. 1971. Receptive-Expressive Emergent Language Scale. Tree and Life Press, Gainesville, FL.

Carroll, J.B. 1964. Language and Thought. Prentice-Hall, Inc., Englewood Cliffs, NJ.

Carrow, E. 1973. Test of Auditory Comprehension of Language. Learning Concepts, Austin, TX.

Carrow, E. 1974. Carrow Elicited Language Inventory. Learning Concepts, Austin, TX.

Crabtree, M. 1963. The Houston Test for Language Development. The Houston Test Publishers, Houston.

Danwitz, M.W. 1981. Formal versus informal assessment: Fragmentation versus holism. Top. Lang. Disord. 1:95–106.

Darley, F. 1979. Evaluation of Appraisal Techniques in Speech and Language Pathology. Addison-Wesley Publishing Co., Menlo Park, CA.

Davis, J.M. 1977. Reliability of hearing impaired children's responses to oral and total presentations of the Test of Auditory Comprehension of Language. J. Speech Hear. Disord. 42:520–527.

Dever, R.B. 1968. A comparison of the results of a revised version of Berko's text of morphology with the free speech and mentally retarded children. Unpublished doctoral dissertation, University of Wisconsin, Madison.

Dever, R.B., and Gardner, W.I. 1967. Performance of normal and retarded boys on Berko's test of morphology. Lang. Speech, 13:162–181.

DiSimoni, F. 1978. Token Test for Children. Teaching Resources, Hingham, MA.

Dunn, L.M., and Dunn, L.M. 1981. Peabody Picture Vocabulary Test-Revised. American Guidance Service, Circle Pines, MN.

Emery, M.L. 1975. A comparison of three language comprehension tests. Unpublished master's thesis, Kansas State University, Manhattan.

Ervin, S.M. 1964. Imitation and structural changes in children's language. In: E.H. Lenneberg (ed.), New Directions in the Study of Language. MIT Press, Cambridge.

Fluharty, N.B. 1978. Fluharty Preschool Speech and Language Screening Test. Teaching Resource Corp., Boston.

Foster, C.R., Giddan, J.J., and Stark, J. 1972. Assessment of Children's Language Comprehension. Consulting Psychologist Press, Palo Alto, CA.

Fraser, C., Bellugi, U., and Brown, R. 1963. Control of grammar in imitation, comprehension, and production. J. Verb. Learn. Verb. Behav. 2:121–135.

Gardner, M.F. 1979. Expressive One-Word Picture Vocabulary Test. Academic Therapy Publication, Novato, CA.

Goldsworthy, C. 1982. Multilevel Informal Language Inventory. Charles E. Merrill, Columbus, OH.

Hammill, D.D. 1980. Test of Early Language Development. Slosson Educational Publications Inc., East Aurora, New York.

Hammill, D.D., Brown, V.L., Larsen, C.S., and Wiedorholt, J.L. 1980. Test of Adolescent Language. Slosson Educational Publications, East Aurora, NY.

Hannah, C., and Gardner, D. 1974. Hannah and Gardner Language Screening Test. Joyce Publications, Northridge, CA.

Hedrick, D., Prather, E., and Tobin, A. 1976. Sequenced Inventory of Communication Development. University of Washington Press, Seattle.

Hood, L., and Lightbown, P. 1978. What children do when asked to "Say what I say": Does elicited imitation measure linguistic knowledge? All. Health Behav. Sci. 1:195–219.

Horstmeier, D.S., and MacDonald, J.D. 1978a. Environmental Prelanguage Battery. Charles E. Merrill, Columbus, OH.

Horstmeier, D.S., and MacDonald, J.D. 1978b. Ready, Set, Go: Talk to Me. Charles E. Merrill, Columbus, OH.

Hubbell, R.D. 1981. Children's language disorders: An integrated approach. Prentice-Hall, Inc., Englewood Cliffs, NJ.

Johnson, W., Darley, F.L., and Spriestersbach, D.C. 1963. Diagnostic Methods in Speech Pathology. Interstate Printers, Danville, IL.

Jorgensen, C., Barrett, M., Huisingh, R., and Zachman, L. 1981. The Word Test. Linguasystems, Inc. Moline, IL.

King, M. 1975. Comparison of three global language tests. Unpublished master's thesis, Kansas State University, Manhattan.

Kirk, S.A., McCarthy, J.J., and Kirk, W.D. 1968. Illinois Test of Psycholinguistic Ability: Revised Edition. University of Illinois Press, Urbana.

Klee, T.M., and Ratusnik, C.M. 1980. Northwestern Syntax Screening Test: A short form. J. Speech Hear. Disord. 45:200–208.

Kretschmer, R.R., and Kretschmer, L.W. 1978. Language Development and Intervention in the Hearing Impaired. University Park Press, Baltimore.

Kuczaj, S., and Maratsos, M. 1975. What children can say before they will. Merrill-Palmer Q. 21:89–112.

Larson, G.W., and Summers, P.A. 1976. Response patterns of preschool-age children to the Northwestern Syntax Screening Test. J. Speech Hear. Disord. 41:486–497.

Lee, L. 1966. Developmental sentence types: A method for comparing normal and deviant syntactic development. J. Speech Hear. Disord. 31:311–320.

Lee, L.L. 1971. Northwestern Syntax Screening Test. Northwestern University Press, Evanston, IL.

Lee, L.L. 1974. Developmental Sentence Analysis. Northwestern University Press, Evanston, IL.

Lee, L.L. 1977. Reply to Arndt and Byrne. J. Speech Hear. Disord. 42:323–327.

Lee, L., and Canter, S. 1971. Developmental sentence scoring: A clinical procedure for estimating syntactic development in children's spontaneous speech. J. Speech Hear. Disord. 36:315–340.

Lenneberg, E. 1967. Biological Foundation and Language. John Wiley & Sons, New York.

Leonard, L.B., Prutting, C.A., Perozzi, J.A., and Berkley, R.K. 1978. Nonstandardized approaches to the assessment of language behaviors. Am. Speech Hear. Assoc. 20:371–379.

Longhurst, T.M. (ed.). 1974. Linguistic Analysis of Children's Speech. Arno Press, New York.

Longhurst, T.M. 1979. Assessment of Children's Language Comprehension (ACLC). In F. Darley (ed.). Evaluation of Appraisal Techniques in Speech and Language Pathology. Addison-Wesley Publishers, Menlo Park, CA.

MacDonald, J.D. 1978a. Environmental Language Inventory. Charles E. Merrill, Columbus, OH.

MacDonald, J.D. 1978b. Oliver: Parent-Administered Communication Inventory. Charles E. Merrill, Columbus, OH.

Marquardt, T.P., and Saxman, J.H. 1972. Language comprehension and auditory discrimination in articulation deficient kindergarten children. J. Speech Hear. Res. 15:382–389.

McCarthy, D. 1970. McCarthy Scales of Children's Abilities. Psychological Corp., New York.

McDade, H.L., Simpson, M.A. and Lamb, D.E. 1982. The use of elicited imitation as a measure of expressive grammar: A question of validity. J. Speech Hear. Disord. 47:19–24.

McNeill, D. 1966. Developmental psycholinguistics. In: F. Smith & G. Miller (eds.), The Genesis of Language. MIT Press, Cambridge, MA.

McNeill, D. 1970. The Acquisiton of Language: The Study of Developmental Psycholinguistics. Harper & Row, New York.

Mecham, M.J. 1971. Verbal language development scale. American Guidance Service, Circle Pines, MN.

Mecham, M., Jex, J., and Jones, J. 1967. The Utah Test of Language Development. Communication Research Associates, Ogden, UT.

Menyuk, P. 1964. Syntactic rules used by children from preschool through first grade. Child Dev. 35:533–546.

Menyuk, P. 1969. Sentences Children Use. MIT Press, Cambridge.

Miller, J.F. 1978. Assessing children's language behavior. In: R.L. Schiefelbusch (ed.), Bases of Language Intervention. University Park Press, Baltimore.

Miller, J.F. 1981. Assessing Language Production in Children. University Park Press, Baltimore.

Miller, J.F., and Chapman, R.S. 1981. The relationship between age and MLU-M. J. Speech Hear. Res. 29:154–161.

Miller, J.F., and Yoder, D. 1975. The Miller-Yoder Test of Grammatical Comprehension: Experimental Edition. University of Wisconsin, Madison, WI.

Muma, J.R. 1978. Language handbook: Concepts, assessment, and intervention. Prentice-Hall, Inc., Englewood Cliffs, NJ.

Mumm, M., Secord, W., and Dykstra, K. 1980. Merrill Language Screening Test. Charles E. Merrill, Columbus, OH.

Newcombe, F., and Marshall, J.C. 1967. Immediate recall of sentences by subjects with unilateral cerebral lesions. Neuropsychologia 5:329–334.

Newcomer, P.L., and Hammill, D.D. 1977. The Test of Language Development. Empiric Press, Austin, TX.

Prather, E.M., Breecher, S.V.A., Stafford, M.L., and Wallace, E.M. 1980. Screening Test of Adolescent Language. University of Washington Press, Seattle, WA.

Prutting, C. 1979. Process. J. Speech Hear. Disord. 44:3–30.

Prutting, C.A., Gallagher, T.M., and Mulac, A. 1975. The expressive portion of the NSST compared to a spontaneous language sample. J. Speech Hear. Disord. 40:40–48.

Ratusnik, D.L., and Koenigsknecht, R.A. 1975. Internal consistency of the Northwestern Syntax Screening Test. J. Speech Hear. Disord. 40:59–68.

Reynell, J. 1969. Reynell Developmental Language Scales. N.F.E.R. Publishing Co., Ltd., Windsor, England.

Riley, G. 1971. The Riley Articulation and Language Test. Western Psychological Services, Los Angeles.

Rodgers, W. 1976. Picture Articulation and Language Screening Test. Word Making Productions, Salt Lake City, UT.

Ruder, K., Smith, M.D., and Hermann, P. 1974. Effect of verbal imitation and comprehension on verbal production. In: L. McReynolds (ed.), Developing Systematic Procedures for Training Children's Language (ASHA Monograph 18). American Speech-Language-Hearing Association, DC.

Semel, E.M., and Wiig, E.H. 1980a. Clinical Evaluation of Language Functions. Charles E. Merrill, Columbus, OH.

Semel, E., and Wiig, E. 1980b. Language Assessment and Intervention for the Learning Disabled. Charles E. Merrill, Columbus, OH.

Siegel, G. 1975. The use of language tests. Lang. Speech Hear. Serv. Schools. 4:211–217.

Sinclair, S., Khan, L., and Saxman, J. 1977. Do differing test conditions predict equivalent language ages? Paper presented at Boston University Conference on Language Development, Sept. 5, 1982, Boston.

Slobin, D., and Welsh, C. 1971. Elicited imitation as a research tool in developmental psycholinguistics. In: C. Lavatelli (ed.) Language Training in Early Childhood Education. University of Illinois Press, Urbana.

Snow, C. 1981. The uses of imitation. J. Child Lang. 8:205–213.

Stephens, M.I. 1977. The Stephens Oral Language Screening Test. Interim Publishers, Peninsula, OH.

Striffler, N., and Willig, S. 1981. The Communication Screen. Communication Skill Builders, Tucson, AZ.

Swisher, L., and Aten, J. 1981. Assessing comprehension of spoken language: A multifaceted task. Top. Lang. Disord. 1:75–85.

Templin, M. 1957. Certain Language Skills in Children: Their Development and Interrelationships. University of Minnesota Press, Minneapolis.

Tyack, D., and Gottsleben, R. 1974. Language Sampling, Analysis and Training. Consulting Psychologists Press, Palo Alto, CA.

Wechsler, D. 1974. Wechsler Intelligence Scale for Children—Revised. Psychological Corp., New York.

Weiner, P.S. 1972. The perceptual level functioning of dysphasic children: A following study. J. Speech Hear. Res. 15:423–438.

Werner, E.O., and Kresheck, J.D. 1978. Structured Photographic Language Test. Janelle Publications, Sandwich, IL.

Wiig, E.H., and Reach, M.A. 1975. Immediate recall of semantically varied "sentences" by learning disabled adolescents. Percept. Mot. Skills 40:119–125.

Wolski, W. 1962. Michigan Picture Language Inventory. University of Michigan Speech Clinic, Ann Arbor, MI.

Zachman, L., Huisingh, R., Jorgensen, C., and Barrett, M. 1977. Oral Language Sentence Imitation Diagnostic Inventory. Linguisystems, Inc., Moline, IL.

Zimmerman, I., Steiner, V., and Evatt, R. 1969. Preschool Language Scale. Charles E. Merrill, Columbus, OH.

chapter

3

Clinical Assessment

New Perspectives

John R. Muma

Speech and Hearing Sciences
Texas Tech University
Lubbock, Texas

contents

Clinical assessment, particularly language assessment, is in a period of major change. This change reflects an important maturational phase in the various clinical fields, i.e., speech pathology, special education, learning disabilities, mental retardation, autism, and deaf education. It is basically a shift from authoritarianism and absolutistic thinking to relativism (Kagan, 1967). For example, clinical disorders had been identified and treated according to diagnostic categories and labels from an authority. However, according to the White Conference on Classification and Labeling (Hobbs, 1974 a,b; Mercer, 1972), absolutistic orientations and authoritarianism are not recommended. Some clinical diagnostic categories and labels are detrimental to appropriate clinical services. Ample testimony to this fact can be seen in the numerous class action legal suits across the country, especially in mental retardation.

The clinical fields are currently going through a new maturational phase that parallels that of psychology about 2 decades ago (Kagan, 1967). Specifically, clinical behavior is no longer viewed in terms of products of underlying systems and processes, nor is behavior segmented and isolated into so-called simple units. The trend in the 1980s is to regard clinical behavior in terms of systems and processes in order to maintain its contextual integrity and to identify individual differences. This shift is evidenced most clearly and strongly in the replacement of descriptive clinical assessment procedures for traditional psychometric normative assessment procedures.

SHIFT FROM NORMATIVE TO DESCRIPTIVE PROCEDURES

The era of normative testing in clinical assessment is waning. Psychometric norms lack power and appropriateness in clinical assessment. They lack power because they do not deal adequately with the seven basic issues of clinical assessment (Muma and Muma, 1979; Muma, 1981; Muma, 1983; Muma, et al., 1982). These issues are: 1) the clinical complaint; 2) problem versus no problem; 3) individual differences; 4) the nature of the problem; 5) the prognosis; 6) intervention implications; and 7) accountability.

Descriptive assessment procedures are more powerful in dealing with these basic issues than psychometric normative procedures. Psychometric normative procedures are weak in dealing with appropriateness because they are *a priori* in nature and product-oriented, whereas descriptive procedures preserve the basic principles of behavior: relativity, conditionality, complexity, dynamism, individual differences, and ecological validity. Ironically, psychometric norms obscure these basic principles. Accordingly, traditional clinical assessment forces individuals to conform to a group vis-à-vis test performance. The result is an assessment process claimed to be "diagnostic" because it follows a classification and labeling process.

At least a decade ago, psychologists shifted away from studying products, status variables (with their attendent norms), and level of performance on intelligence or achievement tests with their respective norms (Kagan, 1967). Interest shifted to alternative cognitive styles that contribute to level of performance (Holtzman and Gardner, 1960; Kagan et al., 1963; Kagan, 1966; Kagan and Kogan, 1970). According to Hess and Shipman (1965), processes are more important than products. Thus, psychologists became more interested in *how* a person performed rather than *what* he or she did (Bowerman, 1974; Cromer, 1974). As for intelligence testing, it was recognized that intelligence and achievement tests merely tap summative products of underlying cognitive, indeed, even social and cultural systems (Cattell, 1963; Guilford, 1967; Wechsler, 1975). Moreover, some important cognitive capacities are not tapped by such tests. Psychologists, especially those concerned with the design and utilization of intelligence and achievement tests, have shifted away from the use of normative tests. They are now attempting to assess various kinds of cognitive style.

NORMATIVE QUANTIFICATIONS IN CLINICAL ASSESSMENTS

The applied fields, on the other hand, have continued to place an inordinate reliance on psychometric norms in clinical assessment. This reliance is clearly evidenced in attempts to deal with accountability. Unfortunately, accountability from a quantification point of view is both premature and misguided in the behavioral sciences (Siegel, 1975). It is premature and misguided mainly because there is no such thing as a definitive test in the behavioral sciences. Behavior is relative, conditional, complex, and dynamic rather than isolatable, categorical, simplistic, and static. In clinical assessment, normative quantification procedures merely categorize behavior. The more important issue of defining the nature of a problem in terms of underlying processes is not broached. One must not be duped into thinking that *data* necessarily constitute *evidence*. Nevertheless, traditional accountability rests on the premise that data always constitute evidence.

Cazden (1972) and three of her former students, Bissell (1970), Moore (1971), and Bartlett (1972) showed that data do not necessarily constitute evidence. They reviewed several preschool language intervention programs, along with measures such as the Illinois Test of Psycholinguistic Abilities (Kirk et al., 1968), Peabody Picture Vocabulary Test (Dunn, 1959), and various intelligence or achievement tests. They observed that those programs that made the most significant gains

were most operational. Apparently, product-oriented assessment procedures measure the operational quality of programs rather than actual
gains in the participating children. This is an interesting paradox. On
the one hand, significant gains are obtained but the gains have no lasting
effects in developing cognitive-linguistic skills in children. On the other
hand, the significant gains apparently index the operational quality of
the program.

CLINICAL ASSESSMENT AND CLINICAL ACCOUNTABILITY

Inasmuch as the applied fields are being pressed for evidence on accountability, it is imperative that relevant assessment issues are fully
understood. It is necessary that obtained data be relevant to the seven
basic issues of assessment. Otherwise, obtained data may be nothing
more than a *numbers game*. To continue the analogy, data must be
relevant to the seven basic issues of clinical assessment in order to
play the *clinical evidence game*. Unfortunately, much of what is currently being done under the guise of accountability in the form of individualized educational programming (IEP) is nothing more than a
numbers game.

Professionals in the applied fields must be more adequately trained
in the use of descriptive assessment procedures so that the assessment
process can more adequately deal with the evidence game. Inasmuch
as most practicing clinicians are not trained in descriptive procedures,
it may be wise to deal with accountability in the same way as two other
related professions—medicine and clinical psychology. In these fields,
accountability is dealt with procedurally by peer review. That is, a
medical doctor or clinical psychologist is accountable to the public to
the extent that he or she is accountable to peers. Doctors and psychologists need only show what procedure they undertook in dealing
with a client. If their peers concur that the procedures were appropriate, they have established necessary accountability. This approach
to accountability is much better than the numbers game approach simply because it allows for individual differences not only in the client
but in the actual procedures employed and, more importantly, provides
for a systems and processes orientation. The peer review approach to
accountability is based upon three premises: 1) acceptable or typical
disposition of cases; 2) individualized cases and circumstances; and 3)
a lack of definitive tests and measures. Medicine and clinical psychology are as much art as science. The peer review is both appropriate
and needed.

The field of mental retardation presents a very interesting and
unfortunate circumstance. On the one hand, mental retardation is part
of psychology. Therefore, the field of mental retardation would seem

to be on the forefront of the shift away from normative to descriptive procedures. On the other hand, mental retardation is dominated by a medical model. For example, medical doctors must direct most programs for the retarded. The medical model is one that has historically operated from a taxonomy; this influence was especially evidenced in the taxonomic and psychometric orientations of the *American Association on Mental Retardation*, most notably in the latest definition of mental retardation (Grossman et al., 1973) and in the poorly conceived AAMD Adaptive Behavior Scale (Nihira, et al., 1974). Grossman et al. virtually ignored the available psychological literature in revising the definition of mental retardation. The current definition promotes and perpetuates the psychometric concept of intelligence, which is woefully outdated and inappropriate. Other more substantial and appropriate models are available (Garrison, 1966). There was a gesture to provide for adaptiveness in the definition. However, the essential issue of adaptiveness was operationally distorted by the AAMD Adaptive Behavior Scale. Adaptiveness is distorted because behavior is categorized, quantified, and removed from context. Consequently, two of the essential issues of adaptivensss—(relativity and conditionality) were undermined. These issues have been considered elsewhere (Baumeister and Muma, 1975; Muma and Baumeister, 1975). The point here is that the field of mental retardation has not evidenced the shift from a product or taxonomic orientation to a systems and processes orientation. The assessment process by virtue of the use of intelligence tests, development profiles and the *AAMD Adaptive Behavior Scale* is nothing more than a numbers game rather than an evidence game in clinical assessment.

Even though the clinical fields in America have a strong commitment and reliance on normative assessment, such commitment and reliance are inappropriate and open to serious question. This argument is in line with the reasons for the shift in psychology away from a normative orientation to a relativistic orientation (Kagan, 1967). The next section deals with two of the seven essential functions of clinical assessment: 1) the resolution of the problem/no problem issue; and 2) the subsequent characterization of the nature of the problem. The argument developed here promotes the view that descriptive procedures are more powerful and appropriate than psychometric normative procedures. Then, some representative descriptive procedures for cognitive, linguistic, and communicative systems are presented.

THE PROBLEM/NO PROBLEM ISSUE

Clinical assessment has two essential functions: 1) establishing the existence or nonexistence of a problem (the problem/no problem issue);

and 2) determining the nature of an existing problem. Most clinical assessments deal with the problem/no problem issue. And, it is typically done from a psychometric normative (quantitative or taxonomic) perspective.

Inasmuch as psychometric norms are categorical or summative (quantification), they are most useful in resolving the problem/no problem issue. If behavior is aberrant, a problem exists. On the other hand, if behavior is within normative limits, no problem exists. Unless repeated samples of behavior are taken and compared to a norm (a practice that virtually never happens in the course of a typical clinical assessment), the one-sample, normative comparison is vulnerable to a serious statistical problem involving the standard error of measurement. The standard error of measurement is particularly sensitive to extreme scores and large variances, both of which characterize clinical groups. For example, Baumeister (1976) stated that the most outstanding characteristic of the mentally retarded population is heterogeneity. Thus, the use of psychometric norms in clinical assessment is open to serious questions from a statistical perspective. Clinical groups are by definition extreme groups (although only extreme groups for some variables) and they are characteristically heterogeneous.

Given the standard error of measurement problem, there is some question whether or not a single-sample, normative assessment has sufficient power to resolve the problem/no problem issue. Statistically, a clinician is faced with what is known as Type I and Type II errors, both of which occur especially when dealing with large variances and extreme scores, such as clinical scores. A Type I error occurs when it is concluded that something (a problem) exists when in fact it does not exist. For example, a child might obtain an aberrant score and a clinician would conclude he has a problem. However, the aberrant performance may be attributable to a variety of extraneous variables rather than what the test presumably measures. He may not actually have a problem even though his performance was aberrant. Indeed, repeated testing may reveal that the aberrant performance was atypical of his averaged performance over several tests. A Type II error occurs when we conclude that something (a problem) does not exist when in fact it does exist (McNemar, 1962). For example, if a child obtains a score within normal limits, a clinician may conclude that he has normal capacities for the domains of the test. However, the child may actually have a problem and the test is not identifying the problem. Repeated testing may reveal the problem. In short, psychometric normative measures lack power in resolving the problem/no problem issue on a single performance.

Although there are serious statistical questions about psychometric normative clinical assessment, there are other limitations as well.

Psychometric norms result in a categorized assessment on three counts: 1) each norm is a category itself, whereby underlying processes are summarized; 2) the yes/no resolution of a problem is a categorizing process whereby more substantial issues about individual differences are lost; and 3) an individual's performance is viewed as exclusively intrinsic to him or her, thereby reducing the assessment process to intrapersonal variables while ignoring interpersonal variables. These are serious limitations in clinical assessment. In regard to the categorized nature of norms, clinicians are prone to conclude that relevant underlying systems and processes are aberrant when a product is aberrant. This is an unwarranted conclusion, especially in cognition and language because there is no direct one-to-one relationship between products and underlying systems and processes (Bowerman, 1974; Bloom and Lahey, 1978; Bates, et al. 1979). For example, three individuals can obtain the same scores on the ITPA for three very different reasons. The yes/no resolution of a problem results in only a hit-or-miss proposition, with virtually no discernible intervention implications. Indeed, most clinicians believe that the intervention implications are to provide activities in the area that was aberrant. This, unfortunately, is only a similar argument to the original product-oriented, hit-or-miss assessment process. It is a serious mistake in clinical assessment to reduce the process down to intrapersonal variables vis-á-vis test performance. Both intra- and interpersonal variables influence behavior (Cazden, 1967; Bruner, 1981). To arbitrarily reduce the assessment process to intrapersonal variables, especially in terms of products, is to invite serious distortion and misrepresentation. In summary, psychometric normative procedures are not very powerful in clinical assessment.

The field of psychology, except for mental retardation, has shifted away from the use of psychometric normative measures because of their categorical nature. Psycholinguists are now more concerned about relativity, conditionality, complexity (Kagan, 1967; Deese, 1969; Bowerman, 1974; Bloom and Lahey, 1978), and dynamism (Jenkins, 1974). They are more interested in patterns of behavior as evidence of underlying systems and processes than products. And consequently, they are more concerned about behavior in natural contexts (Bronfenbrenner, 1979; Brooks and Baumeister, 1977; Proshansky, 1976) than test performance.

A clinical complaint is the original statement of a problem by the person who refers an individual for clinical assessment. This complaint, with follow-up interviewing and observation, offers much more promise in resolving the problem/no problem issue than psychometric normative procedures. The complaint is not only specific to an individual but may extend beyond an individual's performance to the "eye of the complaintant" or other interpersonal or environmental variables. For example, a problem may in fact exist but it may not be so much in the individual's behavior as in the values of a complaintant—an anxious mother who may be too critical, a teacher who thinks that nonstandard dialects should be "corrected," a school psychologist who relies on level of performance measures to classify children retarded or learning disabled, or a learning disabilities specialist who regards such things as digit memory span, PPVT scores, ITPA scores, and mean length of utterances as definitive measures of verbal capacities and skills.

With all of the limitations of normative assessment in the clinical fields, it is surprising that so much reliance is placed on them in America, especially when considering that better alternatives are available. In regard to the problem/no problem issue, the clinical complaint with follow-up interviewing and observation constitutes a more significant assessment approach simply because it is more relevant to the particular needs of a particular individual and extends beyond an individual. Normative procedures could be viewed from two perspectives: 1) as screening procedures rather than assessment procedures, per se; and 2) as supportive procedures to further substantiate other information in what McCaffrey (1969) called a "convergent assessment strategy." A convergent assessment strategy is one in which several different measures sharing a common domain are used to partial out various aspects of a problem. In any event, normative procedures should be subordinate to more powerful and directly relevant clinical assessment procedures, namely descriptive procedures.

Nature of a Problem: A Descriptive Perspective

The resolution of the problem/no problem issue is only an initial step in a much more complex enterprise. The more substantial issue in clinical assessment is an account of the nature of a problem. This is the second essential function of clinical assessment. The nature of the problem is best handled through descriptive procedures concerning an individual's knowledge and command of various underlying intra- and interpersonal systems and processes.

The Value of Descriptive Procedures

Descriptive procedures are more informative because they deal with: 1) systems and processes rather than categories; 2) intra- and interpersonal systems rather than just intra-personal systems; and 3) individual differences rather than group similarities. The most crucial distinction between normative and descriptive clinical endeavors is that the latter provides alternatives that are directly relevant to individual needs while the former does not. In a systems and processes approach, an attempt is made to describe the nature of various cognitive-linguistic-communicative systems available to an individual rather than simply counting or quantifying various products. Moreover, co-existing systems and processes are taken into account as evidence of contextual influences, and in intervention, such systems offer a means for exploiting alternatives.

Coexisting systems and processes are important because cognitive-linguistic-communicative systems and processes are naturally inextricably related. When psycholinguists attempt to isolate one domain from another in assessment or intervention, they are not only vulnerable to distortion and misrepresentation but also lose the best opportunities to get to the heart of the problem.

Cognitive systems and operations can be considered separately from linguistic and communicative systems and operations, but the converse is not true. Linguistic systems and processes must be considered in the context of underlying cognitive systems and processes. For example, according to Chomsky (1968), language is but one aspect of cognition. Bloom (1970, 1973) showed that it is necessary to consider the referents that are being coded in language in order to appreciate what the code is about. Olson (1970) demonstrated that a linguistic code is determined to a great extent by available referents. Brown (1973) argued that labelling or coding is a function of the particular needs for being explicit. Schlesinger (1971 a,b) pointed out that communicative intent is a significant determiner of verbal behavior. And of course, we talk about what we know; obviously, concept development and other aspects of cognition underlie verbal behavior (Nelson, 1973, 1974; Wells, 1974; Bloom and Lahey, 1978; Bates, et.al. 1979; Bruner, 1981).

Just as it is necessary to consider cognitive systems and processes in assessing linguistic behavior (semantic, syntactic, and phonological systems), it is also necessary to consider cognitive and linguistic systems and processes in assessing communicative behavior (encoder/decoder functions, code matrix, role-taking, deixis, communication game, alternative referents, alternative codes, etc.). The hierarchical relationship between cognition, grammar, and communication is as follows:

COGNITION → LANGUAGE → COMMUNICATION

A common error in clinical assessment is to ignore the hierarchical relationship between cognition, grammar, and communication. Typically, the various domains are isolated. Syntax is separated from semantics, resulting in the usual assessment of verbal forms in terms of sentence types, parts of speech, mean length of utterance, or vocabulary size. Phonology is usually separated from syntax. Indeed, clinicians have artificially dichotomized phonology and semantics-syntax in the respective "diagnostic" categories of articulation disorders and language disorders. Phonology or speech articulation and discrimination were considered independent of language, e.g., "an articulation problem not a language problem." For a long time, clinical fields regarded language as vocabulary and sentence-building, essentially equating syntax with language. Some attempt was made to regard vocabulary as somehow related to semantics, but cognition was mysteriously ignored. However, the literature in the 1970s showed that the more the various domains are isolated one from another, the more likely a clinician is to misunderstand and misrepresent an individual's verbal difficulties. Bowerman (1976) held that the distinction between cognition and semantics is more apparent than real and that semantics and syntax are inextricably related.

Assessment of Language Modalities

Another major clinical error is the inordinate emphasis on language modality differences when commonalities are much more substantial and important. The clinical fields have emphasized modality differences, i.e., expressive language, receptive language, auditory language, visual language, etc. This is unfortunate, because it has swayed the clinical assessment process toward modality differences. Modality differences pertain to the surface structure of language. Priority should be not on modality differences but on modality commonalities. All modalities share essentially the same underlying cognitive-linguistic systems and processes. For example, the cognitive-linguistic systems and processes for making a sentence negative are the same for all modalities. This is true for virtually the whole grammatical system, except for some surface structure variations. There are relatively minor differences between modalities: phoneme/grapheme correspondences, segmentation devices, trafficking rules, etc.

The ITPA (Kirk et al., 1968) deals with some intermodality differences, but more substantial psycholinguistic abilities are not broached. Inasmuch as the ITPA does not deal with specific cognitive-linguistic systems and processes but merely quantifies modality performance, it should be regarded as a performance measure rather than an abilities measure. It seems that the ITPA is misnamed. The Peabody Picture Vocabulary Test (PPVT, Dunn, 1959), for example, is a test of highly questionable value. In addition to its limitations by virtue of being a normative test, the PPVT is not a test of vocabulary simply because it misses the essential issue of word or lexical knowledge, i.e., referential, intentional, and combinatorial meanings. Specifically, a single word has many referents, and one referent has many words. The PPVT simply does not deal with this dynamic issue. It may be nothing more than a numbers game. Yet, it is one of the most widely used clinical assessment instruments.

There are several aspects of speech articulation that not only exemplify a segmentation error in clinical assessment but define the importance of contextual influences. Clinicians are prone to not only separate speech from "language" (even though they are inextricably related), but they also isolate phonemes, even though there is a substantial literature that shows the importance of the phonetic contexts. The coarticulation literature is replete with evidence that phonetic contexts are primary determinants of speech sound production and perception. Moreover, clinicians have imposed adult distinctive feature systems on child speech in clinical assessment (McReynolds and Houston, 1971; McReynolds and Sherman, 1972). However, the literature in child phonology does not support adult feature systems. Indeed, the feature systems in child speech are quite different from those in adult speech (Renfrew, 1966; Ladefoged, 1972; Daniloff and Hammarberg, 1973; Ingram, 1973, 1974, 1976; Oller, 1973; Vennemann and Ladefoged, 1973; Daniloff and Hammarberg, 1973; Oller and Kelly, 1974; Panagos, 1974; Compton, 1975).

Locke's (1980) review of the various published speech discrimination tests showed that very little, if any, provision had been made for discriminations attendant to child variations. In the Wepman (1958) test for example, only two of 40 discriminations were relevant to child phonology. Thus, the current status of clinical work in speech articulation might be summarized as follows: 1) phonemes are usually treated as phonetic entities rather than products of phonetic contexts; 2) "error patterns" are viewed in terms of adult categories (omissions, substitutions, and distortions) rather than child variations; 3) phonetic features and variations, such as blunting, fronting, voicing, cluster reduction, reduplication, and weak syllable deletion in child phonology are not recognized, whereas adult features are used to describe child phonology; and 4) available speech sound discrimination tests do not provide for discriminations attendant to child phonology. Moreover, phonological influences apparently extend beyond the phonological domain into syllabic structure, stress, intonation, memory processing, and syntactic structure. For instance, Menyuk (1968) showed that some articulation errors are intraceable to inflection rules.

The traditional phoneme-oriented approach to articulation disorders has several major limitations. It exemplifies taxonomic, product-oriented, normative clinical assessment procedures in cognition and language. The nature of a problem issue can best be handled by descriptive procedures, because they provide a means of identifying an individual's abilities by accounting for his systems and processes as they function naturally.

The goal of descriptive procedures is to obtain a pattern of behavior on a given process so that legitimate inferences can be made about the underlying systems. The pronominal system offers a good illustration that descriptive evidence is both more powerful and relevant than taxonomic psychometric normative procedures in clinical assessment. The normative approach would sample behavior to ascertain which and how many pronouns an individual presumably has. These data are then compared to a developmental norm, and a conclusion is drawn that the individual is normal (no problem) or not normal (problem) for this assessment category.

Descriptive procedures, on the other hand, are quite different. An attempt is made to define the nature of a person's pronominal system. This is done not only by identifying the various pronominal forms used but also the linguistic and referential conditions of their use. Linguistically, a descriptive procedure maps out patterns of co-occurring structures. This provides evidence of the linguistic contexts of pronominal usage for an individual. For example, one individual may use the pronoun "it" for noun phrases in the subject of unmodified, transitive sentences, whereas another individual may use "it" as a generalized or glossed noun phrase filler for all subject noun phrases. (A variety of other co-occurrences may obtain for other individuals.) Referentially, the concept of anaphoric reference is very important to the pronominal system and is its main function. Anaphoric reference is the pronominal function of maintaining a previous referent without having to restate explicitly the referent each time. The following two sentences show anaphoric use of *he, her,* and *she.* "The boy saw a pretty girl. *He* asked *her* for a date but unfortunately *she* already had plans." It is one thing to keep anaphoric reference maintained for one or two repeated referents, but it is more difficult to deal with several repeated references to the same referent or intervening competitive referents. Descriptive evidence about the nature (linguistic systems, co-occurring systems, and referential command) of the pronominal system is much more informative than to merely state an individual is within or outside of a norm. Moreover, descriptive evidence provides directly relevant intervention alternatives—exploitation of various linguistic and referential contexts.

MAP: MUMA ASSESSMENT PROGRAM

Muma and Muma (1979) developed a comprehensive clinical assessment program based upon descriptive procedures. The program is called MAP (Muma Assessment Program). The object of MAP is to sufficiently describe, or map out, an individual's command of given cognitive-linguistic-communicative systems so that legitimate inferences can be made about underlying systems and processes. This kind of descriptive approach is regularly used by the major authorities on language development (Bloom, Brown, Bellugi-Klima, Bowerman, Greenfield, Slobin, McNeill, Ervin-Tripp, etc.), cognitive development (Bruner, Piaget, Kagan, Donaldson, Anglin, etc.), and communicative development (Flavell, Bruner, Glucksberg, Bates, Dore, Halliday, etc.). The most productive literature on developmental processes is based upon descriptive procedures. Given that the descriptive literature is so productive, the clinical fields should utilize the descriptive procedures available in the language development literature to develop clinical assessment procedures. This is what MAP is about. The authors have simply compiled and slightly modified a number of descriptive procedures that show promise for clinical assessment.

DOMAINS OF MAP

MAP contains descriptive procedures for three major domains: cognitive, linguistic, and communicative systems. Although each domain is presented separately, it must be emphasized that all of them are naturally inextricably related. In keeping with the hierarchical relationship portrayed on p. 66, it must be remembered that cognitive systems have priority over linguistic and communicative systems.

MAP, like other descriptive procedures, such as the Uzgiris and Hunt (1975) Piagetian assessment procedures, departs from the traditional clinical assessment policies about testing. In traditional assessment, a test is given and conclusions are drawn about test performance. In descriptive procedures, data sampling is done, but no conclusions or inferences can be made until a discernible *pattern* has been established. Administering an assessment procedure does not mean that an individual has been assessed. In contrast, the traditional assessment position is that when a test is administered, an individual has been tested. Furthermore, in traditional assessment, sample size is established a priori. For example, language sample size is usually 50 or 100 utterances. However, sample size in a descriptive procedure is not set a priori. It is necessary to sample an individual's behavior in several contexts and to obtain a sufficiently large sample to establish *patterns* of target systems of interest.

ASSESSMENT OF COGNITIVE ABILITIES

The MAP procedures include the following areas in cognition: 1) Piagetian sensorimotor skills; 2) Bruner cognitive processing stages;

3) perceptual or dimensional salience; 4) technology of reckoning; 5) cognitive distancing; 6) primacy-recency memory functions; 7) rule- / nonrule-governed learning; 8) categorization-mediation; 9) production deficiency and mediation deficiency; and 10) cognitive tempo. All of these cognitive skills are related to language learning and acquisition in a general way. Cognitive skills with specific relationships to language learning include semantic functions and relations and communicative intents. These aspects are incorporated in the linguistic and communicative components of MAP. The sensorimotor skills that are especially relevant are: causality, anticipation, object permanence, alternative means, and deferred imitation. Additionally, preoperational reversibility is important for the early communicative dialogues. Causality, anticipation, and object permanence are especially important because they index early representational skills—skills that are prerequisite to word learning (Bloom and Lahey, 1978). Alternative means are important because they are cognitive analogs to the fundamental principle of language: one word has many referents and one referent has many words. Reversibility is also germane to this principle.

Bruner Cognitive Processing Stages

The Bruner (1964, 1966) three-stage cognitive processing model is very important because it portrays the emergence of cognitive skills culminating in the acquisition of verbal representation. The first stage is *motoric* or *enactive processing*; the second is *iconic processing*; and the third is *symbolic processing*. It is necessary to know the predominant cognitive processing mode of an individual so that his or her intervention program can be oriented to it. Moreover, the developmental sequence provides a means for assessing and sequencing the intervention process. Motoric processors finger, touch, feel, pat, mouth, or, in various other ways, learn through direct manipulation of proximal stimuli. Once mobile, they convert distal into proximal stimuli for motoric processing. Motoric processing is evidenced clinically by mentally retarded, aphasic, autistic, and learning-disabled individuals. Iconic processors attend to perceptual attributes of things, i.e., color, size, shape, number, and position. Their classifications evidence a perceptual dominance. Symbolic processors attend to inherent functions properties—properties shared by items because they are categorized according to adult properties. For example, a motoric processor is interested in a teddy bear because he likes to feel, touch, pat, or mouth it. An iconic processor is interested in a teddy bear because of its size, shape, color, or position, whereas a symbolic processor possesses a classification that includes "teddy bearness." The symbolic processor regards a teddy bear as another instance of his or her concept of a special kind of toy.

Perceptual or Dimensional Salience

Perceptual or dimensional salience (Odom and Corbin, 1973) is an inordinately strong orientation on a particular perceptual domain. It is evidenced most strongly at preschool ages. Moreover, it was Muma and Muma's clinical experience with a few individuals that perceptual salience fluctuates on a daily basis. For example, an individual may be strongly oriented on color one day, but, the next day, may not show that orientation. Another interesting clinical note is that perceptual salience is so strong that it overrides some other cognitive skills, particularly iconic/symbolic processing and rule- /nonrule-governed learning. It is conceivable that perceptual salience is influential in the behavior of autistic and learning-disabled individuals.

Technology of Reckoning

Technology of reckoning (Bruner, 1964) refers to an individual's emerging cognitive abilities to deal effectively with his or her constantly varying experience. Initially, an individual deals with single attributes; then, a few or several attributes; then, coordinated clusters of attributes; and finally, integrated attributes. Moreover, an individual's ability to reckon with his or her experiences is first manifest for *dynamic* and subsequently *static* attributes. Dynamic attributes are those that change, whereas static attributes remain constant. For example, a child's concept of a drinking glass is learned first through dynamic attributes of "drinking glass," i.e., contains a liquid, pours a liquid, holds a liquid while drinking, can be held by one of two hands, etc. The static attributes are secondary and incidental. Interestingly enough, the applied fields attempt to teach static attributes, such as colors, sizes, and shapes, both directly and before dynamic attributes. This policy probably makes the learning more difficult rather than easier.

Cognitive Distancing

Cognitive distancing (Piaget, 1962) refers to an individual's emerging cognitive development, which provides a means for becoming progressively removed from direct stimulation and increasingly reliant on internal representation of past experience in order to deal with present experience. Cognitive distancing has been operationally defined by the continuum of objects to pictorials to words. Actual objects (as opposed to representational objects) provide opportunities for action patterns toward them. Action patterns constitute the earliest means of classification. Accordingly, actions on actual objects constitute a low level of cognitive distancing. Pictorials provide a secondary level because they give prototypic information. And, words provide a tertiary level because they are labels which must cue the underlying concept. This has implications for both assessment and intervention. In assessment, it means that various assessment procedures may yield different results, depending on their level of cognitive distancing. For example, Burger and Muma (1980) showed that aphasics have less difficulty classifying actual objects than pictorials of the same objects. Clinically, intervention dealing with real objects rather than picture and word is more successful with children who are autistic, mentally retarded, and learning-disabled.

Primacy-Recency Memory Functions

Primacy-recency memory functions have been well-documented in the literature on memory and the language acquisition literature (Ervin-Tripp, 1973; Slobin, 1973). At first glance, the procedure looks like a memory span task because a subject is given one item per second and, at the end, is asked to recall what the items were. However, it is not a memory span task. Indeed, memory span as an index of memory capacity was shown to be highly confounded and nonproductive 40 years ago (Blankenship, 1938), even though the applied fields continue to try to make something of it. Primacy-recency functions are obtained when there is a memory overload problem and there is no discernible structure to the material. The first part of the string is recalled (primacy effect) and the last part is recalled (recency effect). The importance of this comes when an individual is presented structured material, particularly one of his or her own spontaneous utterances removed from context, but regards it as unstructured. However, the best evidence of primacy and especially recency effects comes from spontaneous utterances as described by Ervin-Tripp and Slobin.

Rule- /Nonrule-Governed Learning

Rule- /nonrule-governed learning pertains to the literature on two-choice discrimination learning—specifically, the studies of the Kendlers (1970) on mediation. It is called rule- /nonrule-governed learning because it entails a procedure in which an individual is given a series of bits of information that (only when put together) result in a solution. Individuals who construct rules for the information perform differently than those who do not. There are three stages to the procedure: *initial set, reversal shift,* and *nonreversal shift.* The reversal shift provides evidence that an individual is flexible in his or her thinking by virtue of an ability to shift to a new criterion. The nonreversal shift provides evidence that the person is a flexible thinker by virtue of an ability to shift to a new domain.

Categorization-Mediation

Categorization-mediation deals with a cognitive process that is the heart of language. Language is built on a person's categorization of his or her experiences. Wells (1974) defined language acquisition as children's attempts to match their cognitive organization derived from their experiences to the organization of their language. Brown (1956) held that first language learning is "a process of cognitive socialization," involving "the coordination of speech categories with categories of the nonlinguistic world" (p. 247). Lenneberg (1967) said that categorization is central to language and referred to " . . . concept-formation, the primary cognitive process and naming (as well as acquiring a name), the secondary cognitive process." Categorization-mediation in MAP entails three dimensions: prototypic knowledge, extension or overlap, and mediating agents and mechanisms. Moreover, the assessment process deals with high utility concepts. Utilizing the concept of focal and peripheral exemplars, an individual is given opportunities to show that he or she knows several high-utility concepts. If performance pattern is limited only to focal exemplars, the individual is credited with having prototypic knowledge of a given concept. If performance includes peripheral exemplars with focal exemplars, he or she is credited with having prototypic knowledge and extended knowledge of a given concept. If performance is idiosyncratic, the assessment issue changes to an inquiry into which mediating agents or mechanisms will lead to learning a concept. Mediating agents include: the individual, siblings, peers, parents, or anyone with whom he or she may identify in modeling. Mediation mechanisms include: action patterns, naming or labeling items, class names, and focal or peripheral exemplars.

Production Deficiency and Mediation Deficiency

Production deficiency and mediation deficiency (Moely et al., 1969) are two interesting difficulties evidenced in preschool-aged children. In production deficiency, children can reliably perform a cognitive skill (such as cluster items in memory or categorization), but they are unreliable in producing labels. In mediation deficiency, a child can produce labels for things but the labels do not mediate functional categories.

Cognitive Tempo

Cognitive tempo refers to thinking style, specifically impulsivity and reflectivity. Impulsive thinkers are quick to respond but have a relatively high error rate. Reflective thinkers take more time to respond because they consider alternatives; consequently, they have relatively few errors. Cognitive tempo can be observed in play. The number of toy changes per unit of time may index impulsivity or reflectivity. Intervention for impulsive individuals should be devoted to improving reflective skills, whereas intervention for reflective individuals could focus on the acquisition of classification skills, linguistic skills, and communicative skills.

ASSESSMENT OF LINGUISTIC SYSTEMS

The MAP program contains descriptive procedures for linguistic systems. The specific linguistic systems are not separated as they are for the cognitive systems of MAP. The MAP program describes the following linguistic domains: 1) speech acts; 2) semantic functions and relations; 3) syntax; 4) and phonology; The Halliday (1975), Dore (1975), and Bruner (1975) models are used to account for various kinds of language functions. Specifically, an individual's repertoire of language functions are mapped to ascertain which, if any, are limited or missing. Brown's (1973) five stages are used as a general framework to describe an individual's development. It should be stressed however, that Stages IV, V, and, possibly, III may undergo substantial revision. Nevertheless, Stage I deals with semantic functions and relations for one- and two-word utterances. Once utterances go beyond two words, the assessment process deals with semantic/syntactic mechanisms. The early issues pertain to modulations of meaning, which are mostly accomplished by various inflectional rules and the determiner system. Syntactic analysis entails an individual's command of various phrase structure rules and transformational operations. Accordingly, the syntactic analysis deals with the following systems: nominal, determiner, auxiliary, verbal, adjectival, adverbial, pronominalization, relativization, recursiveness, and derivation.

An interesting new area of descriptive analysis involves co-occurring systems. New systems are learned in the context of old systems (Muma, 1981; Muma and Muma, 1979), a principle that was first espoused by Slobin (1973) when he defined an intimate relationship between form and function in language learning. Specifically, he indicated that new forms first appear with old functions, and new functions first appear with old forms. Co-occurrences are particularly important in clinical assessment. They define the linguistic conditions that are needed by a particular individual as he or she attempts to learn a particular aspect of a new system. For example, one person may first try to learn adjectives with animate nouns, whereas another may first attempt adjectives with inanimate nouns or something else.

The MAP program also deals with some special aspects of language learning. These pertain to the identification of language learning loci such as: consecutive single-word utterances; spontaneous imitations; invented words and glossing; buttressing; buildups; consecutive slightly varied utterances; and alternative language learning styles, such as imitative/ nonimitative, expressive/referential, pronominal/ nominal, and object noun phrase/subject noun phrase.

In phonology, the descriptive procedures deal with various phonotactic rules found in child phonology (Ingram, 1976). These rules include: weak syllable deletion, consonant clusters reduction, voicing, open syllable and simplication, fronting, and blunting.

ASSESSMENT OF COMMUNICATIVE SYSTEMS

The communication section of MAP deals with an individual's array of speech functions, according to the Halliday, Bruner, and Dore models. It deals with encoder–decoder functions, role-taking, alternative referents, deixis, adjusted messages, code matrix, and communication game. These communicative functions pertain to an individual's ability to not only produce and comprehend a message in terms of available reference and communicative intent but to adjust messages and take the perspective of the other in both production and comprehension.

SUMMARY

In summary, the MAP program provides descriptive procedures for clinical assessment of cognitive, linguistic, and communicative systems. These areas are amplified elsewhere (Muma, 1978, 1981; Muma et al., 1982).

It should be stressed that descriptive procedures are much more productive in comparable amounts of time than normative procedures. We have a standing challenge in our clinic at Texas Tech that, given the same amount of time to do descriptive procedures as it took doing psychometric normative tests, a clinician will not only obtain more information, indeed, more relevant information, but will also obtain information that is more easily translated into appropriate intervention implications from descriptive procedures. It is simply not true that descriptive procedures are prohibitively time consuming. It is the technician-oriented clinician who asserts that descriptive procedures are prohibitively time consuming. The most persuasive argument is simply a demonstration.

REFERENCES

Bartlett, E. 1972. Selecting preschool language programs. In: C. Cazden (ed.), Language in Early Childhood Education. National Association for the Education of Young Children, DC.

Baumeister, A., and Muma, J. 1975. On defining mental retardation. J. Spec. Educ. 9:293–306.

Bissell, M. 1970. Programs for promoting language skills in early childhood. Panel discussion. National Association for the Education of Young Children.

Blankenship, A. 1938. Memory span: a review of the literature. Psychol. Bull. 35:1–25.

Bloom, L. 1973. One Word at a Time: The Use of Single-Word Utterances before Syntax. Mouton, The Hague.

Bloom, L., and Lahey, M. 1978. Language Development and Language Disorders. John Wiley & Sons, New York.

Bowerman, M. 1974. Discussion summary: Development of concepts underlying language. In: R. Schiefelbusch, and L. Lloyd (eds.), Language Perspectives—Acquisition, Retardation, and Intervention. University Park Press, Baltimore.

Bowerman, M. 1976. Semantic factors in the acquisition of rules for word use and sentence construction. In: D. Morehead and R. Morehead (eds.), Normal and Deficient Child Language. University Park Press, Baltimore.

Brooks, P., and Baumeister, A. 1977. A plea for consideration of ecological validity in the experimental psychology of mental retardation: A guest editorial. Am. J. Ment. Defic. 81:407–416.

Brown, R. 1956. Language and categories. Appendix in: J. Bruner, J. Goodnow, and G. Austin, A Study of Thinking. John Wiley & Sons, New York.

Brown, R. 1973. A First Language: The Early Stages. Harvard University Press, Cambridge, MA.

Bruner, J. 1964. The course of cognitive growth. Am. Psychol. 19:1–15.

Bruner, J. 1975. The ontogenesis of speech acts. J. Child Lang. 2:1–19.

Bruner, J., Olver, R., Greenfield, P. et al. 1966. Studies in Cognitive Growth. John Wiley & Sons, New York.

Burger, R., and Muma, J. 1980. Cognitive distancing in mediated categorization in aphasia. J. Psycholing. Res. 7:37–47.

Cattell, R. 1963. Theory of fluid and crystallized intelligence: A critical experiment. J. Educ. Psychol. 54:1–22.

Cazden, C. 1967. On individual differences in language competence and performance. J. Spec. Educ. 1:135–150.

Cazden, C. 1972. Language in early childhood education. National Association for the Education of Young Children, DC.

Chomsky, N. 1968. Language and Mind. Harcourt Brace Jovanovich, New York.

Compton, A. 1975. Generative studies of children's phonological disorders a strategy of therapy. In: S. Singh (ed.), Measurement Procedures in Speech, Hearing, and Language. University Park Press, Baltimore.

Cromer, R. 1974. Receptive language in the mentally retarded: Processes and diagnostic distinctions. In: R.L. Schiefelbusch and L. Lloyd (eds.), Language Perspectives—Acquisition, Retardation, and Intervention. University Park Press, Baltimore.

Daniloff, R., and Hammarberg, R. 1973. On defining coarticulation. J. Phon. 1:239–248.

Deese, J. 1969. Behavior and fact. Am. Psychol. 24:515–522.

Dore, J. 1975. Holophrases, speech acts, and language universals. J. Child Lang. 2:21–40.

Dunn, L. 1959. Peabody Picture Vocabulary Test. American Guidance Service, Circle Pines, MI.

Ervin-Tripp, S. 1973. Some strategies for the first two years. In: T. Moore (ed.), Cognitive Development and the Acquisition of Language. Academic Press, New York.

Garrison, M. (ed.). 1966. Cognitive models and development in mental retardation. Am. J. Ment. Defic. Monogr. Suppl. 70.

Grossman, H., Warren, S., Begab, M. et al. 1973. Manual on Terminology and Classification in Mental Retardation (1973 Revision), American Association on Mental Deficiency, Special Publication Series No. 2.

Guilford, J. 1967. The Nature of Human Intelligence. McGraw-Hill, New York.

Halliday, M. 1975. Learning how to mean. In: E. Lenneberg and E. Lenneberg (eds.), Foundations of Language Development: A Multi-disciplinary Approach. Academic Press, New York.

Hess, R., and Shipman, V. 1965. Early experience and the socialization of cognitive modes in children. Child Dev. 34:869–886.

Hobbs, N. (ed.). 1974a. The Futures of Children: Categories, Labels, and Their Consequences. Jossey-Bass, San Francisco.

Hobbs, N. (ed.). 1974b. Issues in the Classification of Children: A Sourcebook on Categories, Labels, and Their Consequences. Jossey-Bass, San Francisco.

Holtzman, P., and Gardner, R. 1960. Leveling-sharpening and memory organization. J. Abnorm. Soc. Psychol. 61:176–180.

Ingram, D. 1973. Phonological rules in young children. J. Child Lang. 1:49–64.

Ingram, D. 1974. Fronting in child phonology. J. Child Lang. 1:233–241.

Ingram, D. 1976. Phonological disability in children. Elsevier, New York.

Jenkins, J. 1974. Remember that old theory of memory? Well forget it! Am. Psychol. 29:785–795.

Kagan, J. 1966. Reflectivity-impulsivity: The generality and dynamics of conceptual tempo. J. Abnorm. Psychol. 71:17–24.

Kagan, J. 1967. On the need for relativism. Am. Psychol. 22:131–142.

Kagan, J., and Kagan, N. 1970. Individual variation in cognitive processes. In: P. Mussen (ed.), Carmichael's Manual of Child Psychology. John Wiley & Sons, New York.

Kagan, J., Moss, H., and Siegel, I. 1963. Psychological significance of styles of conceptualization. Monogr. Soc. Res. Child Dev. 28:73–124.

Kendler, H., and Kendler, T. 1970. Developmental process in discrimination learning. Human Dev. 13:65–89.

Kirk, S., McCarthy, J., and Kirk, W. 1968. The Illinois Test of Psycholinguistic Abilities (Revised Ed.). University of Illinois Press, Urbana.

Ladefoged, P. 1972. Phonological features and their phonetic correlates. J. Int. Phon. Assoc. 2:2–12.

Lenneberg, E. 1967. Biological Foundations of Language. John Wiley & Sons, New York.

Locke, J. 1980. The inference of speech perception in the phonologically disordered child. J. Hear. Disord. 45:431–444.

McCaffrey, A. 1969. Convergent methodologies and the study of language usage by children from differing sub-cultural environments. Convention paper, Society for Research in Child Development.

McReynolds, L., and Houston, K. 1971. A distinctive feature analysis of children's misarticulations. J. Speech Hear. Disord. 36:155–166.

McReynolds, L., and Sherman, B. 1972. Distinctive feature generalization in articulation training. J. Speech Hear. Disord. 37:462–470.

Menyuk, P. 1968. The role of distinctive features in children's acquisition of phonology. J. Speech Hear. Res. 11:138–146.

Mercer, J. 1972. The lethal label. Psychol. Today 44.

Moely, B., Olsen, F., Halwas, T., and Flavell, J. 1969. Production deficiency in young children's clustered recall. Dev. Psychol. 1:26–34.

Moore, D. 1971. Language research and preschool language training. In: C. Lavatelli (ed.), Language Training in Early Childhood Education. University of Illinois Press, Urbana.

Muma, J. 1981. Language Primer. Natural Child Publisher (P.O. 3452) Lubbock, TX.

Muma, J., and Muma, D. 1979. Muma Assessment Program. Natural Child Publisher (P.O. 3452), Lubbock, TX.

Muma, J. 1978. Language handbook: Concepts, assessment, intervention. Prentice-Hall, Englewood Cliffs, NJ.

Muma, J., and Baumeister, A. 1975. Programmatic evaluation in mental retardation. J. Spec. Educ. 9:293–306.

Muma, J. Lubinski, R., and Pierce, S. 1982. A new era in language assessment. In: N. Lass (ed.), Speech and Language, Volume 7, Academic Press, New York.

Nelson, K. 1973. Some evidence for the cognitive primacy of categorization and its functional basis. Merrill-Palmer Q. 19:21–39.

Nelson, K. 1974. Concept, word, and sentence: Interrelations in acquisition and development. Psychol. Rev. 81:267–285.

Nihira, K., Forster, R., Shellhaas, M., and Leland, H. 1974. AAMD Adaptive Behavior Scale. American Association of Mental Deficiency, DC.

Odom, R., and Corbin, D. 1973. Perceptual salience and children's multidimensional problem solving. Child Dev. 44:425–432.

Oller, K.D. 1973. Regularities in abnormal child phonology. J. Speech Hear. Disord. 38:36–47.

Oller, K., and Kelly, C. 1974. Phonological substitution processes of a hard-of-hearing child. J. Speech Hear. Disord. 39:65–74.

Olson, D. 1970. Language and thought: Aspects of a cognitive theory of semantics. Psychol. Rev. 77:257–273.

Panagos, J. 1974. Persistence of the open syllable reinterpreted as a symptom of language disorder. J. Speech Hear. Disord. 39:23–31.

Piaget, J. 1962. Play, Dreams, and Imitation in Childhood. W.W. Norton, New York.

Proshansky, H. 1976. Environmental psychology and the real world. Am. Psychol. 31:303–310.

Renfrew, C. 1966. Persistence of the open syllable in defective articulation. J. Speech Hear. Disord. 31:370–373.

Schlesinger, I. 1971a. Learning grammar: From pivot to realization rule. In: R. Huxley and E. Ingram (eds.), Language Acquisition: Methods and Models. Academic Press, New York.

Schlesinger, I. 1971b. Production of utterances and language acquisition. In: D. Slobin (ed.), The Ontogenesis of Grammar. Academic Press, New York.

Siegel, G. 1975. The high cost of accountability. ASHA 17:796–797.

Slobin, D. 1973. Cognitive prerequisites for the development of grammar. In: C. Ferguson and D. Slobin (eds.), Studies of Child Language Development. Holt, Rinehart and Winston, New York.

Uzgiris, I., and Hunt, J. 1975. Assessment in infancy: Ordinal scales of psychological development. University of Illinois Press, Urbana.

Vennemann, T., and Ladefoged, P. 1973. Phonetic features and phonological features. Lingua 32:61–74.

Wechsler, D. 1975. Intelligence defined and undefined: A relativistic appraisal. Am. Psychol. 30:135–139.

Wells, G. 1974. Learning to code experience through language. J. Child Lang. 1:243–269.

Wepman, J. 1958. Auditory Discrimination Test. Language Research Associates, Chicago.

Section

II

Perspectives on Language Training in Developmental Language Interventions

This section presents examples of developmental psycholinguistic approaches to language remediation, ranging from infant intervention to intervention with school-age children, and encompasses such language-impaired categories as mentally retarded and hearing-impaired. Each chapter discusses the psycholinguistic bases for the type of intervention presented in that particular chapter.

Recently, considerable emphasis has been placed on the study of pragmatics in the normal acquisition of language (Bates, 1976; Rees, 1978). These research efforts are just beginning to be translated into intervention approaches (Schiefelbusch and Bricker, 1981). The shift from the teaching of syntactic structures to a pragmatically based communication strategy represents a radical departure from early psycholinguistically based language intervention programs (Stremel and Waryas, 1974). Waryas and Stremel-Campbell's (1978) pragmatically oriented language training program represents an initial foray into a long-term involvement by language clinicians and developmental psycholinguists into redefining the goals and directions of much of language intervention research. No longer can the psycholinguist and/or language clinician be committed only to the study of the acquisition of *linguistic competence*. A more encompassing interest, the acquisition of *communicative competence*, is becoming evident in much of the recent developmental psycholinguistic literature. As just mentioned, the language intervention literature is already beginning to accommodate this shift in emphasis. This line of research promises to continue and expand in the future. The emphasis on the assessment of communicative competence stressed in the assessment section of this volume attests to the fact that the intervention literature is accompanying that of developmental psycholinguistics in this shift of emphasis.

Chapter 4 by Roberts and Schaefer provides a preliminary view on where *early intervention research* may be headed. They have identified three general factors that should be considered when developing early intervention programs: 1) the relationship between cognitive abilities and the emergence of language; 2) the form of linguistic input to the child; and 3) modification of the child's productions. As Roberts and Schaefer are careful to point out, the data base for early intervention is, in the 1980s, being extrapolated from the psycholinguistic literature concerning the cognitive prerequisites to normal language development. Roberts and Schaefer provide some preliminary directions for incorporating these basic developmental research data into a systematic early intervention schema. However, application of such data to direct early intervention research is lacking. The future should witness a substantial effort by the developmental interventionists to systematically integrate the ''pre-linguistic'' language acquisition data into a developmental approach to early intervention.

The cognitive/semantic basis of language acquisition is the focus of Chapter 5 by Leonard. In this chapter, Leonard discusses the developmental psycholinguistic aspects of *semantic notions* and how these may play a role in the early language intervention approaches with handicapped children. He distinguishes between cognitive notions and semantic notions and provides a rationale for the selection of which semantic notions to train and in what sequences. Semantic notions in this context refer to the relational meanings attached to communicative expressions, involving actions on objects, attributes of persons and objects, possessors of objects, and other meanings that extend beyond the simple labeling of entities in the environment. Leonard discusses his approach to training such semantic notions. He emphasizes the importance during training of structuring nonlinguistic events that represent the types of relationships to which the semantic notion (being trained) refers. The emphasis on nonlinguistic events parallels the more overtly pragmatic-based approaches to language intervention. Leonard's examples in the training of semantic notions combine the communication system components of pragmatics, cognition, semantics, and syntax stressed in the assessment chapters by Muma and Longhurst.

Chapter 6, by Smith, Ruder and Stremel-Campbell, explores the interdependence and/or independence of linguistic structures that function as target behaviors in language training. The behavioristic and psycholinguistic views on the bases for developing training sequences are discussed. Ample data are provided to show the utility of interdependencies between linguistic structures and how such interdependency may be used in achieving generalization in language training.

Chapter 7 of this volume discusses applications of psycholinguistic data to the training of metacognitive and metalinguistic skills to language-impaired youngsters. The discussion details the utility of training these skills, the point being that such skills are basic to the acquisition of communicative competence and that language intervention programs should be so designed that these skills are included as essential targets for assessment and/or training. In his concluding comments, Kretschmer reiterates the relationship of such a training approach to the developmental psycholinguistic perspective. In doing so, he clearly identifies metacognition and metalanguage as essential components of an applied psycholinguistics.

The final chapter in this volume, by Weber-Olsen and Ruder, reviews in detail the pros and cons of various language training programs. These are discussed within the context of what Bricker and Bricker (1974) referred to as the "language game," a game frequently played between psycholinguists and behaviorists—a game that is notable for its lack of established rules or methods for determining a winner. The authors summarize their review of the language game by noting that current research has changed the *language game* to a *communication game* (Prutting, 1982) and that there seems to be a convergence of behavioristic and psycholinguistic thought in practice, if not in principle. The remedial logic/developmental logic may thus be more of a pseudo-issue than a real discrepancy in intervention approaches.

REFERENCES

Bates, E. 1976. Language and Context: The Acquisition of Pragmatics. Academic Press, New York.
Bricker, W.A., and Bricker, D. D. 1974. An early language training strategy. In: R.L. Schiefelbusch and L.L. Lloyd (eds.), Language Perspectives— Acquisition, Retardation, and Intervention. University Park Press, Baltimore.
Prutting, C. 1982. Pragmatics as social competence. J. Speech Hear. Disord. 47:123–134.
Rees, N. 1978. Pragmatics of language: Applications to normal and disordered language development. In: R.L. Schiefelbusch (ed.), Bases of Language Intervention. University Park Press, Baltimore.
Schiefelbusch, R.L., and Bricker, D.D. 1981. Early Language: Acquisition and Intervention. University Park Press, Baltimore.
Stremel, K., and Waryas, C. 1974. A behavioral psycholinguistic approach to language training. In: L. McReynolds (ed.), Developing Systematic Procedures for Training Children's Language, ASHA Monograph #18.
Waryas, C., and Stremel-Campbell, K. 1978. Grammatical training for the language-delayed child: A new perspective. In: R.L. Schiefelbusch (ed.), Language Intervention Strategies. University Park Press, Baltimore.

chapter 4

Cognitive Abilities and Infant Language Intervention

Kenneth Roberts

Human Development and Family Life
University of Kansas
Lawrence, Kansas

Ronald Schaefer

Linguistics and African Languages
University of Benin
Benin City, Nigeria

contents

A major component of any language intervention program is the substantive content that is to be trained. Ideally, the content should derive from a strong data base to ensure its relevance to the language learning process. Most available data on language acquisition are from studies focusing on the period when the child already exhibits linguistic behavior (Brown, 1973; Bloom, 1973; Bowerman, 1973; Nelson, 1973; Bloom et al., 1975; Braine, 1976; Greenfield and Smith, 1976). Consequently, most language intervention programs are concerned only with this period of development (Miller and Yoder, 1974; MacDonald and Blott, 1974; MacDonald et al., 1974; Lee et al., 1975). These programs assume that certain necessary, or at least facilitative, cognitive and other prelinguistic abilities already exist upon entry into training. Consequently, there is a shortage of language intervention programs concerned with the potentially language-related abilities predominating from birth to about 2 years of age.

In the past several years, however, there has been considerable interest in the nonlinguistic, cognitive bases of language acquisition (Sinclair-de Zwart, 1971, 1973; Nelson, 1973; Slobin, 1973, Brown, 1973; Clark, 1973b, 1974; Bates et al., 1975; Bates, 1976, 1979; Bates et al., 1977; Bowerman, 1978a). The cognitive achievements receiving primary attention are those that occur in children from birth to 2 years of age. This interest is broadening the data base associated with the first 2 years of life, a period considered by many to include the acquisition of certain potentially prerequisite behaviors for language learning. If language acquisition is shown to be dependent upon or facilitated by the acquisition of certain nonlinguistic, cognitive abilities during the first 2 years of life, then it would necessitate the language interventionist to establish or facilitate the development of these abilities. Furthermore, it would require the initiation of intervention early in infancy, preferably at birth or soon after—well before the appearance of actual linguistic behavior. The importance of this approach to training has been emphasized by Bricker and Bricker (1974, 1976) and Horton (1974). Horton (1974) stated that in the early postbirth period, the infant is maximally pliable, and intervention during this period may have its most significant effects. Moreover, by intervening at birth or soon after, the nature of intervention shifts from remedial to preventative. Most current programs are decidedly remedial, thus requiring a clear indication of language delay for entry into the program (Tjossem, 1976). However, intervention in very early infancy, when the child is most plastic, could reduce or eliminate deficits in cognitive or other language-related abilities and, hence, reduce or eliminate associated language delay (Bricker and Bricker, 1974; Horton, 1974; Tjossem, 1976). A corollary of this shift from remedial to preventative intervention is that the population of interest shifts from one of *diagnosed* language delay to one that is *high risk* for language delay.[1] Although a detailed understanding of the interactive variables contributing to the occurrence of high-risk circumstances is lacking, there are nevertheless some major variables, such as retardation, hearing impairment, neurological impairment, etc., that are associated with language delay. When such circumstances exist, the normal development of language and language-related cognitive abilities is at risk.

This discussion focuses on cognitive development, one aspect of the developmental period from birth to 2 years, and its role in infant language intervention. This, of course, is not to suggest that cognitive development is *the* language-related variable developing in this period. The effects of the development of normal mother-infant interaction (both verbal and nonverbal), pragmatic abilities, infant vocalization, etc. are equally important, and the harmonious interaction among all of these variables is surely required for effective language acquisition.

Specifically, this discussion is limited to the relationship between cognition and language and its implications for infant language intervention. The available evidence on the cognition-language relationship is reviewed and evaluated for the choice of program content; then, conclusions are drawn about the strength of this data base.

COGNITION AND LANGUAGE

The early intervention programs focusing on the period from birth to 2 years generally consider cognitive intervention an important aspect of training (Bricker and Bricker, 1974, 1976). But what is the nature of the data base on which this cognitive intervention rests? What is known about the relationship between cognitive development and language acquisition? Ingram (1977) pointed out that an exact statement of the language-cognition relationship requires a firmer grasp of the "what" and "when" of both linguistic and cognitive development.

There are at least three major positions regarding the relationship between cognition and language (see Bates et al, 1977, for a discussion of other possible relationships):

1. *Language determines cognition*   This claim has been labeled linguistic determinism and maintains that the segmentation of reality is arbitrary; that is, language determines how a person's environment and world view are structured. The Whorfian hypothesis is often cited as an example of such a claim.

---

[1] See Tjossem (1976) for a discussion of the factors relevant to the definition and identification of high-risk infants.

2. *Cognition determines language*   In direct opposition to linguistic determinism, this claim has been termed "cognitive determinism" (Schlesinger, 1977). Here, language is seen as mapping previously acquired nonlinguistic, cognitive knowledge. This is perhaps the most widely held position among psycholinguists in the 1980s. Piagetian psychology generally is thought to exemplify this position (see Bates et al., 1977, for a different interpretation).

3. *Interaction of cognition and language*   Although cognition may in some cases precede language, there are other cases where linguistic input can function to trigger the development of a nonlinguistic concept and/or provide information regarding the language-specific boundaries of a concept. Embodying elements of the above two positions, this position (Bowerman, 1976, 1980; Schlesinger, 1977) has been labeled "interactionist" (Bowerman, 1976) and represents the belief that both linguistic and cognitive determinism overstate the issue. Instead, a bi-directional characterization of the relationship is deemed more appropriate.

There are two issues that have implications for interpreting the available data:

1. *The exact specification of what is meant by "cognition"*   Bowerman (1978b) distinguished two aspects of cognition. One involves the notion of "concepts" and their potential relationship to language acquisition. The notion "concepts" refers variously to specific meanings, semantic intentions, relations, cognitions, categories, etc. that can be *directly* coded in speech. Action, agent, possession, categories of real world objects, etc. are examples of concepts. The other aspect involves the notion of the deeper cognitive achievements recognized by Piagetian theory, such as the development of object permanence, casuality, space, and time. These do not have direct realizations in speech. Cromer (1976) made a similar distinction between what he termed "cognitions" (meanings) and "cognitive structures." If a distinction is made between the two senses of cognition, it follows that each may possess a unique relationship to language acquisition and, consequently, each may have differing implications for language training.

2. *The relationship between certain linguistic advances (e.g., acquisition of first words, abrupt increases in vocabulary, etc.) and the achievement of general cognitive stages, like the sensorimotor substages of Piaget*   Here, the concern is not with particular cognitive structures (e.g., object permanence) at a particular level of development (e.g., Stage 6) but rather with the general level of cog-

nitive achievement of a child when all of the sensorimotor, cognitive structures are considered.

The following sections examine some of the current psycholinguistic research bearing on the relationship of language acquisition to: 1) Piagetian sensorimotor achievements; 2) cognitive concepts; and 3) general cognitive stages.

PIAGETIAN SENSORIMOTOR ACHIEVEMENTS

Cognitive Structures and Language

The "rediscovery" of the work of Jean Piaget has provided a description of certain cognitive abilities that may be prerequisite for language. The following focuses on work examining the relationship between Piagetian sensorimotor abilities and language acquisition.

Mental Representation: Object Permanence   Mental representation is the cognitive ability most often cited as a possible prerequisite to language (Sinclair-deZwart, 1971; Bowerman, 1974, 1978a). The achievement of mental representation is manifested in the near simultaneous appearance of Stage 6 object permanence, deferred imitation, symbolic play, and language. Language, because it is a system of arbitrary signs, represents the crowning achievement of mental representation in that it frees representation from the temporal constraints of actions, from the restriction to immediate events, and it allows simultaneous representation of all aspects of an event (Piaget and Inhelder, 1969).

Bloom (1973) suggested that mental representation is prerequisite to two aspects of language development: the increased use and stability of substantive words[2] and the appearance of syntax (two-word combinations). With regard to substantive words, Bloom noted that at 18 months (the average age associated with Stage 6 object permanence and the onset of the preoperational period), her daughter, Allison, showed a dramatic increase in the use and stability of substantive words. Before 18 months, substantive words were few in number and tended to drop out of Allison's repertoire after a short period of time. However, function words were used frequently and showed no mortality in the period before 18 months. Bloom concluded that mental representation was prerequisite to the *changes* in the use and stability of substantive words, but was not prerequisite to the use of function

---

[2] Substantive words refer to classes of objects, such as chairs or cars. Function words are inherently relational and may be applied in a variety of contexts (e.g., "more," "no," "away," "gone," and "up,").

words because function words were frequent and stable before 18 months. This conclusion implies that the major role of mental representation is not necessarily in the onset of language but in certain later changes in linguistic behavior. Bloom further suggested that the mental representation of the intersecting relationships between objects and events must be achieved in order for word combinations to begin.

Bowerman (1978a) questioned Bloom's claims. Bowerman pointed out that Bloom's data lacked independent cognitive evidence for the achievement of mental representation and that this precludes any strong claim as to the exact relationship between mental representation and certain linguistic behaviors. Furthermore there is evidence that conflicts with Bloom's proposed link between mental representation and substantive and function words. Huttenlocher (1974), in a study of the development of language comprehension, found that mental representation (as reflected in the ability to locate absent objects occupying a permanent position) appeared at about 14 to 15 months in her subjects. This was a period when the children used at most only one or two object words, yet understood several. Her findings place the appearance of mental representation before the onset of function words and before or coincident with object words. Huttenlocher's findings are more consistent with mental representation as a prerequisite to function words and the onset of language use. Huttenlocher suggested that the instability of substantive words is attributable not to undeveloped representational abilities (as suggested by Bloom) but rather to a decrease in the salience of certain words.

Also investigating comprehension, Goldin-Meadow et al. (1976) found that their subjects, like Bloom's daughter Allison, exhibited a sudden increase in the use of substantive words. However, Goldin-Meadow et al. (1976) noted that their children understood many words before this increase, at a time when they produced few words or none. Although they collected no independent cognitive data, Goldin-Meadow et al. (1976) argued that a:

> . . . vocabulary comprehender (regardless of whether or not he is a vocabulary producer) must possess some permanent representation of objects and actions in order to understand words.

Consistent with Huttenlocher (1974), this places mental representation before both the change in the use of substantive words and the appearance of function words. Because the children were comprehending many words at a time when few or none were being produced (and because a comprehender must have some mental representation), mental representation is more plausibly associated with the onset of language, specifically language comprehension.

In a study of object permanence and productive language, Corrigan (1978) used modified Uzgirus and Hunt (1975) tasks and found that a relationship between object permanence and language was evident only at certain points in the development of cognition and language. Corrigan segmented object permanence into a series of ranks, from Rank 1 (sensorimotor Stage 4) to Rank 15 (the beginnings of Stage 6) and finally to Rank 21 (preoperational stage object permanence). She found that there was a general correspondence between Rank 15 (Stage 6) and the onset of single-word utterances. This suggests that the entry to Stage 6 object permanence is important to the onset of productive language. Although it is not certain what level of object permanence or mental representation Bloom (1973) was referring to with regard to Allison's sudden increase in substantive words, Corrigan (1976, 1978) did find that Rank 21 object permanence generally corresponded to an increase in vocabulary. This lends some support to Bloom's (1973) claims of the relationship of object permanence to certain *changes* in language, although it does not negate the relationship of lower levels of object permanence to the onset of language. Corrigan also found that semantic functions expressing nonexistence and recurrence appeared *after* Rank 21 object permanence was achieved. This finding is contrary to Bloom's (1973) claim that mental representation was not necessary for the use of function forms. Moreover, Corrigan found no difference in the frequency between function and substantive forms before object permanence and no greater mortality for substantive than function forms before object permanence.

Bates et al. (1975, 1977) presented evidence that is in accord with the above studies. They found that one-half of their subjects exhibited Stage 6 cognitive abilities at about 12 months of age, a time when the children were barely producing words. In addition, Bates et al. (1975) found Stage 6 object permanence to precede the referential use of words. Both observations are consistent with representation being related to the initiation of language production.

Most recently, Smolak (1982) reported that children in the early stages of producing words tend to be functioning in Stage 6 of object permanence. She concluded that object permanence may facilitate language—in particular, the beginnings of language production.

The findings of the above studies provide counterevidence to Bloom's (1973) claim that mental representation is a prerequisite for certain changes in substantive word use but not necessary for function words. The findings suggest that mental representation in terms of object permanence occurs coincident with or before word use and, thus, may be prerequisite or facilitative to the onset of productive language. These data, then, could be used to corroborate a position of cognitive determinism.

Mental Representation: Imitation and Symbolic Play   Equally important to the development of the symbolic function are imitation and symbolic play. Morehead and Morehead (1974) emphasized the prerequisite status of sensorimotor Stage 6 imitation (internalized imitation) to the development of the symbolic function. They pointed out that, for Piaget, representation presupposes a signifier that is differentiated from the signified (Piaget and Inhelder, 1969). Morehead and Morehead (1974) further contended that deferred imitation marks the first indication of representation. The primary precursors to the appearance of the symbolic function are the imitative developments in Stages 4 and 5. In support of this, Morehead and Morehead (1974) cited evidence from Bloom (1973). They noted that Allison's first use of "away" at 10 months followed repeated statements of "Let's throw it away," an example of imitation (Stage 4) requiring a model to be present. Morehead and Morehead pointed out, however, that Allison was quickly able to move on to use the word in new but familiar contexts without the necessity of a model (Stage 5 imitation). Such early imitations allow for the subsequent jump to an internalization of action schemes that manifest themselves first in deferred imitation, indicating a differentiation of signifier and signified. There is some correlational evidence that supports the proposed importance of imitation. Bates (1979) and her colleagues found imitation to be a good predictor of the beginnings of language (nonreferential and referential words)[3] in children from 9 to 13 months of age. Although not providing support for the importance of Stage 6 imitation, the studies of Ingram (1975) and Corrigan (1976) described the abilities of single children, suggesting the potentially important role of lower levels of imitation in language learning. Ingram (1975) found that one of his four subjects produced her first words in sensorimotor Stage 4 and her first multiword combinations by Stage 5. Ingram suggested that the advanced imitative abilities of this child stood out as the most plausible explanation of her advanced language abilities. Similarly, Corrigan (1976) found one of her three subjects using syntax before Stage 6 object permanence. Corrigan reported that, her subject, like Ingram's subject, exhibited advanced imitative abilities. Evidence such as this suggests the importance of sensorimotor imitation in the onset of language.

A number of studies examined the relationship between symbolic play and language. In addition to deferred imitation, Morehead and Morehead (1974) noted that Stage 6 symbolic play is also important to

---

[3] Nonreferential words are not used in association with any specific object. For example, Bates et al. (1977) noted that words used as general request forms (e.g., "Mama" used as a request form for any listener) are nonreferential in nature. Referential words, on the other hand, are used more specifically to refer to particular objects or events.

the development of the symbolic function because in symbolic play, the child comes to " . . . substitute objects or events (signifiers) for other objects or events (the signified)" (p. 174). Bates (1979) found that play (both symbolic and combinatorial) could be used to predict the appearance of nonreferential and referential words. Moreover, Bates and her colleagues found play to strongly predict communicative gestures (giving, showing, communicative pointing, and ritualized request), some of which were, themselves, strong predictors of language. McCune-Nicholich (1981), reviewing the evidence on the relationship between five levels of symbolic play and various linguistic milestones, concluded that the evidence supports the existence of structural correspondences between the two domains. In a longitudinal study of six children from 10 to 16 months, Veneziano (1981) investigated the relationship between pretend and symbolic play behaviors and the appearance of consistently used sound sequences that eventually became conventional words. Although these data did not allow a clear statement regarding the primacy of one domain over another, Veneziano concluded that the data suggest a temporal interrelationship between pretend and symbolic play and a large increase in the use of consistent or conventional sound sequences. Specifically, it was hypothesized that the relationship is one of interaction. Corrigan (1982) examined the relationship between specific play and language behaviors in which the same skills were required for performance in each domain. Of specific interest was the use of animate and inanimate components in both play and language at four age levels between 19 and 28 months. She found that the number of animate and/or inanimate components in pretend play was associated with the number of animate and/or inanimate components in a language imitation task. Furthermore, play tended to be more advanced than language in terms of the number of animate and/or inanimate components. She concluded that pretend play showed a systematic relationship to language in an imitation task. Finally, Steckol and Leonard (1981), in apparently the only training study focusing on very young children, found that training on the Uzgiris and Hunt schemes for Relating to Objects Scale (Stage 5) led to improved use of imperative and declarative performatives. However, they also found that of four subjects who failed to complete Stage 5 training on schemes for relating to objects, two showed performative usage. They concluded that evidence was provided for a relationship between certain sensorimotor abilities and communicative development. However, the authors also noted that a causal relationship was not supported and that Stage 5 performance on schemes for relating to objects was not *necessary* for communicative development.

Mental Representation: Evidence from Delayed Populations   Evidence reviewed thus far has been primarily correlational. As a supplement to correlational evidence, Bates (1979) and her colleagues suggested using evidence from language deficient children to determine whether nonlinguistic deficits relate to language delay. There are a number of studies that address this question.

Snyder (1978) found in her study that of the six Uzgiris-Hunt scales, only the Stage 6 Means-Ends Scale differentiated the language-delayed children from the normal children. She concluded that language-delayed children are characterized by a specific deficit in representing the dynamic aspects of symbolization. More directly, the deficit seems not to involve the representation of *static objects* but rather the inability to represent the relationship between the word (symbol) and the end result brought about by the use of that word. This inability results in a failure of the language-delayed child to *anticipate* the end result.

A similar explanation of deficient language in dysphasic children was suggested by Inhelder (1966). In her study, the dysphasic children exhibited normal operational thought, but figurative knowledge (of which certain language characteristics and other manifestations of the symbolic function are a part) was found to be deficient. The symbolic imagery of dysphasic children was noted to be "static" in quality rather than anticipatory. This is quite similar to Snyder's (1978) finding of a representational deficit that precludes the child being able to anticipate the end result of using a verbal performative.

Data reported by Morehead (1972) also indicated a representational deficit in language-delayed children. Morehead replicated a study by Lovell et al. (1968) and found that language-delayed children evidence a delay in symbolic play behavior. Like Inhelder (1966), Morehead used subjects who were more linguistically advanced (MLU 2.00) than Snyder's (1978) subjects. His results, therefore, do not actually link symbolic play to the onset of language. Nevertheless, Morehead's results do suggest that a relationship may exist between symbolic play and language acquisition.

Folger and Leonard (1978), on the other hand, presented evidence that is not as strongly supportive as the arguments of Morehead (1972). Folger and Leonard used the Uzgiris and Hunt (1975) scales as their cognitive measures and found that performance on the Relating to Objects Scale and symbolic play did not relate with any degree of precision to the appearance of the bulk of referential words or two-word combinations. They found that language-disordered children using single words and two-word combinations did not differ in their performance on the Relating to Objects Scale or in symbolic play. The same was true for normal children. They concluded that Stage 6 symbolic play showed at best only a very general relationship to referential words or two-word combinations.

Mental Representation: Counterevidence   The evidence discussed thus far has been, on the whole, supportive of a relationship of mental representation to the onset of language and, thus, generally consistent with a cognitive determinist position. However, there are data suggesting that mental representation is not necessary to language acquisition. Ingram (1975), in a study of the relationship between general cognitive stages and language acquisition, found that one of his four subjects produced her first words in sensorimotor Substage 4. In fact, by Stage 5, the onset of multiword utterances had begun. This is inconsistent with the hypothesis that Stage 6 mental representation is necessary for the beginnings of language. Ingram reported that this particular child was highly imitative, and the mother's efforts in training imitation could have contributed to the child's advanced linguistic abilities. Corrigan (1976) reported similar findings. She found, in a study of the relationship between object permanence and language, that one of her three subjects began using word combinations before attaining Stage 6 object permanence. Corrigan's subject also exhibited advanced imitative abilities. Again, the necessary nature of at least Stage 6 mental representation to the onset of language is clearly contradicted.[4] Moreover, Snyder (1978), in her study of normal and language-delayed children, found that Stage 6 object permanence, as well as imitation, was not predictive of the use of verbal performatives.

In a review of the observations of Piaget and several other diary studies, Ingram (1977) arranged the data into chronological sequences—one for behaviors reflecting cognitive functioning and another reflecting language behavior. He found that the first word productions tend to appear in Stage 5. Two dairy studies for which comprehension information was available further reported the comprehension of many words during this stage. Ingram's (1977) analysis is contrary to the hypothesis that Stage 6 cognitive abilities are necessary for the onset of language. He did, however, note some support for the co-occurrence of Stage 6 object permanence and rapid growth in vocabulary.

Finally, Miller et al. (1980), in a study of the relationship between specific language milestones and both general levels of cognitive func-

---

[4] Recall that mental representation has several manifestations (see p. 9). The above evidence is usually cited as representing contradictory evidence considering that representation is manifested primarily by object permanence (see Bowerman, 1978a). In the brief discussion of the importance of imitation to language learning, it was suggested that the same evidence could be interpreted as an indication of the importance of the imitative manifestation of representation to language, albeit not necessarily Stage 6 imitation. This serves as an example of the desirability (to be discussed later) of precisely defining the ability on the cognitive side if the specifics of the relationship between cognition and language are to be uncovered.

tioning and performance on specific cognitive tasks, found that Stage 6 object permanence was not necessary in order to comprehend words for absent people and objects. Moreover, when the effects of age were considered, no single sensorimotor subscale was found to be significantly related to overall comprehension. Age, rather than sensorimotor performance, seemed to be the better predictor of overall comprehension. The authors pointed out, however, that this does not mean that cognitive functioning is unrelated to comprehension but rather that the individual influence of certain sensorimotor abilities may not be as strong as previously thought (Corrigan, 1978; Folger and Leonard, 1978). Other factors, such as social level and linguistic input, may also play a significant role.

Mental Representation: Relationship to Syntax   In addition to a relationship between mental representation and the increased use and stability of substantive words, Bloom (1973) hypothesized that representation is linked to the appearance of syntax. That is, the ability to represent the intersecting relationships between objects or events was linked to the ability to combine words. Bowerman (1978b) cited two lines of objection to Bloom's hypothesis: 1) there is evidence for representation long before the appearance of syntax (i.e., associated with the onset of language); and 2) there is evidence for word combinations before any indication of fully developed object permanence or other manifestations of representation (e.g., Huttenlocher, 1974; Bates et al., 1975; Ingram, 1975; 1977; Corrigan, 1976; Goldin-Meadow et al., 1976). Moreover, Bates et al. (1977) argued that the onset of syntax is not associated with the appearance of mental representation but rather with a gradual increase in the *span* of an already developed representational ability.

Means-Ends   Piaget's concept of causality has been less investigated than mental representation. Bates et al. (1975) examined the relationship between certain cognitive, social, and communicative developments. The socio-communicative developments of interest were *proto-declarative* and *proto-imperative* intentions. Proto-imperatives were defined as the use of an adult to obtain some end, for example, an object. Proto-declaratives, on the other hand, were defined as the use of an object to obtain adult attention. The cognitive developments were inferred from loosely structured assessment tasks, designed to measure the Piagetian structures of object permanence, imitation, groups and spatial displacements, and means-ends. Bates et al. found Stage 5 means-ends to co-occur with Stage 5 social sequences, specifically, the onset of communicative *intentions* involving the proto-imperative and proto-declarative. They concluded that the proto-imperative and proto-declarative performatives were based on the achievement of sensorimotor Stage 5. A follow-up cross-sectional study (Bates et al., 1977; Bates, 1979) substantiated the findings of their preliminary study. They found that the dynamic causal aspect of cognition, as reflected by the performance on Stage 5 means-ends tasks, once again seemed to play a greater role in the development of communicative intentions than more static object-oriented cognition.[5]

The development of proto-declarative and proto-imperative performatives was also examined by Snyder (1978) in a study of normal and language-delayed children. The Uzgiris and Hunt (1975) assessment scales, along with tasks designed to tap presuppositions and declarative and imperative performatives, were given to both groups of children. She found that only Stage 6 means-ends tasks differentiated the language-delayed from the normal group.

Harding and Golinkoff (1979) examined the relationship of two Stage 5 causality tasks to the *intentional vocalizations* of infants 8 to 14 months of age. Intentional vocalizations were defined as any sequence of behavior that included infant vocalization while making eye contact with the mother. Eye contact accompanied by gesturing and/or looking back and forth was scored as an attempt to direct the adult's attention using intentional vocalization. They found that Stage 5 causality was significantly related to infants' use of intentional vocalizations. It was concluded that Stage 5 causality may be a necessary, although not sufficient, achievement for intentional vocalizations.

Folger and Leonard (1978) investigated the relationship of Stage 6 means-ends performance to the acquisition of referential words and two-word combinations. Using items from the Uzgiris and Hunt (1975) scales, they found that although the majority of children using two-word combinations performed at Stage 6 on means-ends tasks, this finding did not always hold. They found one child who used only single words performing at a Stage 6 level on means-ends and a child using two-word combinations who had not yet achieved Stage 6 performance. These findings are similar to those of Ingram (1975, 1977) and Corrigan (1976) with regard to the relationship between mental representation and syntax. Folger and Leonard (1978) concluded that Stage 6 performance on means-ends tasks could not be related with any degree of precision to the use of two-word combinations. Therefore, although means-ends ability may be important for the appearance of certain performatives, Stage 6 means-ends performance may bear on the acquisition of syntax in only a very general way.

Recently, Steckol and Leonard (1981) examined the relationship of means-ends and symbolic play to performative usage within a train-

---

[5] Recall from the previous discussion concerning mental representation that Bates et al. (1975) found Stage 6 object permanence to co-occur with referential *speech*.

ing paradigm. In contrast to some of the above studies, they found training children on means-ends tasks did not facilitate the use of performatives relative to a control group that received no training. However, the authors noted certain methodological problems in the training of means-ends and concluded that although means-end schemes are clearly not necessary for the acquisition of performatives, future work may demonstrate a facilitative role.

Time and Space   The possible relationship between sensorimotor time concepts and language remains virtually unstudied because it is difficult to investigate the concept of time during the sensorimotor period. As Flavell (1963) pointed out:

> Piaget devotes relatively few pages to this special development, probably for the very good reason that here evidence is exceptionally hard to come by (p. 147).

Similarly, the relationship between sensorimotor spatial concepts and language development remains relatively unexplored, although there is some data of a general nature. Bates et al. (1977), in their cross-sectional study of 25 infants, reported that performance on the spatial relations tasks of the Uzgiris and Hunt (1975) scales was a poor predictor of communication, both gestural and linguistic. This suggests that spatial concepts as measured by the Uzgiris and Hunt tasks had little influence on the development of imperative and declarative performatives.

Cognitive Concepts and Language

Two aspects of cognition were distinguished at the beginning of this chapter: 1) cognitive structures, the deeper, more general underlying cognitive knowledge; and 2) cognitive concepts. Concepts, which have been variously referred to as meanings, semantic intentions, cognitions, categories, etc. differ from the deeper cognitive structures in their more direct codability. At least three major positions exist regarding the possible relationship between concepts and language: 1) linguistic determinism; 2) cognitive determinism; and 3) the interaction between concepts and language to form the final, mature concept.

Linguistic Determinism   The notion that language determines or shapes concepts is most often associated with the Sapir-Whorf hypothesis:

> It is quite an illusion to imagine that one adjusts to reality essentially without the use of language . . . the fact of the matter is that the "real world" is to a large extent unconsciously built upon the language habits of the group (Slobin, 1971, p. 120).

Linguistic determinism maintains that the segmentation of reality into concepts is arbitrary. In effect, an initially undifferentiated reality is organized and categorized for a native speaker by his or her native language. It follows that different languages will lead to different segmentations of reality. The structure of thought, then, varies across language groups (for more detailed reviews see Slobin, 1971; Hoijer, 1974). Evidence supporting linguistic determinism is exemplified by Whorf's (Slobin, 1971) description of the Eskimo's multiple-terminology for snow. Whorf argued that because the Eskimo language has several words for snow, each of which refers to a different "kind" of snow, and English has only one "snow-term," Eskimos conceptualize this domain differently from English-speaking people. The evidence in this case rests solely on the lack of a word-to-word correspondence between Eskimo and English. Brown and Lenneberg (1954) offered experimental evidence supporting a form of linguistic determinism. They found that the codability of a color correlated with the accuracy of recall of that color in a recognition task. The common interpretation of these findings is that memory for color names is facilitated by the linguistic coding of the color. In other words, language facilitates cognition (memory). Actually, a weaker form of the Whorfian hypothesis is supported here (discussed by Slobin, 1971)—that is, language predisposes or facilitates (but does not determine) a speaker's ability to think in particular ways.

Linguistic determinism has come into disfavor as more research has been conducted. For example, studies by Furth (1966) showed that deaf children, despite a lack of verbal language, do not differ significantly in cognitive ability from normal children. These findings are inconsistent with a deterministic view of language. From another perspective, it has been recognized that speakers of one language do understand the concepts expressed by another language, even though word-to-word translation is lacking (Cromer, 1976). For example, the English speaker can certainly come to recognize (and potentially speak of) the Eskimo's different kinds of snow.

Cognitive Determinism   As a result of the above kinds of evidence and in reaction to the nativist claims of Chomskian linguists, investigators turned to a consideration of the conceptual bases of language (Schlesinger, 1977). Essentially, cognitive determinism maintains that the child's concepts are first acquired on a nonlinguistic basis and then mapped by the appropriate linguistic markers (Bloom, 1973; Clark, 1973b; Slobin, 1973; Nelson, 1974). This amounts to a translation from one representational system (conceptual structuring) to another (language) (Bowerman, 1978b). There are several sources of evidence in support of this position, many relating to the very beginnings of language.

Huttenlocher (1974), studying three children's very early comprehension abilities, suggested that a knowledge of meaning (concept, schema) may be prerequisite for attending to the word sounds associated with that meaning. Macnamara (1972), in his theory of the beginnings of language learning, outlined a position in substantial agreement with Huttenlocher:

> Infants learn their language by first determining, independent of language, the meaning which a speaker intends to convey to them (p. 1).

Similarly, Nelson (1973), in her study of 18 infants' first words, adopted the assumption that, at least for the beginnings of word production, the child must first possess the concept. She maintained:

> The child moves from concept to name, from those aspects of the world to which he already attends (and has organized into structural wholes) to the less salient linguistic invariance (p. 101).
> The child must have a schema or concept in order to learn the word that applies to it (p. 98).

Ricks (1972, cited in Cromer, 1976), in a study of children's first words, proposed that the child is an active participant in word-learning and initially attempts only those words for which he or she already has acquired concepts. Ricks found that certain words: 1) occurred only in the presence of the corresponding event; 2) showed overgeneralization; and 3) in contrast to "dada" words (words with very loose referents), were readily imitated. Cromer's (1976) interpretation of the Ricks' study is consistent with cognitive determinism: "The child has a number of concepts which he attempts to use and to generalize to other situations" (p. 294). Moreover, Cromer suggested that the child invents words for the concepts that he or she wishes to express, at least in the sense that the child searches for the linguistic marker that expresses the existing concept. Clark (1973b) proposed that features of word meaning have their origin in prior nonlinguistic, perceptual organization; that is, the semantic features defining initial linguistic categories are primarily derived from the encoding of the child's percepts (Clark, 1973b). Furthermore, the more general semantic features are acquired first, with increasingly specific features being added as development proceeds. Because acquisition consists of the progressive addition of features, the theory assumes that the child's initial use and interpretation of words differs from the adult's (Clark, 1973b). The phenomenon of overgeneralization in word use constitutes the major source of supportive evidence for both the perceptual basis of children's word meanings and the initial discrepancy of those meanings from the adults. Bowerman (1978b) called attention to the inconsistency between the occurrence of overextensions and linguistic determinism. Bowerman reasoned that the child probably hears linguistic labels only in correct contexts; that is, adults do not tend to commit labeling errors in the presence of the child. (However, see Mervis and Mervis, 1982, for an account of maternal mislabeling.) If language determines conceptual organization, then errors by children in category-labeling would not be expected. Bowerman suggested that a plausible explanation for a child's overextension of any linguistic form over a range of situations differing systematically from his or her linguistic experience is the child's unique formulation of a concept on a nonlinguistic basis. Bowerman (1978b) also pointed out the inconsistency between the existence of nonlinguistic strategies and the claims of linguistic determinism. The line of argument is similar to that regarding overgeneralization. If language determines conceptual level, then nonlinguistic strategies should play no role in language development. However, the important role of nonlinguistic strategies in language development was suggested by several investigators (Clark, 1973a, 1975; Strohner and Nelson, 1974; Chapman, 1978). That such strategies exist is most consistent with cognitive determinism.

Brown (1973) provided evidence for cognitive determinism from later language development. He reported on three children, Adam, Eve, and Sarah, who used unmarked verbs in four different senses: imperative ("Get book"), past ("Book drop"), intention or prediction ("Mommy read"), and present temporary duration ("Fish swim"). These senses were suggested by the context of the children's utterances and the glosses of the parents. Subsequent development showed that these four senses first came to be marked in a way consistent with the adult markings. In other words, the use of contextual cues suggested the children had some notion or knowledge of these four senses of verbs, even though the children at first did not mark these senses linguistically. The subsequent marking of just these senses suggests that the rich interpretation was correct and that a nonlinguistic knowledge of these senses did exist before their linguistic marking. Similarly, Brown found that the interrogative intention seemed to arise in Stage I speech, marked initially by rising intonation. Only later did the children begin to mark questions by transposing the subject and verbal auxiliary. Finally, Brown discussed an example provided by Bloom (1973), involving possession. Bloom noted that names like "Mama" and "Dada" were initially used by Allison when the corresponding person was present or in reference to objects associated with these persons. Later, after acquiring the names of the objects, Allison sometimes referred to these objects by the object's name and sometimes by the possessor's name. At the time of this shift in naming, Allison may have had some concept of possession, although an appropriate linguistic marker was not yet used.

Slobin (1973) also cited supportive evidence for cognitive determinism from bilingual children (Mikeš and Vlahović, 1966; Mikeš, 1967). By age 2, two children acquiring both Hungarian and Serbo-Croatian exhibited control of several Hungarian case endings indicating locative relations. At the same time, they showed little evidence of controlling locative expressions in Serbo-Croatian. Slobin argued that because the linguistic marker was present in Hungarian, knowledge of locative relations could be attributed to the children. However, because control of the locative marker in Serbo-Croatian was absent, would it be concluded that the children lacked the locative concept? The children's control of the Hungarian locative marker strongly suggests that they had the concept, even though they failed to mark it in Serbo-Croatian. Slobin argued that such evidence clearly demonstrates that surface form may not reflect the underlying concepts that are present but that the use of contextual cues will allow interpretations crediting children with such concepts before their linguistic marking.

Interactionist Position: Linguistic Determinism Revisited   Even though a sizeable collection of data supports claims of cognitive determinism, advocates of this position would probably reject the notion that language *never* has any effect on conceptual development (Bowerman, 1980). The typical viewpoint is that the effects of language are observed later; it is the beginnings of language that depend on prior concepts (Nelson, 1973; Bowerman, 1980). However, this position is confronted with conflicting data that suggests that language may affect conceptual development, even in the very early stages of language development.

Several investigators questioned whether conceptual development is sufficient to explain language (Blank, 1974; Cromer, 1976; Bowerman, 1976; Schlesinger, 1977). Both linguistic determinism and cognitive determinism overstate the case. Cromer (1974), for instance, proposed a weak cognitive hypothesis—that cognitive abilities are necessary but not in themselves sufficient to explain language acquisition. Specific linguistic abilities may also be functioning in the learning process. Cromer's reconsideration of the strong conceptual bases for language acquisition in favor of a weaker posture seems to have been motivated by recent evidence, best interpreted in terms of linguistic determinism. However, similar evidence prompted other investigators to accept an even stronger and more explicit hypothesis. Bowerman (1978b) reviewed some of the recent phenomena that are difficult to explain solely in terms of cognitive determinism. She pointed out that an appeal to conceptual development alone cannot explain the transition from nonlinguistic, cognitive organization to the corresponding linguistic categories and the forms that mark them. Bowerman (1976, 1978b) and Schlesinger (1977) maintained that nonlinguistic categorization of the environment is distinct from linguistic categorization. What is needed is a description of the mechanism by which nonlinguistic organization is translated into language-specific categories. Conceptual abilities alone do not explain the translation mechanism; they simply provide the input to it. Both Bever and Mehler (in Discussion, Sinclair-deZwart, 1971) made a similar point with regard to the translation of cognitive structures into language categories.

A second issue cognitive determinism must contend with is linguistic elaboration. Imagine that a child has acquired a concept, for example, rudimentary questioning, and begins to mark it with an incipient linguistic marker, for example, rising intonation. In the course of language development, the child will exhibit various linguistic advances in marking his questions (see Brown, 1968, for some proposed stages of development in questions). What is the motivation for these linguistic advances? The nonlinguistic concept is not a probable candidate because it was observed to be present before linguistic elaboration. That is, each linguistic advance does not seem to coincide with an associated conceptual advance. A clear example from very early language development is provided by Bloom's (1970) discussion of the three meanings of negation—nonexistence, rejection, and denial. Nonexistence was the first meaning to be expressed with a linguistic form. Rejection and denial appeared later and were initially expressed with the simple forms used to mark nonexistence. As development progressed, nonexistence came to be marked by a more complex linguistic form. Because no change in the concept of nonexistence was associated with this increase in grammatical complexity, conceptual influences could not have determined the linguistic changes (see Cromer, 1976, for further examples and discussion).

Another problem for cognitive determinism is the apparent existence of purely syntactic devices that the child must master. Consider, for example, the device of particle movement: "The boy put his coat on"/"The boy put on his coat." Particle movement is an optional rule with no effect whatsoever on meaning—a purely syntactic device having no semantic or nonlinguistic perceptual basis. The rule is governed by purely formal aspects of the system. Schlesinger (1977) also noted that certain linguistic categories, such as gender, and certain grammatical rules, such as agreement, extend beyond those characteristics of language that are required for the expression of nonlinguistically attained concepts. Similarly, Cromer (1976) cautioned against ignoring the possible existence of specific linguistic abilities bearing on language learning. Some anecdotal evidence by Dore et al. (1976) is related to Cromer's point. They found evidence for what they termed "presyntactic devices" (mechanisms for extending the length of what is essentially a single-word utterance), like reduplication ("car car") and prefixing a word with a meaningless phonetic element (/a/ more; /te/ bottle). The presyntactic devices do not express structural meaning; rather, they serve as "linguistic placeholders" to:

> . . . allow for a transition from single word utterances to syntax without requiring the child to deal with the conceptual content or semanticity of structural meaning (p. 24).

There are several other sources of evidence for the role of language in concept development. Carter (1975) provided an example from very early language development. She traced the development in one child of the morphemes "more" and "mine" from the gestural level to the semantically differentiated use of these words. She found that the child consistently differentiated m-initial monosyllables on a phonetic level *before* distinguishing their meanings. Carter concluded that the differentiated production of the m-initial monosyllables (similar to Blank, 1974, discussed below) was a necessary step in sorting out their underlying concepts.

> It appears that in this case the establishment of their individuality as distinct sounds was necessary to pave the way for their subsequently developing individuality of meaning (p. 236).

Blank (1974) described a similar situation for later language development, where children also seem to use production in discovering underlying concepts. She noted that children usually use their sensorimotor abilities (action, imitation, etc.) to organize and assign meaning to the physical world; that is, the child can arrive at the meaning by attempting several possible actions in response to a word or by imitating the adult model that constitutes the appropriate response to the word. However, in the case of such words as "why" and "how," gestural (action) correlates, visual cues as to their meaning do not exist. In such cases, sensorimotor strategies fail. Blank maintained that the child, faced with such failure, must produce the words and utilize adult reactions to them as a guide to their underlying concepts. The child, then, does not possess the concept initially; rather, the use of the word indicates active hypothesis-testing—and active searching for the concepts underlying "why" and "how." Finally, Bowerman (1980) provided clear examples from data on her daughters of how language might influence conceptual development from the earliest stages of language acquisition. Consider the description of Christy's acquisition of "hi" at 18 months. Christy had used "hi" as a greeting for some time. Her mother then initiated a game in which she put a finger puppet on the end of her own finger and said "hi," as if the puppet was greeting Christy. The concept that resulted in association with "hi" was one of "something resting on or covering the hand or foot"—an interesting, although admittedly peculiar, concept by adult standards. Bowerman suggested that the most plausible explanation for the formation of this unexpected concept is that the word "hi," in its particular context, led Christy to interpret it in connection with something on the finger (later generalized to the covering of other appendages such as feet) rather than in its known sense of a greeting. It appears that the use of "hi" may have stimulated Christy to formulate a new or additional hypothesis regarding the concept underlying "hi." A similar example is found with Bowerman's daughter Eva, also at 18 months. Eva first acquired the word "kick" in the sense of kicking a ball. Bowerman felt that rather than attribute the learning of "kick" to some special nonlinguistic salience involved in "kicking," a more plausible explanation is that frequent modeling of the word "kick" in this context highlighted the kicking of the ball and provided it with some special salience for Eva. From examples such as "hi" and "kick," Bowerman concluded that even during the earliest stages of language acquisition, language can stimulate a search for a corresponding concept.

The evidence presented above persuasively shows that language can influence conceptual development, even to the point of stimulating, early in acquisition, the initial formation of some concepts. However, such evidence certainly does not require a return to strong linguistic determinism, as described in the first part of this section. Several investigators (e.g., Bowerman, 1976, 1980; Schlesinger, 1977) adopted an interactionist position. Schlesinger (1977) clearly described this position. He proposed that two problems must be addressed to account for conceptual and language development: 1) the interpretation problem; and 2) the categorization problem. The interpretation problem refers to the necessity of nonlinguistically organizing, structuring, and categorizing the environment. This nonlinguistic structuring is a prerequisite to language learning and does not require linguistic input. The categorization problem, on the other hand, refers to the linguistic categorization of objects, states, processes, events, etc. coded by a particular language. Here, linguistic input is needed; cognitive determinism alone cannot explain the categorization problem. Schlesinger argued that to complete conceptual development by delineating the conceptual boundaries marked by a particular language (i.e., to solve the categorization problem), linguistic input is required. That is, a concept can be partially formed on a nonlinguistic basis, but the concept's completion in terms of the specification of concept boundaries requires experience with the language. Consider the concept of agent. When a mother hands a bottle to her child, she is, no doubt, the agent. But when she is simply holding the bottle, is she still functioning as the agent? Is the bottle an agent that is holding or "containing" the milk? Only linguistic input can delineate concept boundaries and allow solution of the categorization problem. As stated, the interpretation problem can conceivably be explained within cognitive determinism. But cognitive determinism need not necessarily be invoked to explain interpretation. As Schlesinger (1977) put it:

> What is claimed here is merely that in effect the formation of a given concept may be triggered off by linguistic input, not that the latter is indispensable for it (p. 161).

Recently, Schlesinger (1982) argued that the primary emphasis in word learning is best placed on the linguistic component. He pointed out that there is a notable lack of independent evidence for nonlinguistic categorization before language. This raises serious questions as to whether prelinguistic categories even exist. Consequently, there is no compelling evidence that nonlinguistic categorization is necessary to an account of word learning. Schlesinger, in fact, argued that it is not. Instead, a nonlinguistic concept is simply a concomitant of learning words. What remains unresolved from attempts to explicate the relationship between nonlinguistic concepts and early word learning is: 1) whether children form nonlinguistic categories at all *before* language; and 2) whether such nonlinguistic categories, in fact, serve to facilitate word learning (Schlesinger, 1982).

To summarize, a substantial body of evidence is available in support of both linguistic and cognitive determinism. At best, each position alone functions only as a partial explanation of language development. The position that seems most consistent with the available data is the interactionist position advocated by Schlesinger (1977) and Bowerman (1976, 1980). Recently, however, Schlesinger (1982), based on the lack of independent evidence for prelinguistic categorization, advocated that primary emphasis in an account of word learning be placed on the linguistic component.

General Cognitive Stages and Language

In Piaget's theory, major achievements at any sensorimotor substage are held to represent an intergrated totality. The attained structures of a substage show a high interdependence, as if each formed partial processes within a total system (Flavell, 1963) (however, see Bates, 1979, for an alternative discussion of this). Consequently, a number of investigators have been interested in the attainment of a *general* stage of cognitive functioning (e.g., Stage 5) as important in the achievement of certain language milestones. However, as Ingram (1977) pointed out, very few studies have attempted to investigate the role of general cognitive stages in language acquisition.

Attainment of general Stage 6 functioning, i.e., the culmination of the sensorimotor period, has been suggested as prerequisite to language. Sinclair-deZwart (1971) viewed the achievements of the sensorimotor period as a necessary attainment for the acquisition of language. Similarly, Brown (1973) noted:

> The intellectual achievement of the first 18 months of life, what Piaget calls the sensorimotor period, seems to be just the necessary prerequisites for the semantic relations expressed by the word order in English in Stage 6 (p. 151).

Brown went on to speculate on what particular sensorimotor abilities underlie a number of the semantic relations found in Stage 1. Slobin (1973), drawing on Piagetian theory and the universality of early sentence meanings, proposed that the child will express only what he already knows: " . . . the pacesetter in linguistic growth is the child's cognitive growth . . . " (Slobin, 1973, p. 184).

Ingram (1975, 1977) attempted to examine the relationship between general cognitive stages and language by defining a general cognitive stage as the occurrence of a *cluster* of behaviors primarily reflecting the performance level of a particular stage (e.g., Stage 5). Using this definition of general cognitive stage, Ingram arranged the observations of Piaget and several turn-of-the-century diarists into chronological sequences—one sequence for language and one for a wide variety of cognitive behaviors. Comparison indicated that for most of the children, the initial production of words in small numbers was marked by Piaget's Stage 5. Furthermore, for those studies containing information on comprehension, the observations indicated a substantial number of words were *comprehended* during Stage 5. Comparing the diary results to previously gathered linguistic data from his own studies, Ingram suggested that sensorimotor Stage 5 is associated with what he termed Period 1, a period of single words used in a variety of functions (see Ingram, 1974). He suggested that Stage 6 is associated with Period 2, a lengthy period where single words are propositionally complex (see Ingram, 1971, 1974). Based on his findings he concluded that "certain linguistic milestones occur along with certain sensorimotor stages (p. 25). However, he strongly cautioned against overinterpreting such findings, reiterating a justly conservative conclusion that the findings only indicate that certain linguistic and cognitive developments occur contiguously. Any interpretation attributing prerequisite or precursory status to cognitive stages is unwarranted.

In more recent work, the achievement of general Stage 6 sensorimotor functioning as necessary to various language milestones has not been supported. Citing a number of "multimeasure" studies, Bates and Snyder (1983) concluded that for normal and language-delayed children, there is not clear evidence that a general Stage 6 level of functioning is related to the beginnings of language use. Similarly, McCune-Nicholich (1981) noted that a high correlation between Piagetian sensorimotor stages and language has not received strong support. Miller et al. (1980) found no evidence that Stage 6 sensorimotor functioning was necessary to the development of comprehension of one- and two-word utterances. Veneziano (1981), based on her findings of a developmental progression in symbolic play abilities, suggested that analyses of representation in terms of general Stage 6 functioning are probably not sensitive enough to identify those relationships holding between representation and language.

EVALUATION OF THE EVIDENCE

The inclusion of cognitive intervention as part of early language intervention should rest on clear evidence that the former contributes to the effectiveness of the latter. To the degree that such evidence is unavailable, it is incumbent upon the clinician to be aware of such limitations and their implications for the use of cognitive intervention with infants. This section evaluates the strength of the data base provided by psycholinguists regarding cognition's relationship to learning language.

Five criteria are proposed as guidelines to evaluate the existing data base from which cognitive intervention content is drawn: 1) evidence should originate primarily from studies establishing causal links between domains; 2) measurement of cognitive functioning should be independent of language behavior; 3) cognitive abilities, including the various levels of attainment, as well as linguistic behavior should be precisely defined so that the predicted relationships between abilities in the two domains are clearly specified; 4) the tasks used to tap cognitive abilities have acceptable validity as measures of those cognitive abilities; and 5) evidence from training studies bearing on the effects of cognitive intervention on language teaching should be carefully considered. To the degree that studies fail to meet these five criteria, the strength of the data base underlying infant cognitive intervention would be correspondingly weakened. How well, then, do the studies from developmental psycholinguistics meet the proposed criteria?

Evidence Establishing Causal Relationships

Does the psycholinguistic literature on cognitive structures and concepts provide evidence for causal relationships? For the most part, the answer is no. The studies of cognitive structures are mostly correlational (Ingram, 1975, 1977; Corrigan, 1976, 1978; Bates et al., 1977; Bates, 1979). Correlational data are particularly problematic for specifying direct relationships between cognition and language. For example, Bates et al. (1977) cautioned that correlational studies provide only very weak evidence for dependence relationships because any correlational finding is always subject to explanation in terms of a third, unrelated factor.

In recognition of the problems associated with evidence resulting from correlational designs, Bates (1977, 1979) and her colleagues suggested supplemental sources of evidence. For instance, the use of normal and language-delayed children allows independent groups, differing only in their language development, to be compared on performance of cognitive tasks. Although studies of this type do not provide cause-effect information, they do allow the examination of whether the delayed development of a certain cognitive ability is associated with delayed language development. Several studies of this type do exist (Inhelder, 1966; Morehead, 1972; Snyder, 1978; Folger and Leonard, 1978). Unfortunately, the studies by Inhelder (1966) and Morehead (1972) dealt with linguistically advanced children, and hence, the findings have only general implications for the choice of early cognitive content. Bates et al. (1977) also suggested training studies as a source of supplemental evidence. Steckol and Leonard (1981) apparently provided the only training study that examines sensorimotor abilities and early language milestones.

Psycholinguistic studies of cognitive concepts are either primarily descriptive and correlational in nature (Brown, 1973; Clark, 1973b; Blank, 1974; Huttenlocher, 1974; Carter, 1975; Bowerman, 1980) or presented as theoretical or logical arguments regarding the concept-language relationship (see Macnamara, 1972; Nelson, 1973; Bowerman, 1978a,b). Slobin (1973), however, described evidence from two bilingual girls acquiring Hungarian and Serbo-Croatian that constitutes a kind of experimental evidence because the languages form two levels of an independent variable, with each child serving as her own control. The literature, in general, lacks causal studies of the relationship between cognition and language. Without a solid foundation of experimental studies, particularly training studies, the choice of cognitive content for intervention with high-risk infants becomes, at best, one of principled conjecture.

Independent Cognitive Evidence

Numerous investigators invoked independent measurement of cognitive functioning as necessary for an accurate evaluation of the relationship between cognition and language (Bowerman, 1978a; Siegel, 1978; Moore and Harris, 1978). How well do psycholinguistic studies meet this independent measurement criterion? A number of studies of cognitive structures (Morehead, 1972; Bates et al., 1977; Corrigan, 1978; Folger and Leonard, 1978; Snyder, 1978; Bates, 1979; Harding and Golinkoff, 1979; Miller et al., 1980; Veneziano, 1981) were successful in this regard and, as a result, their findings allow more reliable conclusions regarding cognition's relationship to language. On the whole, investigations of Piagetian cognitive structures do very well at meeting this criterion.

However, most studies on cognitive concepts do *not* meet the independent measurement criterion (Brown, 1968; Bloom, 1973 as discussed by Brown, 1973; Clark, 1973b; Blank, 1974; Carter, 1975; Bowerman, 1980). Work directed toward determining the role of cognitive concepts before language depended primarily on the *linguistic* data of already verbal children. Such language-dependent measures provided little direct insight into the existence, nature, and role of nonlinguistic concepts that may exist before early language milestones (Rice, 1980). The failure to use independent measures of cognitive concepts considerably weakens the current knowledge base on this aspect of cognition and its role in early language learning.

This failure is primarily attributable to the difficulties in measuring concepts or categories *nonlinguistically* (Rice, 1980; Schlesinger, 1982). Clearly, techniques to measure concepts independent of language are needed. Although sorting tasks have been used as a nonlinguistic measure of concepts or categories (Ricciuti, 1965; Nelson, 1977; Rice, 1980; Starkey, 1981; Sugarman, 1981), this method presents several problems:

1. It has been successful primarily with infants 12 months or older. Consequently, it may not be useful in investigations focusing on the prelinguistic period, the period in which the role of prior nonlinguistic concepts in early language learning can be most directly examined.
2. It is unclear from sorting whether a child has *category* knowledge or is simply using a strategy of *immediate* perceptual comparison of items (Rice, 1980; Schlesinger, 1982).

3. Sorting does not ensure representation of category information, a common criteria for category knowledge (Schlesinger, 1982).

Recently, multiple habituation paradigms and familarization techniques have been used to study category formation processes in infants (Cohen and Strauss, 1979; Strauss, 1979, 1981; Ross, 1980; Caron et al., 1982). These paradigms are successful with young infants and should prove useful in directly investigating nonlinguistic categories and their relationship to language.

However, it is impossible from the present evidence to characterize the relationship between cognitive concepts or categories and language. Faced with such a notable lack of independent evidence for prior nonlinguistic categories, there is not, as yet, compelling evidence either way regarding the necessity of such categories to an account of early language learning. There is clearly a need for adequate measuring techniques, particularly those that would be useful in the prelinguistic period of development.

Precise Definition

Corrigan (1978, 1979) pointed out that the definition of a cognitive ability determines when it is attained and, therefore, whether or not it is determined to relate to a linguistic achievement. Different criteria yield different results. Siegel (1978) presented a similar argument regarding the assessment of preoperational cognitive structures. Bates (1979) and her colleagues pointed to the use of different operational definitions of object permanence to explain conflicts between their findings and those of other investigators. Moreover, Corrigan (1979) noted that to achieve an understanding of the cognition-language relationship requires a precise statement of which cognitive abilities will be related to which linguistic abilities.

With the exception of Corrigan's (1976, 1978) work, studies of cognitive structures, like object permanence and means-ends, have not given great attention to precise definition. Rather, cognitive functioning has been defined in terms of a single stage of performance on a particular sensorimotor task or in terms of a general level of functioning across a number of sensorimotor tasks. Perhaps as a result of overly general definitions, studies have captured some indications of a relationship between sensorimotor structures, but with conflicting results regarding the details of the nature of the relationship. When cognitive and linguistic behaviors were precisely specified (e.g., Corrigan, 1978, 1981) very *specific* relationships of only moderate strength emerged between cognition and language.

Outside of sorting tasks, precise operational definitions of nonlinguistic cognitive concepts have not been employed. This directly reflects the heavy reliance of psycholinguistics on *linguistic* evidence for inference about prior *nonlinguistic* concepts. Because direct measurement of the nonlinguistic concept is seldom undertaken, an operational definition of a nonlinguistic concept is not needed. The lack of a precise statement of what constitutes direct evidence for a nonlinguistic concept clearly makes it difficult to specify the nature of the relationship between concept and language.

Validity of Cognitive Measurement

A fundamental aspect of any successful scientific endeavor is the adequacy of the measurement employed. Particularly critical to the study of human behavior, and certainly the complexities of the relationship between cognition and language, is the validity of the measuring device used. Does the device actually reflect the cognitive or linguistic ability of interest? Obviously, to the extent that there are questions regarding the validity of a measuring device, there is also a risk that a particular relationship between cognition and language, as measured, has not actually been demonstrated. Consequently, there is like risk that training on that cognitive ability may not be relevant for language acquisition.

Recently, a few investigators began to examine validity in the measurement of cognitive functioning. Their interest focused primarily on the tasks used to measure object permanence. Cornell (1978) emphasized that contingencies within a search task can affect the child's performance such that an explanation of search errors first requires a careful task analysis. He described several task requirements that could influence performance. Citing a study by Gratch et al. (1974), Cornell (1978) noted that successive search behavior seems to be related to the infant's attention and direction of gaze during the interval between the final displacement and search behavior. Furthermore, the tendency of a child to continue search (perseverate) at the location where he or she has experienced success most often could account for search errors. Bertenthal (1977) reported data indicating that the sequential, invisible, displacement tasks commonly used to assess object permanence do not actually tap representation, but rather reflect simple *persistence* of search behavior. That is, it is not necessary to attribute representation to the child who sequentially searched, but only that the child demonstrated the requisite persistence in searching. Bertenthal concluded that evidence from research using this type of task to examine the relationship between cognition and language is subject to question. Similarly, Corrigan (1981) examined invisible displacement and systematic search procedures in terms of certain task factors. From her findings, she concluded that invisible displacement procedures and systematic search tasks do not require representation, but rather are best explained in terms of sensorimotor search strategies. Most recently, Bates and Snyder (1983) pointed out that the wide range of findings on the relationship of object permanence to early word learning simply underscores the importance of careful task analysis. It seems that there is a growing consensus that for the common tasks used to assess object permanence, there are task factors unrelated to representation that may interfere with task performance. Additional research of this type is clearly needed. At present, the available evidence on cognitive abilities should be approached with some measure of caution and with a clear awareness that nontrivial questions regarding basic measurement remain.

Training Studies

Training studies contribute evidence directly relevant to establishing the functional relationship between the training of a particular cognitive ability and a particular linguistic ability (Bates, 1979; Bates and Snyder, 1983). However, as Leonard (1979) pointed out, training studies are hard to do and are virtually nonexistent in the psycholinguistic literature. Apparently, Steckol and Leonard (1981) provided the only training study involving cognitive abilities and early language. Rice (1980) reported a training study on the relationship between cognitive categories of color, as measured by a sorting task and the learning of color terms. It is clear that the available evidence using a training strategy is minimal at this time. However, despite the difficulties they present, training studies offer the strongest possible demonstration of the dependence of one domain upon another, and thus research efforts utilizing this strategy are needed.

Conclusion

The consensus of most investigators seems to be that there is an important relationship between certain Piagetian cognitive structures and language acquisition. This is particularly true of symbolic play and means-ends abilities. Although a number of studies support the relationship between object permanence and certain language milestones, when more precise characterizations of the relationship are attempted, opinion becomes much more divided (Corrigan, 1978). The findings related to Stage 6 object permanence do not strongly support a prerequisite or correlational relationship to first words (Bates et al., 1982; Bates and Snyder, 1983). However, there is suggestive evidence that the *completion* of Stage 6 object permanence relates to a sudden increase in vocabulary (Bloom, 1973; Ingram, 1975; Corrigan, 1978). There has been little support for the achievement of general Stage 6 functioning as necessary for language (Bates and Snyder, 1983;

Ingram, 1975, 1977; Miller et al. 1980; McCune-Nicholich, 1981; Veneziano, 1981). Rather, where relationships exist, specific sensorimotor abilities are involved.

There seems to be much less consensus regarding the relationship of cognitive concepts to early language development. Three major positions are discernible. Cognitive determinism remains strong in psycholinguistics (Nelson, 1973, 1977; Clark, 1973b, 1975). An ample body of evidence can be garnered in support of this position. In response to data conflicting with cognitive determinism, several investigators (e.g., Schlesinger, 1974, 1977; Bowerman, 1976, 1980) suggested adopting an interactionist position that embodies principles of both cognitive and linguistic determinism. More recently, Schlesinger (1982) seemed to move more toward a linguistic determinist position, arguing that the notion of "prelinguistic concept" is not necessary to an account of early word learning, but rather that such nonlinguistic concepts are simply concomitants of learning words.

With the application of the five evaluative criteria proposed earlier, it becomes clear that the nature and existence of the particular relationships reflected in any of the positions currently held is not strongly documented. In general, problems of measurement are the major obstacles. Nearly all of the data relating to sensorimotor cognitive structures are correlational. This provides only very weak evidence regarding dependence relationships (Bates et al., 1977); although training studies are direct sources of data regarding dependence and are particularly important sources for those concerned with early intervention, only one such study is apparently available (Steckol and Leonard, 1971). On the whole, the lack of precise definition of cognitive structures, themselves, and of the specification of what linguistic ability is related to what cognitive ability have led to troublesome variability in the available data (Corrigan, 1978, 1979; McCune-Nicholich, 1981). Although studies of cognitive structures have generally used independent cognitive measures, serious questions regarding the validity of these measures have been raised (Bertenthal, 1977; Cornell, 1978; Corrigan, 1981). Work directed toward the role of nonlinguistic cognitive concepts has suffered from a pervasive lack of independent measurement of nonlinguistic concepts. This failure to devise language independent measures supersedes all of the other criteria proposed. As Schlesinger (1982) forcefully argued, the lack of independent evidence for the existence of nonlinguistic categories before the onset of language by itself raises serious questions as to the necessity of such categories to an account of word learning.

It seems clear that very little is known in the 1980s about the nature and extent of any existing relationship between cognition and language, although suggestive data have given rise to a variety of positions. On the basis of the strength of currently available data, it cannot be said with confidence whether cognition and language do, in fact, enter into a dependence relationship or, instead, represent independent systems with mutually exclusive bases (see Bates et al., 1977, for a discussion of the latter possibility). The dilemma regarding the dependence relationship between the two domains is particularly acute when considering the role of nonlinguistic concepts in word learning. This is not to say that cognition and language are not related in some important way, but rather that the existence of any relationship has not, as yet, been strongly documented.

The major implication of this state of affairs for infant language intervention is that the interventionist must be cautious in adopting cognitive content for training. However, although the documentation is not very strong at this time, this does not warrant the exclusion of cognitive content for training. Correlational studies provide at least some evidence for a *possible* dependence relationship as do some of the language dependent data on the role of cognitive concepts. In the 1980s, inclusion of such content seems to be more prudent and less of a risk to training outcome than exclusion. However, the current state of the evidence warrants a healthy skepticism by the interventionist and an avoidance of wholehearted acceptance of any particular role of cognition or set of cognitive contents. What is at issue are the expectations an interventionist may reasonably entertain about the effect of cognitive intervention on language training. From the present data base, it is not clear what these expectations should be. Most investigators believe a modicum of cognitive sophistication must be achieved for language learning to proceed (e.g., Schlesinger, 1977). What is not yet clear is which particular cognitive abilities at what level relate to which linguistic abilities, what the nature and extent of such a relationship might be, and how much the training of certain cognitive abilities influences the training of language. Attention to future research on cognition and language, particularly training studies, and the charting of the effects of cognitive training on language in the clinician's own training program may be the most productive approach at present. Only through such a critical approach can the particulars of the cognition-language relationship and its specific role in early intervention be revealed.

COGNITIVE CONTENT IN EARLY LANGUAGE INTERVENTION PROGRAMS

With the above caution in mind, the sensorimotor structures of Piaget and relevant nonlinguistic cognitive concepts represent a reasonable starting point for the cognitive content of an infant language intervention program. However, the inclusion of such content raises important issues about training that were not addressed in the preceding sections: 1) Can these cognitive abilities be trained?; 2) Which cognitive abilities should be focused on when intervening with infants?; and 3) How might a clinician go about training these abilities in infants?

Cognitive Abilities: Can They Be Trained?

To include cognitive abilities in an intervention program is to, first of all, assume that they *can* be trained. The trainability of the deeper, Piagetian cognitive structures has been a subject of longstanding debate between Piagetian psychologists and advocates of learning theory. Obviously, implications of the research on cognition and language for training must rest on the fundamental requirement that cognitive abilities are trainable. The debate on trainability has focused primarily on later cognitive structures (e.g., concrete operations); however, the same logic would presumably apply to the deeper cognitive abilities of the sensorimotor period. Briefly, the positions are as follows: Within the Piagetian framework, constraints are imposed on both *what* can be trained and *how* a clinician can train it (Brainerd, 1978). Deeper cognitive structures cannot be trained in the sense of the initial establishment of a cognitive structure. The child must initially acquire the cognitive structure through his or her own active construction of reality. Training can be effective only after some minimal construction of the cognitive structure has taken place.

Investigators advocating learning theory approaches have taken an opposite view. These investigators maintain that the deeper cognitive structures *can* be trained. Although the issue is not resolved, learning theory approaches provide some evidence for the trainability of certain cognitive structures and, hence, the feasibility of cognitive intervention (see Brainerd, 1978, for discussion). The trainability of cognitive concepts seems less controversial. A sizeable literature from learning theory has dealt with concept formation and categorization suggesting categorization to be trainable.[6] In summary, if infant intervention is to include a focus on cognitive abilities that have been implicated as relevant to language learning, then those cognitive abilities must be approached as trainable. Fortunately, data exist that supports the trainability of both the deeper Piagetian cognitive structures and the more "superficial" cognitive concepts.

---

[6] Rosch (1975a, 1977) leveled criticism at studies of concept formation because of their use of arbitrary categories with discreet, well-defined boundaries; rather, category members are better characterized in a decreasing degree of membership with reference to a central, prototypical exemplar. However, these particular criticisms do not affect the conclusion that these concepts are trainable. Rosch, herself, used learning paradigms in research on the internal structure of categories (see Rosch, 1973).

What to Train: Speculation on a Cognitive Content

There are two major considerations in determining program content (Ruder, 1978): 1) the particular perspective of language taken by an interventionist; and 2) the appropriateness of the content to the target population of the program. Implicit in the present discussion is a developmental psycholinguistic perspective of language in which the concepts and forms acquired by the normally developing child are considered to provide a reasonable first approximation of the content for an intervention program. The target population is prelinguistic infants who are high risk for language delay. It has been suggested that cognitive developments during the period from birth to 2 years represent some of the most important developmental phenomena that bear on the onset of language and, therefore, constitute crucial content in an infant language intervention program.

Piagetian Sensorimotor Abilities

What deeper cognitive structures should be included as part of an infant language intervention program? Stage 6 object permanence does not appear to be necessary for the appearance of first words (Bates and Snyder, 1983). If, however, the language training goal is to increase early vocabulary, data from Corrigan (1978) and Ingram (1975) suggest Stage 6 object permanence would be a reasonable cognitive intervention goal. Well-developed imitative abilities have been implicated in explaining the appearance of language *before* a Stage 6 level of functioning (Ingram, 1975; Corrigan, 1976). Probably the most consistent evidence in support of a relationship between cognition and language comes from studies of symbolic play. However, the definitions and tasks used to assess symbolic play vary widely in these studies (McCune-Nicholich, 1981). Consequently, although results are generally positive, there is little to guide the clinician in determining what level or characterization of symbolic play is related to what linguistic advance. Similarly, Stage 5 means-ends has generally been found to relate well to the use of performatives (Bates et al., 1975, 1977; Bates, 1979) and the appearance of the intentional vocalizations (Harding and Golinkoff, 1979). However, in the only early training study available, training Stage 5 means-ends did not facilitate the use of performatives (Steckol and Leonard, 1981).

Categorization

Fundamental to the early linguistic knowledge acquired by children is the ability to structure their environment into manageable portions, i.e., the ability to categorize. The fundamental nature of categorization has been argued by Rosch (1977):

One of the most basic functions of an organism is the cutting up of the environment into classifications by which non-identical stimuli can be treated as equivalent.

The ability to use or comprehend combinatorial structure requires some concept of what constitutes *agents*, *actions*, and *objects of actions* and linking these categories to linguistic forms. Likewise, the ability to use or comprehend object or event names, usually the first linguistic ability noted in children, requires a knowledge of objects and/or event categories. Consequently, program content aimed at cognitive concepts can be approached in terms of the acquisition of categorization skills, specifically the nonlinguistic categorization abilities underlying the initial object and event names acquired by children.

Which object and/or event categories should be the focus of training for a particular child? This is not an easy question to answer in absolute terms because of the complications introduced by individual differences. Children vary in the way they choose to organize experience. For example, Nelson (1973) suggested that some children tend to see the function of language as labeling objects (*referential*). Thus, they tend to acquire general nominals, while other children tend to view language as a way to deal with people and manipulate the environment (*expressive*). These children tend to acquire relational terms, pronouns, etc. Individual differences must be considered when choosing the kinds of categories to be included in training for a particular child (see Rosenblatt, 1975, for potential ways for predicting individual style).

Choice of Categories   Even though an absolute listing of training categories is complicated by individual differences in children, a number of considerations provide an initial pool of potential training categories and a set of criteria by which to narrow that pool to a set of categories appropriate for a particular child. An initial pool of possible categories could be identified by choosing those object and event categories that are frequently early acquisitions of normally developing children. Nelson (1973), in a study of early lexical acquisition, found that for general nominals, the names of animals, food items, toys, vehicles, and household items predominated in that order for the first 10 words acquired.[7] By the time 41 to 50 words were acquired, the names for foods, body parts, clothing, animals, and household items were most frequent. The most frequent names for members of these early categories were:

---

[7] Nelson pointed out that both the names for animals and vehicles might have referred to toys.

Food—"juice," "milk," and "cookie"
Animals—"dog," "cat," "duck," "horse," "bear," "bird," and "cow"
Toys—"blocks," "ball," and "doll"
Vehicles—"car," "boat," and "truck"
Household items—"clock," "light," "blanket," "chair," and "door"
Clothing—"shoes," "hat," and "socks"

Nelson found that there was greater agreement among children for the first 10 words acquired than for the last 10 (of the 41 to 50 words acquired). The most common words in the first group of 10 words were "Mommy," "Daddy," "dog," "hi," and "ball." This kind of information provides a beginning in the choice of specific lexical categories, even though, as Nelson herself pointed out, children show a good deal of individual variation in their early vocabularies.

Several guidelines can be used to individualize the choice of lexical categories.

What Object and Event Categories Would Be Salient for the Infant[8] Nelson (1973), examining the content of early words, suggested that the first words acquired tend to mark categories of objects on which the child can act ("shoes," "ball," "dog," "juice") or those that do something (move or change) that the child observes (such as dogs, cats, trucks, or clocks). Thus, the ability to interact with or observe movement and change in an object is highly salient to children and stimulates the acquisition of those categories and their labels. In fact, Nelson (1973) pointed out that labels conspicuously missing from very early vocabularies are those referring to things that are simply "there," even though these objects may be frequently encountered by the child.

What Objects and Actions Will Likely Be Useful To Know and Talk About? Lahey and Bloom (1977) suggested that the frequency with which a child encounters certain objects or actions influences the utility of knowing about them. However, frequency alone may not always determine the utility of a category and its eventual label (Nelson, 1973). Lahey and Bloom (1977) also suggested considering the child's interest in certain objects or actions. For infants, this may translate into the objects and actions that seem to recruit attention.

---

[8] Because the population of concern here is primarily the prelinguistic infant in the first year of life, there is the problem of how to predict what is going to develop some degree of salience. This dilemma of predicting is also true of the other considerations in choosing training categories. It seems that the best that can be done is to use developmental data as a "ballpark" estimate of important categories. Specific category choices probably must follow the best guess of the interventionist, based on a consideration of the particulars of the child's environment.

What Objects and/or Actions Would Be Important in Expressing the First Semantic Relations? That is, from a knowledge of the infant's environment, what are likely objects and actions that might be placed into relations, such as *agent + action, action + object, locative + possession,* etc. (Brown, 1973; Greenfield and Smith, 1976)? As an example, Daddy's coffee cup that is placed routinely on the table by his chair may be an object that is likely later to occur in a possessive relationship and, therefore, the category, "cup," may have potential utility for the infant in the future.

In choosing initial training categories it is also very important to choose categories in which content or structure is easily and clearly demonstrable in the nonlinguistic context (Lahey and Bloom, 1977). Actions involving gross movements (e.g., washing, throwing, kissing, or tickling) may carry a higher probability for successful infant participation, and, therefore, may be more appropriate than actions associated with fine movements. Similarly, objects that are of some size so that their shape and other attributes are more easily recognized may be preferred over small or caricatured objects that may obscure important attributes. Furthermore, larger objects are probably more easily manipulated and explored by the infant than very small ones.

What Is the Theoretical Framework of Category Structure and Formation Being Used? This last consideration is very important in determining the nature of a training content focusing on categorization. It is to the interventionist's advantage to have some concept of the principles that are commonly used in structuring stimuli into categories. Hopefully, the ultimate effect of training would be the stimulation of general categorization strategies that parallel identified principles of category structure and formation.

PROTOTYPE THEORY: A THEORY OF CATEGORY STRUCTURE

Rosch (1975a, 1977, 1978) proposed a set of categorization principles, which she suggested are responsible for cultures partitioning the real world in their characteristic ways. Although her research concentrated on color and noun categories, the proposed principles may be applicable to other linguistic categories as well (e.g., deVilliers, 1980). Rosch proposed that natural categories are formed around discrete prototypes that represent a best example of a basic level category (as opposed to superordinate or subordinate levels).[9] Basic level categories

---

[9] An example of a basic level category would be "car." A corresponding superordinate category would be "vehicles," including trucks, buses, cars, etc. A subordinate category would be "Volkswagen," a particular subcategory of "cars."

represent the level of abstraction at which the various members of a category have the most attributes in common with each other. And it is the prototype or best exemplar of, say, the basic level category "car," that brings together the highest number of attributes common to all exemplars of "car." For example, a standard four-door Chevrolet probably brings together more attributes associated with "car" than does an Indianapolis-type racer, although both are "cars." It is the basic level categories that should, according to Rosch's model, be acquired first (Rosch, et al., 1976), and it is the prototype that forms the foundation of a basic level category. All other basic level category members are organized around the prototype in decreasing degrees of membership. That is, some members are better exemplars of the category than others.

Rosch (1978) suggested that two principles may account for the prototypical structure of natural categories: 1) cognitive economy; and 2) the perceived structure of the world. Cognitive economy (a very important principle because infants' cognitive abilities are relatively limited) is achieved when categories map the perceived world as closely as possible, thereby giving the most information for the least cognitive effort. According to Rosch, the attributes to be found in the perceived world are not arranged in an arbitrary fashion. Rather, certain attributes tend to co-occur with other attributes to form "clusters" of attributes, the occurrences of which are correlated with each other. For example, wings are much more likely to occur with feathers than with fur. Wings and feathers are highly correlated. This tendency of attributes to co-occur nonindependently results in information-rich bundles of perceptual and functional attributes that form natural discontinuities in the perceived world. These discontinuities stand out; they have a natural salience and high informational redundancy. It is at these information-rich discontinuities that category prototypes are mapped onto the perceived world; hence, it is the prototype that maximizes cognitive economy. The nature and origin of prototypes and the notion of internal category structure may prove important for training categorization in infants.

Recent data from psycholinguistics indicate that, like adults, very young children seem to utilize prototypical category structure. Anglin (1977) found that young children tend to learn the category membership of good category exemplars before poor ones, a finding consistent with prototypical category structure. Rosch et al. (1976) found that 3-year-old children, when given the opportunity to sort at a basic object level, did so much more frequently than at a superordinate level. From studies of very young children's overextensions of words, it seems that such overextensions are based on the identification of a prototypical referent. Words are then applied to referents having one or more features in common with the prototype (Clark, 1975; Bowerman, 1976, 1980; Rescorla, 1980).

Very recently, work in the area of infant categorization has suggested that 10-month-old babies can form a category of schematic face and that they seem to abstract a prototype from a series of nonprototypical faces (Sherman, 1981; Strauss, 1979, 1981). Moreover, Bornstein and his colleagues reported categorization of color and the presence of color prototypes in three- to four-month-old babies (Bornstein, 1975, 1976, 1978; Bornstein et al., 1976). These data provide a preliminary indication that Rosch's model can be profitably applied to categorization in infancy.

Two implications stem from the adoption of Rosch's prototype theory as a framework within which to pursue training. First, the guidelines proposed as a basis for category choice should be applied to the choice of basic level categories rather than superordinate or subordinate level categories. Second, the specific referents used to begin training should be the prototypical exemplar/s of the selected basic level categories. For example, if "car" is a basic level category of choice, the initial training exemplar/s should not be a peripheral member, such as an Indianapolis race car, but rather a more standard passenger car.

But how can it be determined which specific exemplar/s of a basic level category is/are prototypical, and which more peripheral? One approach is to utilize Rosch's own procedures of adult judgments. She simply provided adults with a list of exemplars from a basic level category (e.g., the category, "bird"), and asked them to rate the exemplars on a 7-point scale (1 = good exemplar; 7 = poor exemplar). The exemplar/s that had an average rating closest to 1 was/were considered to be the prototype (see Rosch, 1975b). This rating scale also allowed an estimate of the "distance" of other category exemplars from the prototype and could prove important in determining the training sequence of other category members. Anglin (1977) found that adult judgments of prototypes correlate well with the knowledge that preschool children have regarding category membership. That is, it is the prototypical members that preschoolers have learned. This suggests that adult judgments of prototypicality may, indeed, provide a valid index in which category members are also learned first by children.

Summary

What the choice of possible training categories should be cannot be set down in absolute terms. However, considerations such as developmental data, potential category salience and utility, and the ease of nonlinguistic demonstration of a category should provide ways to identify and individualize those categories that seem appropriate for a particular child. Furthermore, applying Rosch's prototype theory, categories of choice would be at a basic level of abstraction. Training would begin with referents identified as being prototypical exemplars of the selected categories. The prototypical referents of a category could be identified through adult rating.

TRAINING THE SELECTED COGNITIVE ABILITIES

After a cognitive content has been selected, the training procedures must be determined. The lack of data on training procedures for cognitive abilities in very young infants makes this a difficult task. Consequently, certain qualifications are in order before offering any speculations on how training might proceed:

1. *Most evidence supporting the successful training of certain cognitive abilities has come primarily from children in Piaget's preoperational stage (see Brainerd, 1978)* The training of sensorimotor abilities has received much less attention (Steckol and Leonard, 1981). Consequently, the procedures explained here must be regarded only as suggestions for ways in which a clinician might approach the training of certain cognitive abilities.

2. *Data regarding nonlinguistic categorization abilities in very young infants and how these abilities might be trained are very limited* The few studies available have focused primarily on highly salient stimuli, such as faces (Cohen and Strauss, 1979; Strauss, 1979, 1981; Sherman, 1981) and facial expressions (Caron et al., 1982) or on color (Bornstein, 1975). Infants show categorization of facial stimuli at about $7\frac{1}{2}$ months of age (Cohen and Strauss, 1979) and color categorization has been documented as early as 4 months (see Bornstein, 1978). Nonface categories (e.g., animal) have been documented at about 12 months of age (Ross, 1980; Husaim and Cohen, 1981). However, virtually no data are available regarding the categories of objects or events that are commonly associated with the earliest lexical items, the category-relevant attributes that recruit infant attention, or the training of categorization in prelinguistic infants. Moreover, the available infant categorization studies place little emphasis on relating categorization to issues in early language development (e.g., the role of such categorization in establishing initial word-object associations).

3. *Categorization in the high-risk infant may differ from the normal infant* The high-risk infant presents special problems that may require a shift in emphasis regarding content and, as a conse-

quence, a parallel shift in training procedures. Little information regarding categorization skills in high-risk infants is available.

4. *Only recently has the model of categorization presented here begun to be applied to infant categorization (e.g., Bornstein, 1976; Strauss, 1979, 1981; Sherman, 1981)* Predictions made by the model have implications for the structure of an infant training program; nevertheless, these predictions require further substantiation regarding their applicability to infants.

Training Model   The first concern relating to training methodology is the choice of a general training model or framework. The framework suggested here is the experimental analysis of behavior. Based on the arguments by Brainerd (1978) suggesting that learning-based approaches showed more training and generalization effects than Piagetian self-discovery procedures in establishing behaviors in very young infants (e.g., Rheingold et al., 1959; Todd and Palmer, 1968; Routh, 1969), the principles of the experimental analysis of behavior provide a workable technology for training cognitive structures and concepts.[10]

This technology provides a principled system of feedback or reinforcement (e.g., use of various reinforcement schedules, response cost), aimed at establishing behaviors efficiently with maximum maintenance and generalization and a workable framework for program development and evaluation (see Ruder, 1978 for further discussion of program development and evaluation). An experimental analysis of behavior requires precise operational definitions of terminal behaviors and the component tasks and sequence that lead to eventual attainment of the terminal behaviors. These explicit definitions allow objective and quantitative data to be compiled and can be used to judge the attainment of training or generalization criteria. In turn, quantitative data allow the evaluation of content, procedures, and sequence and the incorporation of appropriate modifications, if needed.

Training Cognitive Structures

Several guidelines for training should prove effective in establishing sensorimotor cognitive abilities.

1. Identify and formulate operational definitions for the terminal objectives and component tasks. Also, construct an initial sequencing of these tasks. These principles have already been mentioned in connection with an experimental analysis of behavior.
2. Training should coincide as much as possible with the child's environment and his or her interactions, thus maximizing the saliency

---

[10] See Reese (1966) for a clear discussion of the experimental analysis of behavior.

of training and contributing to increased generalization and maintenance of behaviors.

3. Use modeling to initially establish cognitive abilities. The effectiveness of modeling or "observational learning" has been discussed by Brainerd (1978) with respect to certain postsensorimotor cognitive abilities.

4. Use consequation, both positive and negative, during training. This is also part of an experimental analysis of behavior. Brainerd (1977) discussed the effectiveness of feedback (termed "simple correction") in the training of postsensorimotor cognitive abilities.

How might the above principle be applied to the training of sensorimotor abilities? First, the terminal objectives for the cognitive contents of interest (e.g., means-ends or symbolic play) would be formulated. For example, the terminal objective for symbolic play might be for the infant to use a stick as a spoon when pretending to eat. Once the end point of training is identified, the subtasks and sequence that would gradually build toward terminal behaviors can be defined. For sensorimotor abilities, the sequence in which these abilities emerge is determined by the theory. Brainerd (1977) pointed out that Piagetian stages are logically determined; subsequent stages incorporate a preceding stage plus "something more." Thus, an invariant order is logically assured. Sequencing, then, is a matter of training from, say, Stage 1 play behaviors through Stage 6 play behaviors.

Once the sequence is determined, then it must be decided what training subtasks are to be used at each sensorimotor stage. An obvious approach would be to tailor tasks closely to the observational examples given by Piaget as illustrating abilities at successive stages of development. Observational anecdotes are provided throughout Piaget's works on the development of intelligence in infancy (Piaget, 1952, 1954, 1962). A more accessible source of example tasks, drawn from the original observational anecdotes of Piaget, may be found in Uzgiris and Hunt (1975). This is an assessment battery that has sequentially organized a number of tasks spanning the range from Stage 1 to Stage 6 for all of the sensorimotor contents except time. Suggestions are provided for objects and directions for structuring each task. Although designed as assessment tasks, the same or similarly constructed tasks could prove useful in training target cognitive abilities.

Once the general structure of possible subtasks is formulated (e.g., following Uzgiris and Hunt, 1975), the tasks must be individualized for a particular child. Training should coincide as closely as possible with the child's environment. There are several components to consider in achieving this correspondence. First, the objects and materials used in the training tasks should be those that occur in the child's environment or those in which the child has demonstrated an interest. For example, in the training of symbolic play behaviors, it is obvious that toys and the play behaviors, themselves, must be interesting and relevant to the child in order to gain and maintain productive interaction on the child's part. The choice of such objects and activities depends on the interventionists' knowledge of each child's environment and the objects, etc., in which the child takes an interest. The interventionist must remain flexible regarding the use of certain objects and materials. Infants may quickly lose interest in an object and, consequently, the training task as a whole may suffer in effectiveness. The interventionist must be constantly aware of objects and activities that are interesting to the child so that appropriate changes in the task objects and materials can be made. Training conducted in the home would maximize the correspondence between training and the child's environment. This would be the ideal situation; however, the clinic setting could be arranged to resemble the infant's home environment. That is, chairs, a sofa, lamp, etc. could be spatially arranged to resemble the infant's home surroundings.

Having defined terminal objectives, subtasks and sequencing, and having identified the specific objects and materials to be used in training, actual training of behaviors must begin. Brainerd (1977) discussed two tutorial procedures that have met with some success in the training of certain postsensorimotor abilities: 1) observational learning (*modeling*); and 2) simple correction (*consequation*). Modeling here refers to another child or the interventionist showing the infant what an appropriate response would be for a particular task. Consequation refers to the positive or negative feedback provided by the interventionist or parent contingent upon the behavior of the infant in a task. Examples of positive consequences given after an appropriate response are a smile, clapping, tickling, or even an interesting facial expression or vocalization by the interventionist or parent. The specific nature of the consequences to be used (both positive and negative) must be individually determined for each child.

How might training be structured to utilize modeling and consequation? The following hypothetical example helps to clarify this:

Suppose the level of symbolic play at which the child substitutes one object for another (e.g., a stick for a spoon) is the terminal objective. The task is for the child to use a popsicle stick as a spoon when pretending to eat from a bowl. Currently, the child uses only a toy spoon in this task. A model of the appropriate play behavior would be given to the child. The game of "eating" would be initiated, and the interventionist would direct the infant's attention to another participating trainer. Instead of a toy spoon, the other trainer would dip a popsicle stick into a bowl and pretend to eat. He or she would be reinforced for good "eating" behavior. This could be repeated several times or alternated with trials where the infant is allowed to participate in the pretend eating. If modeling alone did not produce reasonably frequent occurrences of appropriate play to be reinforced, modeling could be successfully supplemented by "prompting" and/or "put-through" procedures. For example, the child could be prompted to substitute the popsicle stick for the toy spoon by being handed the popsicle stick as he or she initiates the pretend eating sequence. Positive feedback would be provided if the infant accepted the stick. This prompt would be gradually faded out until the infant was selecting the stick himself or herself. Another possibility, if necessary, would be to actually "put the child through" or "physically assist" the correct behavior. Here, at the initiation of the "eating" sequence, the trainer could place the stick in the infant's hand and, while holding the infant's hand, dip the popsicle stick into the bowl and then bring the stick to the infant's mouth to "eat." The degree of physical assistance would be gradually faded. A number of tasks requiring similar object substitution would be trained to promote generalization of this level of play.

Training Categorization

The training principles listed for sensorimotor cognitive abilities are also applicable to categorization skills. The overall goal in training categorization skills is to establish some equivalence in responding to all members of a category. For children who have some language abilities, response equivalence has usually been in terms of using the same word to label the members of a particular category while using a different word when confronted with members of another category. Another common response is to point to the appropriate category member associated with different words. However, for prelinguistic infants, the nonlinguistic as well as linguistic response repertoires are much more limited. One behavioral response that might be used with very young infants is visual orientation or head turning, e.g., right versus left (see Husaim and Cohen, 1981, for a description of a differential head-turning procedure used with 10-month-olds). Adopting such a response and its dichotomous nature suggests that training can be structured in terms of a choice task (Category A versus Category B), using right-left head turning as a "nonlinguistic naming" response for exemplars of Category A versus Category B. For the simultaneous training of two object categories, the terminal objective might be: When exemplars of categories A and B are randomly presented one at a time, the infant will turn or orient to the right when presented with an exemplar of Category A and to the left when presented an exemplar of Category B. Subtasks leading to this terminal behavior would first be concerned with establishing direction of head turning or visual orientation as a discriminative response to the two categories.

Unlike the sequencing of sensorimotor abilities, the training sequence of category content can take many forms. Which categories to train first out of the several finally chosen may result in making an arbitrary choice. At this point, one category may be as good as another. However, one useful factor in determining a sequence is the infant's apparent interest level in the objects constituting the chosen training categories. The degree of visual attention or manipulation stimulated by certain objects may help determine which categories receive training first.

The sequencing of the category referents during training might also take several forms. One possibility is to successively train single exemplars for each category. Here, the clinician begins with the prototype of each category and adds, one at a time, increasingly less prototypical exemplars until the infant responds appropriately to all target exemplars. Another possibility is to train appropriate responding to the prototype, then train a peripheral exemplar. Following this, the clinician alternately trains to criterion a more prototypical member and then a more peripheral member. Essentially, category training would be accomplished by working from "both ends" of the category toward a point midway between the prototype and the most peripheral member. An alternative to training successive single exemplars is to train two or three exemplars of a particular category as a group (one exemplar being the prototype) and then introduce, one at a time, the remaining exemplars to complete the category.

At this point, the formulation of terminal objectives, possible training sequences, and choice of specific categories have been made. How might the actual training of discriminative head turning proceed? The two training principles suggested previously were modeling, with the supplementary procedures of prompting and "putting-through," and the use of feedback or consequation. Again, a hypothetical example can best illustrate how these principles could be translated into training procedures.

Suppose that the two initial training categories are "bird" and "car" and training was to proceed by introducing exemplars of each category one at a time, beginning with the prototype and progressing to the most peripheral member. The initial task would be to establish discriminative head turning. Prompting and positive consequences can be used to do this. For example, the infant might be seated in the mother's lap facing the interventionist. The specific objective of this subtask would be to train a right head turn for "bird" and a left head turn for "car." The interventionist would present the "bird" prototype, first giving the infant an opportunity to clearly see it and then making it "fly."[11] The interventionist would then put the bird behind him or her, out of the child's view. As the bird is withdrawn, a prompt to the infant's right

---

[11] The demonstration of "flying" serves two functions. First, it makes the object dynamic, thus increasing its salience for the child. Second, it shows the child a salient movement associated with the object. Thus, the infant would have access to both perceptual attributes of the object, itself, and functional attributes.

would be activated to gain his attention in that direction. This prompt, for example, might consist of a small whistle or other noisemaker, set off to the right and activated by air from a squeeze bulb that the mother operates. When the infant turns to the right to locate the noise, the mother could hold out a toy (such as a doll, teddy bear, or other interesting object) in the right visual field and shake or wave it, etc. The toy, which should be interesting to the infant, would function as the positive consequence for looking to the right. The corresponding sequence of events would be used when the prototypical car is presented. The interventionist could present the car prototype and then perform a salient function (e.g., pushing the car on the floor). The child would be prompted by the noisemaker to turn to the left as the car is withdrawn by the interventionist. Upon the infant's turning to the left, the mother would hold out the toy as a positive consequence for turning left. When the child reliably and appropriately responds to the prompting, the prompt would begin to be faded out, possibly by gradually reducing the loudness of the noisemaker or gradually increasing the number of trials on which a prompt is not given. When the infant appropriately responds discriminatively to the two prototypes, generalization to untrained exemplars of each category could be assessed. If generalization is not found or is small, training could begin on the most prototypical exemplar to which no generalization was found. During the training of subsequent exemplars, the category exemplars already trained might require periodic presentation in order to maintain appropriate responding on the child's part. Training would proceed in this manner until the terminal objective was reached.

This is only one example of how one can establish equivalence for unique objects. Equivalence in terms of what the infant himself or herself does with objects is another aspect to consider. For example, through imitation, it could be established that particular objects can be used in particular ways and that these uses can be a basis for treating these objects as essentially the same.

Finally, a point needs to be made regarding the preceding example and the training implications of an interactionist position. The above example demonstrates the training of equivalence sets (categories) on a nonlinguistic basis. However, the possibility exists that an early introduction of category symbols (verbal or nonverbal) may facilitate the acquisition of categorization skills. This would be consistent with the interactionist position—the position judged most consonant with available data. However, the acceptance of this position carries implications that complicate matters from a training standpoint. The previous example illustrates one training approach consistent with an interactionist position. Further training implications are worth considering briefly. Schlesinger (1977) acknowledged that minimal nonlinguistic structuring of the environment must be present before linguistic experience can influence categorization.[12] However, for subsequent structuring of a category, either nonlinguistic or linguistic, experience may predomi-

---

[12] However, what constitutes "minimal" structuring has yet to be described.

nate, and which one predominates will likely vary with the particular category. This means that the interventionist must now identify the particular concepts that tend to be learned predominantly through linguistic or nonlinguistic experience. In addition, for any one concept, *children* may vary in whether they tend to learn it through linguistic or nonlinguistic experience. With this possibility, the interventionist must now identify each child's individual approach (linguistic or nonlinguistic) to each target concept. Finally, the interactionist position allows for both linguistic and nonlinguistic experience to be used in structuring the same concept. This adds a third approach that is available to a child in concept formation and which should be assessed by a clinician. Obviously, the interactionist position, although most consonant with current data, admits to a wide variety of possible interactions between nonlinguistic and linguistic experience in category formation. For the interventionist interested in maximally effective training, the issue is the problem of early identification of individual differences—in this case, cognitive styles in language learning, a problem that has received very little attention (but see Bowerman, 1976 for a general discussion of cognitive styles in language learning). More research on individual differences and their early identification is needed before interventionists can find maximum utility in the interactionist position. Clinicians should be sensitive to individual differences so that programming will remain flexible in terms of procedures, materials, etc. in an attempt to maximize benefit to the child.

SUMMARY

This chapter examines the relationship between cognition and the development of language and the implications of this relationship for early language intervention. The psycholinguistic literature on cognition and language was reviewed, both in terms of the relationship of deeper, Piagetian sensorimotor abilities to language and the relationship to language of more "superficial" cognitive concepts (meanings, semantic intentions, semantic relations, categories). Five criteria were proposed as a basis for evaluating the strength of the psycholinguistic data base: 1) evidence should ideally originate from studies establishing causal links between domains; 2) measurement of cognitive abilities should be independent of language; 3) cognitive as well as linguistic abilities should be precisely defined; 4) cognitive measures should be independently validated; and 5) evidence from training studies bearing on the effects of cognitive intervention on language learning should be available. From the review of available evidence it was concluded that investigators believe that an important relationship exists between cognitive abilities and language. This view receives some support from the data. However, applying the five proposed criteria suggested that this view, although intuitively compelling, rests on a relatively weak data base at present. Little is actually known about the existence and extent of any relationship between cognition and language.

It was suggested, however, that such a conclusion does not imply that cognitive content has no place in an intervention program. There is enough correlational data available to indicate that existence of a relationship between cognition and the appearance of language is certainly a possibility. Given this, to exclude cognitive content from an intervention program is not warranted. What the above conclusion *does* imply is that the role of cognitive content that is included in an intervention program should be viewed with a healthy skepticism and attention should be directed to future research on cognition and language.

Finally, speculations were offered regarding a cognitive content and some possible directions for the training of these abilities. It was suggested that certain Piagetian sensorimotor abilities constituted one aspect of cognition on which to focus training. Categorization, a basic aspect of cognition and an ability fundamental to language, was also proposed as an ability that warrants attention in developing a language intervention program for infants. The last section of the chapter dealt with how actual training of the suggested cognitive content might proceed. Several principles of training were suggested, followed by hypothetical examples illustrating how these principles might be applied in a training situation. Because of the lack of research on the training of early cognitive abilities, these examples were intended only as possible starting points for training—examples that might stimulate clinicians to formulate their own procedures by expanding upon or modifying these examples. To reiterate, there is simply very little known at present about effective training procedures for early cognitive abilities. Consequently, in order to deal with high-risk children *now*, much of the burden of developing such procedures rests with individual clinicians.

ACKNOWLEDGMENTS

The authors would like to acknowledge the support of grant HD 00870 from NICHD to the Bureau of Child Research, University of Kansas in the preparation of this manuscript.

REFERENCES

Anglin, J. 1977. Word, Object and Conceptual Development. W. W. Norton, New York.

Bates, E. 1976. Language and Context: The Acquisition of Pragmatics. Academic Press, New York.

Bates, E., 1979. The Emergence of Symbols: Cognition and Communication in Infancy. Academic Press, New York.

Bates, E., Camaioni, L., and Volterra, V. 1975. The acquisition of performatives prior to speech. Merrill-Palmer Q. 21:204–226.

Bates, E., Benigni, L., Bretherton, I., Camaioni, L., and Volterra, V. 1977. From gesture to first word: On cognitive and social prerequisites. In: M. Lewis and L. Rosenblum (eds.), Origins of Behavior: Communication and Language. John Wiley and Sons, New York.

Bates, E., Bretherton, I., Beeghly-Smith, M., and McNew, S. 1982. Social bases of language development: A reassessment. In: H. Reese and L. Lipsitt (eds.), Advances in Child Development and Behavior, Vol. 16. Academic Press, New York.

Bates, E., and Snyder, L. 1983. The cognitive hypothesis in language development. In I. Uzgiris and J. M. Hunt (eds.), Research with Scales of Psychological Development in Infancy. University of Illinois Press, Champaign-Urbana.

Bertenthal, B. 1977. The importance of task analysis. A reexamination of early representation. Paper presented at the meetings of the American Psychological Association, San Francisco.

Blank, M. 1974. Cognitive functions of language in the preschool years. Dev. Psychol. 10:229–245.

Bloom, L. 1970. Language Development: Form and Function in Emerging Grammars. MIT Press, Cambridge, MA.

Bloom, L. 1973. One Word at a Time: The Use of Single Word Utterances Before Syntax. Mouton, the Hague.

Bloom, L., Lightbown, P., and Hood, L. 1975. Structure and variation in child language. Monogr. Soc. Res. Child Dev. 40:2. (Serial No. 160).

Bornstein, M. 1975. Qualities of color vision in infancy. J. Exp. Child Psychol. 19:401–419.

Bornstein, M. 1976. Infants are trichromats. J. Exp. Child Psychol. 21:425–445.

Bornstein, M. 1978. Chromatic vision in infancy. In: H.W. Reese and L.P. Lipsitt (eds.), Advances in Child Development and Behavior, Vol. 12. Academic Press, New York.

Bornstein, M., Kessen, W., and Weiskopf, S. 1976. Color vision and hue categorization in young human infants. J. Exp. Psychol. 2:115–129.

Bowerman, M. 1973. Early syntactic development: A cross-linguistic study with special reference to Finnish. Cambridge University Press, Cambridge, England.

Bowerman, M. 1974. Discussion summary: Development of concepts underlying language. In: R.L. Schiefelbusch and L. Lloyd (eds.), Language Perspectives—Acquisition, Retardation, and Intervention. University Park Press, Baltimore.

Bowerman, M. 1976. Semantic factors in the acquisition of rules for word use and sentence construction. In: D. Morehead and A. Morehead (eds.), Normal and Deficient Child Language. University Park Press, Baltimore.

Bowerman, M. 1977. The acquisition of word meaning: An investigation into some current conflicts. In: N. Waterson and K. Snow (eds.), The Development of Communication. John Wiley & Sons, New York.

Bowerman, M. 1978a. Words and sentences: Uniformity, individual variation, and shifts over time in patterns of acquisition. In: F.D. Minifie and L.L. Lloyd (eds.), Communicative and Cognitive Abilities—Early Behavioral Assessment. University Park Press, Baltimore.

Bowerman, M. 1978b. Semantic and syntactic development: A review of what, when, and how in language acquisition. In: R.L. Schiefelbusch (ed.), Bases of Language Intervention. University Park Press, Baltimore.

Bowerman, M. 1980. The structure and origin of semantic categories in the language learning child. In: M. Foster and S. Brandes (eds.), Symbol as Sense: New Approaches to the Analysis of Meaning. Academic Press, New York.

Braine, M.D.S. 1976. Children's first word combinations. Monogr. Soc. Res. Child Dev. 41:1. (Serial No. 164).

Brainerd, C.J. 1977. Learning research and Piagetian theory. In: L. Siegel and C.J. Brainerd (eds.), Alternatives to Piaget: Critical Essays on the Theory. Academic Press, New York.

Brainerd, C. 1978. Piaget's theory of intelligence. Prentice-Hall, Englewood Cliffs, NJ.

Bricker, W., and Bricker, D. 1974. An early language training strategy. In: R.L. Schiefelbusch and L.L. Lloyd (eds.), Language Perspectives—Acquisition, Retardation, and Intervention. University Park Press, Baltimore.

Bricker, W., and Bricker, D. 1976. The infant, toddler, and preschool research and intervention project. In: T. Tjossem (ed.), Intervention Strategies for High Risk Infants and Children. University Park Press, Baltimore.

Brown, R., and Lenneberg, E. 1954. A study in language and cognition. J. Abnorm. Soc. Psychol. 49:454–462.

Brown, R. 1968. The development of Wh-questions in child speech. J. Verb. Learn. Verb. Behav. 7:279–290.

Brown, R. 1973. A First Language: The Early Stages. Harvard University Press, Cambridge, MA.

Caron, R. F., Caron, A.J., and Meyers, R.S. 1982. Abstraction of invariant face expressions in infancy. Child Dev. 53:1,008–1,015.

Carter, A. 1975. The transformation of sensorimotor morphemes into words: A case study in the development of more and mine. J. Child Lang. 2:233–250.

Chapman, R. 1978. Comprehension strategies in children. In: J.F. Kavanagh and W. Strange (eds.), Implications of Basic Speech and Language Research for the School and Clinic. MIT Press, Cambridge, MA.

Clark. E.V. 1973a. Non-linguistic strategies and the acquisition of word meanings. Cognition 2:161–182.

Clark. E.V. 1973b. What's in a word? On the child's acquisition of semantics in his first language. In: T.E. Moore (ed.), Cognitive Development and the Acquisition of Language. Academic Press, New York.

Clark. E.V. 1974. Some aspects of the conceptual basis for first language acquisition. In: R.L. Schiefelbusch and L.L. Lloyd (eds.), Language Perspectives—Acquisition, Retardation, and Intervention. University Park Press, Baltimore.

Clark, E.V. 1975. Knowledge, context, and strategy in the acquisition of word meaning. In: D. Dato (ed.), Proceedings of the 26th Annual Georgetown University Roundtable: Developmental Psycholinguistics: Theory and Applications. Georgetown University Press, DC.

Cohen, L. and Strauss, M. 1979. Concept acquisition in the human infant. Child Dev. 50:419–424.

Cornell, E. 1978. Learning to find things: A reinterpretation of object permanence studies. In: L. Siegel and C.J. Brainerd (eds.), Alternatives to Piaget: Critical Essays on the Theory. Academic Press, New York.

Corrigan, R. 1976. Patterns of individual communication and cognitive development. Unpublished doctoral dissertation, University of Denver, CO.

Corrigan, R. 1978. Language development related to Stage 6 object permanence development. J. Child Lang. 5:173–190.

Corrigan, R. 1979. Cognitive correlates of language: Differential criteria yield differential results. Child. Dev. 50:617–631.

Corrigan, R., 1981. The effects of task and practice on search for invisibly displaced objects, Dev. Rev. 1:1–17.

Corrigan, R. 1982. The control of animate and inanimate components in pretend play and language. Child Dev. 53:1,343–1,353.

Cromer, R. 1974. The development of language and cognition: The cognition hypothesis. In: B. Foss (ed.), New Perspectives in Child Development. Penguin, Baltimore.

Cromer, R. 1976. The cognitive hypothesis of language acquisition and its implications for child language deficiency. In: D. Morehead and A. Morehead (eds.), Normal and Deficient Child Language. University Park Press, Baltimore.

deVilliers, J. 1980. The process of rule learning in child speech: A new look. In: K. Nelson (ed.), Children's Language, Vol. 2. Gardner Press, New York.

Dore, J., Franklin, M., Miller, R., and Ramer, A. 1976. Transitional phenomena in early language acquisition. J. Child Lang. 3:13–28.

Flavell, J. 1963. The Developmental Psychology of Jean Piaget. D. Van Nostrand, Princeton, NJ.

Folger, M.K., and Leonard, L.B. 1978. Language and sensorimotor development during the early period of referential speech. J. Speech Hear. Res. 3:519–527.

Furth, H. 1966. Thinking without Language: Psychological Implications of Deafness. Free Press, New York.

Goldin-Meadow, S., Seligman, M., and Gelman, R. 1976. Language in the two-year-old. Cognition 4:189–202.

Gratch, G., Appel, K.J., Evans, W.F., LeCompte, G.K., and Wright, N.A. 1974. Piaget's stage IV object concept error: Evidences of forgetting or object conception? Child Dev. 45:71–77.

Greenfield, P.M., and Smith, J.H. 1976. The Structure of Communication in Early Language. Academic Press, New York.

Harding, C., and Golinkoff, R. 1979. The origins of intentional vocalizations in prelinguistic infants, Child Dev. 50:33–40.

Hoijer, H. 1974. The Sapir-Whorf hypothesis. In: B. Blount (ed.), Language, Culture and Society: A Book of Readings. Winthrop, Cambridge, MA.

Horton, K. 1974. Infant intervention and language learning. In: R.L. Schiefelbusch and L.L. Lloyd (eds.), Language Perspectives—Acquisition, Retardation, and Intervention. University Park Press, Baltimore.

Horton, K. 1976. Early intervention for hearing-impaired infants and young children. In: T. Tjossem (ed.), Intervention Strategies for High Risk Infants and Children. University Park Press, Baltimore.

Husaim, J., and Cohen, L. 1981. Infant learning of ill-defined categories. Merrill-Palmer Q. 27:443–456.

Huttenlocher, J. 1974. The origin of language comprehension. In: R.L. Solso (ed.), Theories in Cognitive Psychology: The Loyola Symposium. Lawrence Erlbaum Associates, Potomac, MD.

Ingram, D. 1971. Transitivity in child language. Language 47:888–909.

Ingram, D. 1974. Stages in the development of one-word utterances. Paper presented at the Sixth Annual Stanford Child Language Forum, April, Stanford, CA.

Ingram, D. 1975. Language development during the sensorimotor period. Paper presented at the Third International Child Language Symposium, September, London.

Ingram, D. 1977. Sensorimotor intelligence and language development. In: A. Lock (ed.), Action, Gesture and Symbol: The Emergence of Language. Academic Press, New York.

Inhelder, B. 1966. Cognitive development and its contribution to the diagnosis of some phenomena of mental deficiency. Merrill-Palmer Q. 12:299–319.

Katz, J.J., and Postal. P. 1964. An integrated theory of linguistic descriptions. Research Monograph No. 26. MIT Press, Cambridge, MA.

Lahey, M., and Bloom, L. 1977. Planning a first lexicon: Which words to teach first. J. Speech Hear. Disord. 42:340–350.

Lee, L., Koenigsknecht, and Mulhern, S.T. 1975. Interactive Language Development Teaching. Northwestern University Press, Evanston, IL.

Leonard, L. 1979. Language impairment in children. Merrill-Palmer Q. 25:205–232.

Lovell, K., Hoyle, H., and Siddall, M. 1968. A study of some aspects of the play and language of young children with delayed speech. J. Child Psychol. Psychiatr. 9:41–50.

Macnamara, J. 1972. Cognitive basis of language learning in infants. Psychol. Rev. 79:1–13.

McCune-Nicholich, L. 1981. Toward symbolic functioning: Structure of early pretend games and potential parallels with language. Child Dev. 52:785–797.

MacDonald, J.D., and Blott, J.P. 1974. Environmental language intervention: The rationale for a diagnostic and training strategy through rules, context, and generalization. J. Speech Hear. Disord. 39:244–256.

MacDonald, J.D., Blott, J.P., Gordon, K., Spiegel, B., and Hartmann, M. 1974. An experimental parent-assisted treatment program for preschool language-delayed children. J. Speech Hear. Disord. 39:395–415.

Mervis, C., and Mervis, C. 1982. Leopards are kitty-cats: Object labeling by mothers for their thirteen-month-olds. Child Dev. 53:267–273.

Mikeš, M., and Vlahović, P. 1966. Razvoj gramatickih kategorija u deajem govoru. Prilozi Proucavanju Jezika, II. Novi Sad, Yugoslavia.

Mikeš, M. 1967. Acquisition des categoires grammaticales dans le langage de l'enfant. Enfance 20:289–298.

Miller, J., and Yoder, D. 1974. An ontogenetic language teaching strategy for retarded children. In: R.L. Schiefelbusch and L.L. Lloyd (eds.), Language Perspectives—Acquisition, Retardation, and Intervention. University Park Press, Baltimore.

Miller, J., Chapman, R., Branston, M., and Riechle, J. 1980. Language comprehension in sensorimotor stages V and VI. J. Speech Hear. Res. 23:284–312.

Moore, T., and Harris, A. 1978. Language and thought in Piagetian theory. In: L. Siegel and C.J. Brainerd (eds.), Alternatives to Piaget: Critical Essays on the Theory. Academic Press, New York.

Morehead, D. 1972. Early grammatical and semantic relations: Some implications for a general representational deficit in linguistically deviant children. In: D. Ingram (ed.), Papers and Reports in Child Language Development. Stanford University, Stanford, CA.

Morehead, D., and Morehead, A. 1974. From signal to sign: A Piagetian view of thought and language during the first two years. In: R.L. Schiefelbusch and L.L. Lloyd (eds.), Language Perspectives—Acquisition, Retardation, and Intervention. University Park Press, Baltimore.

Nelson, K. 1973. Structure and strategy in learning to talk. Monogr. Soc. Res. Child Dev. 38:1–2 (Serial No. 149).

Nelson, K. 1974. Concept, word and sentence: Interrelations in acquisition and development. Psychol. Rev. 81:267–285.

Nelson, K. 1977. The conceptual basis for naming. In: J. Macnamara (ed.), Language Learning and Thought. Academic Press, New York.

Piaget, J. 1952. The Origins of Intelligence in Children. International Universities Press, New York.

Piaget, J. 1954. The Construction of Reality in the Child. Basic Books, New York.

Piaget, J. 1962. Play, Dreams and Imitation in Childhood. Norton, New York.

Piaget, J., and Inhelder, B. 1969. The Psychology of the Child. Basic Books, New York.

Reese, E. 1966. Human behavior: Analysis and Application. W.C. Brown, Dubuque, IA.

Rescorla, L. 1980. Overextension in early language development. J. Child Lang. 8:321–326.

Rheingold, H., Gerwitz, M., and Ross, H. 1959. Social conditioning of vocalizations in infants. J. Comp. Physiol. Psychol. 52:68–73.

Riccuiti, H. 1965. Object grouping and selective ordering behavior in infants 12–24 months old. Merrill-Palmer Q. 11:129–143.

Rice, M. 1980. Cognition to Language: Categories, Word Meanings, and Training. University Park Press, Baltimore.

Ricks, D.M. 1972. The beginnings of vocal communication in infants and autistic children. Unpublished doctorate of medicine thesis, University of London, London.

Rosch, E. 1973. On the internal structure of perceptual and semantic categories. In: T.E. Moore (ed.), Cognitive Development and the Acquisition of Language. Academic Press, New York.

Rosch, E. 1975a. Universals and cultural specifics in human categorization. In: R. Brislin, S. Bochner, and W. Lonner (eds.), Cross-Cultural Perspectives on Learning. Halstead Press, New York.

Rosch, E. 1975b. Cognitive representations of semantic categories. J. Exp. Psychol. 104:192–233.

Rosch, E. 1977. Human categorization. In: N. Warren (ed.), Advances in Cross-Cultural Psychology, Vol. 1. Academic Press, London.

Rosch, E. 1978. Principles of categorization. In: E. Rosch and B. Lloyd (eds.), Cognition and Categorization. Lawrence Erlbaum Associates, Hillsdale, NJ.

Rosch, E., Mervis, C., Gray, W., Johnson, D., and Boyes-Braem, P. 1976. Basic objects in natural categories. Cog. Psychol. 8:382–439.

Rosenblatt, D. 1975. Learning how to mean: The development of representation in play and language. Paper presented at the Conference on the Biology of Play, June, Farnham, England.

Ross, G. 1980. Categorization in 1- to 2-year-olds. Dev. Psychol. 16:391–396.

Routh, X. 1969. Conditioning of vocal response differentiation in infants. Dev. Psychol. 1:219–226.

Ruder, K. 1978. Planning and programming for language intervention. In: R.L. Schiefelbusch (ed.), Bases of Language Intervention. University Park Press, Baltimore.

Schaefer, E.S. 1970. Need for early and continuing education. In: V.H. Denenberg (ed.), Education of the Infant and Young Child. Academic Press, New York.

Schlesinger, I.M. 1974. Relational concepts underlying language. In: R.L. Schiefelbusch and L.L. Lloyd (eds), Language Perspectives—Acquisition, Retardation, and Intervention. University Park Press, Baltimore.

Schlesinger, I.M. 1977. The role of cognitive development and linguistic input in language acquisition. J. Child Lang. 4:153–169.

Schlesinger, I.M. 1982. Steps to language. Lawrence Erlbaum Associates, Hillsdale, NJ.

Sherman, T. 1981. Categorization skills in infants. Paper presented at the meetings of the Society for Research in Child Development, Boston.

Siegel, L. 1978. The relationship of language and thought in the preoperational child: A reconsideration of nonverbal alternatives to Piagetian tasks. In: L. Siegel and C.J. Brainerd (eds.), Alternatives to Piaget: Critical Essays on the Theory. Academic Press, New York.

Sinclair-deZwart, H. 1971. Sensorimotor action patterns as a condition for the acquisition of syntax. In: R. Huxley and E. Ingram (eds.), Language Acquisition: Models and Methods. Academic Press, New York.

Sinclair-deZwart, H. 1973. Language acquisition and cognitive development. In: T.E. Moore (ed.), Cognitive Development and the Acquisition of Language. Academic Press, New York.

Slobin, D.I. 1971. Psycholinguistics. Scott, Foresman and Company, Glenview, IL.

Slobin, D.I. 1973. Cognitive prerequisites for the development of grammar. In: C.A. Ferguson and D.I. Slobin (eds.), Studies of Child Language Development. Holt, Rinehart and Winston, New York.

Smolak, L. 1982. Cognitive precursors of receptive vs. expressive language. J. Child Lang. 9:13–22.

Snyder, L. 1978. Communicative and cognitive abilities and disabilities in the sensorimotor period. Merrill-Palmer Q. 24:161–180.

Starkey, D. 1981. The origins of concept formation: Object sorting and object preference in early infancy. Child Dev. 52:489–497.

Steckol, K., and Leonard, L. 1981. Sensorimotor development and the use of prelinguistic performatives. J. Speech Hear. Res. 24:262–268.

Strauss, M. 1979. Abstraction of prototypical information by adults and 10-month-old infants. J. Exp. Psychol. 5:618–632.

Strauss, M. 1981. Infant memory for prototypical information. Paper presented at the meeting of the Society for Research in Child Development, April, Boston.

Stremel, K., and Waryas, C. 1974. A behavioral-psycholinguistic approach to language training. In: L.V. McReynolds (ed.), Developing Systematic Procedures for Training Children's Language. American Speech and Hearing Association, Monograph No. 18. Interstate Press, Danville, IL.

Strohner, H., and Nelson, K. 1974. The young child's development of sentence comprehension: Influence of event probability, non-verbal context, syntactic form, and strategies. Child Dev. 45:567–576.

Sugarman, S. 1981. The cognitive basis of classification in very young children: An analysis of object ordering trends. Child Dev. 52:1,172–1,178.

Tjossem, T. 1976. Early intervention: Issues and approaches. In: T. Tjossem (ed.), Intervention Strategies for High Risk Infants and Children. University Park Press, Baltimore.

Todd, G.A., and Palmer, B. 1968. Social reinforcement of infant babbling. Child Dev. 39:591–596.

Uzgiris, I., and Hunt, J. 1975. Assessment in Infancy: Ordinal Scales of Psychological Development. University of Illinois Press, Urbana, IL.

Veneziano, E. 1981. Early language and nonverbal representation: A reassessment. J. Child Lang. 8:541–563.

Wells, G. 1974. Learning to code experience through language. J. Child Lang. 1:243–269.

chapter 5

Semantic Considerations in Early Language Training

Laurence B. Leonard

Audiology and Speech Sciences
Purdue University
West Lafayette, Indiana

contents

It is now widely recognized that a complete understanding of children's linguistic functioning requires consideration of at least three aspects of their language: 1) the form or structure of the language; 2) the meaning conveyed in the language; and 3) how the language is put to use in a social context. In a sense, these aspects form a chronology of events; in the past decade, each has served as a dominant focus of research in child language, only to be replaced by the next within a few years. However, as emphasis has shifted from one aspect of language to another, a core of important information has been retained—information that is a basis not only for further investigation with normally developing children, but for work with language-handicapped children as well.

This chapter focuses on the aspect of language that deals with meaning—in particular, the meaning derived from relationships between words. After discussing the nature of these meanings in adult and child language, how these meanings can play a role in language intervention with handicapped children is illustrated.

THE NATURE OF SEMANTIC NOTIONS

For years, investigators of early language development have been aware that the young child's speech constitutes much more than labeling entities in the environment. This early speech also involves expressing the disappearance of objects, actions on objects, attributes of persons and objects, possessors of objects, and other meanings. Such relational meanings, or *semantic notions*, cannot be conveyed by word meaning per se. For example, the meaning of a child's utterance such as "Morgan bowl" is not totally contained in the meaning of the words "Morgan" and "bowl" because they provide no means of specifying that the bowl belongs to Morgan.

Semantic notions are often expressed via specific syntactic constructions, but they are not, themselves, syntactic in nature. The notion that an animate experiences some change in mental state, for example, can be conveyed in the construction "Karen anguished over Batman's death" as well as "News of the rejection exasperated Karen." Syntactic considerations may actually obscure distinctions between semantic notions if they are used as the sole means of semantic interpretation. For example, the distinction between an animate instigating some activity and an animate undergoing a change in mental state would be lost if the two utterances "Karen leaped over Batman's car" and "Karen anguished over Batman's death" were interpreted solely on the basis of syntactic structure.

143

Semantic notions do not seem to represent features of specific languages but, rather, of languages in general. Fillmore (1968) suggested that such notions may reflect certain judgments that humans are capable of making about events going on around them. Schlesinger (1971) noted that semantic notions seem to represent cognitively based relations that make a difference linguistically. These points of view prompted some investigators to examine the semantic notions reflected in children's developing speech in order to determine which aspects of cognitive structure children in general find significant for communication (e.g., Slobin, 1970; Edwards, 1973) and how these in turn are developed and organized (e.g., Bowerman, 1973; Leonard, 1976). A number of the semantic notions attributed to children's early speech are presented in Table 1.

Semantic notions are not easy to study. They are not directly observable and must, therefore, be determined by other means. This prob-

Table 1.   Frequently cited semantic notions reflected in children's early speech

Nomination	The naming of an inanimate or animate (*"That's a ring."*)
Recurrence	The awareness of the potential for reappearance of an object or reenactment of an event ("Could I have some *more water* please?")
Denial	The rejection of a proposition ("Vegetarians do *not* eat meat.")
Nonexistence	The recognition of the absence of an object that was once present ("The *furs* were *gone.*")
Rejection	The prevention or cessation of the occurrence of an activity or the appearance of an object (*"Stop* the shouting.")
Action + object	The recognition that an inanimate was receiving the force of an action ("The *grass* was *mowed.*")
Agent + action	The recognition that an animate initiated an activity ("The *boy threw* the football.")
Location	The recognition of a spatial relationship between two objects ("The *billfold* is on the *dresser.*")
Possession	The recognition that an object belongs to or is in the frequent presence of someone or something (*"My shirt* is at the cleaners.")
Attribution	The recognition of properties not inherently part of the class to which the object belongs ("The *room* was *chilly.*")
Experience + experiencer	The recognition that an animate was affected by an event ("The story *frightened Jan.*")
Action + instrument	The awareness that an inanimate was causally involved in an activity. ("The cake was *cut* by *a penknife.*")

lem is compounded by the fact that the precise semantic notions operative for the child and the way in which these notions are organized in his or her linguistic system may not be identical with that of the adult. The difficulties involved in analyzing the semantic notions reflected in a young child's speech may have led a number of investigators to impose their preexisting semantic categorizations on the child's language (Tyler, 1969). Howe (1976) and Duchan and Lund (1979) made a fairly strong case that a number of investigations of the relational meanings of children's two-word utterances have provided instead only information concerning adult interpretations of such utterances.

It seems that children's early word combinations may, in certain instances, reflect broader semantic categories and, in other instances, narrower categories than seen in the adult semantic system. For example, utterances that seem to involve separate notions in the adult system, such as *rejection* (e.g., "No book") and *possession* (e.g., "Daddy book") may for the child fall within a single semantic category of *social prohibition* (Edwards, 1978). In the case of the latter, Braine (1976) found evidence that children's early word combinations may be represented as a small set of positional formulas, each one of which specifies how to combine words to express some relational content. Often, these formulas are much more limited in scope than relations such as *agent* or *location*. Some specify only how a particular lexical item is to combine with other items (e.g., "Boom boom" + X), while others deal with a small set of lexical items sharing a particular semantic feature (e.g., activities involving oral consumption such as "eat" and "bite").

It is clear that evidence of how semantic notions are partitioned in the young child's linguistic system must be carefully utilized. Three types of evidence may be used: 1) differences in the point in time at which two otherwise similar semantic relationships are reflected in the child's utterances; 2) differences in the syntactic coding of utterances reflecting otherwise similar semantic relationships; and/or 3) consistent differences in the nonlinguistic behaviors that accompany the use of utterances, reflecting otherwise similar semantic relationships (Leonard, 1976). Although these types of evidence are useful in arriving at a much more accurate picture of the semantic notions operative for the child, this picture will no doubt only be approximate.

A number of investigators proposed that the emergence of semantic notions in children's speech may be related to the course of their cognitive development. For example, Brown (1973) noted similarities between the tendency of children at the third stage of sensorimotor intelligence, upon seeing a familiar object, to perform in abbreviated fashion the action schema most associated with it, and the semantic notion of *nomination*, a form of recognition through an action of articulation. Children during this same stage also develop a means of preserving events in their surroundings by repeating a behavior that accidentally produced an interesting effect in order to cause the effect to recur. Such occurrences are thought to closely resemble the semantic notion of *recurrence*. Other semantic notions may be related to cognitive development. For instance, the notions *agent* and *object* seem to presuppose the knowledge that the child and others are potential sources of causality and recipients of action; the child conceives of his or her own body as being subject to the actions of things as well as a source of actions that operate on them (Piaget, 1954). This sense of causality is usually not achieved until approximately the fifth stage of sensorimotor intelligence.

Two aspects of the nature of semantic notions suggest the importance of examining the semantic notions reflected in the speech of language-handicapped children.

Aspect 1: Semantic Notions, Although Separable to Some Degree from Syntax, Interact with Syntactic Coding Rules in Important Ways   The emergence of *location* in a child's linguistic system, for example, requires a means of coding this notion in speech. If a child demonstrates difficulty acquiring syntactic structure, then the acquisition of certain semantic notions may be slowed by his or her problems in developing a means to code them. An important finding from an investigation by Morehead and Ingram (1973) illustrates this kind of interaction.

Morehead and Ingram compared the syntactic structure evidenced in the spontaneous speech of normal and language-handicapped children matched for mean length of utterance (MLU). One of the comparisons yielding a difference between the groups involved a comparison of the mean number of lexical categories (e.g., object nouns, locative nouns) per syntactic construction type (e.g., noun + verb + noun). A greater number of lexical categories per syntactic construction type was seen in the speech of the normal children. Such a finding suggests two possible explanations involving semantic notions: 1) language-handicapped children may not yet have acquired certain semantic notions, and because these may have involved new lexical categories, the mean number of lexical categories per construction type would be reduced; or 2) the language-handicapped children may have only partial mastery of certain syntactic constructions and, thus, could not readily apply them to code newly acquired semantic notions involving new lexical categories.

Aspect 2: Semantic Notions Seem To Relate to Cognitive Development   This relationship may prove important in light of investigations suggesting that language-handicapped children may show a specific deficit in the figurative or representational aspect of cognition (see Leonard, 1979). In fact, Morehead and Ingram (1973) attributed the finding in their study, which seemingly pertained to semantic notions, to the fact that language-handicapped children may not use their linguistic systems creatively to produce highly varying utterances, a tendency perhaps relating to a representational deficit.

In summary, a good case can be made for examining the semantic notions reflected in the speech of language-handicapped children. Semantic notions seem quite related to two dimensions of development already suspect in the language-handicapped child—syntax and, more broadly, cognition. Several recent studies were devoted to this kind of examination.

THE SEMANTIC NOTION SYSTEMS
OF LANGUAGE-HANDICAPPED CHILDREN

Leonard et al. (1976) compared the semantic notions in the sampled speech of normal and language-handicapped children, employing a modification of Fillmore's (1968, 1971) case grammar as a method of analysis. The comparisons of importance to this chapter were among: 1) handicapped children and normal children of the same age; 2) handicapped children and younger, normal children; and, to further clarify the nature of any normal-handicapped differences, 3) handicapped children and normal children with equal utterance length.

The results indicated that the semantic notion of *nomination* was evidenced more frequently in the speech of the 3- and 5-year-old language-handicapped children than either the 3- or 5-year-old normal children. In addition, the 3- and 5-year-old handicapped children used utterances reflecting *agent* + *action* more frequently than the three-year-old normals. In turn, each of the two normal groups produced a greater number of utterances containing three or more semantic notions than either the 3- or 5-year-old handicapped children.

Finding differences between the normal and language-handicapped children was not particularly unexpected. However, further analysis was necessary before these differences could be assumed to mean that the semantic notions reflected in the speech of the language-handicapped children were less mature than those reflected in the speech of the normal children rather than simply different in some way. An attempt was made to compare the semantic notions reflected in the speech of normal children and handicapped children matched for MLU. Because MLU has been viewed as a general index of linguistic development, if differences were again noted it could be concluded that the semantic notions reflected in the speech of handicapped children were simply different from, rather then less mature than, those of normal children. In fact, however, no differences were observed.

Although Leonard et al.'s (1976) investigation indicated that the semantic notion systems of language-handicapped children resembled those of younger, normal children, the results could only be viewed as preliminary. A comparison between normal and handicapped children could only be made at one mean utterance length level (approximately 5.00 morphemes).

A subsequent study by Leonard et al. (1978) attempted to shed further light on this issue. This investigation differed from that of Leonard et al. (1976) in two respects. First, comparisons between normal- and language-handicapped children were made at two different levels of mean utterance length. Second, each of these levels represented an earlier period of development than that utilized by Leonard et al.

Semantic notions reflected in the speech of language-handicapped children were compared with those from a matched group of normal children with an MLU ranging from 3.50 to 4.00 morphemes; also, the semantic notions reflected in the speech of language-handicapped children were compared with those from a matched group of normal children with an MLU ranging from 4.40 to 4.90 morphemes. The children's sampled speech was analyzed according to a modification of Fillmore's (1971) revision of case grammar.

Although there were many similarities in the semantic notion systems of the normal and language-handicapped children, some differences were noted. This finding was somewhat unexpected because these two groups of children were matched for MLU; a matching that yielded no differences in the Leonard et al. (1976) study. Utterances reflecting both *agent + action* and *action + object*, relatively early emerging notions (see Bloom, 1970; Bowerman, 1973), were noted more frequently in the speech of the language-handicapped children. On the other hand, *experiencer + experience*, a later emerging notion (see Brown, 1973), was evidenced more frequently in the speech of the normal children. These results, along with an observation of the general distribution of semantic notions in the speech of the two groups, seemed to suggest that the language-handicapped children possessed a less mature semantic notion system than the normal children.

The nature of the differences between the two groups was consistent with an interpretation based along a continuum of presumed maturity of semantic notion development. However, the very finding of differences when the children were matched for MLU introduces a new issue. Language-handicapped children may not only possess less mature semantic notion systems than normal children, but their semantic notion development may lag further behind their development of surface features of language (estimated by MLU).

There is an alternative interpretation of these findings. Examining the use of grammatical morphemes (e.g., article, copula, and auxiliary) in the speech of these two groups of children, features which influence MLU, revealed that the normal children used grammatical morphemes in a greater proportion of obligatory contexts than the language-handicapped children (Steckol and Leonard, 1979). A longitudinal study of normal children showed that grammatical morphemes may appear first in utterances reflecting semantic notions that have been a part of the child's linguistic system for some time (Leonard, 1976). Because the normal children in the Leonard et al. (1978) investigation seemed to have reached a relatively stable point in the development of their semantic notion system, the acquisition of grammatical morphemes in their speech could have been at a more advanced stage than that of the language-handicapped children, whose semantic notion systems were still in a more active state of development. As noted in Leonard (1976), this can also take place in comparisons of two groups of normal children. One unanswered question is applicable to studies of normal children's language as well as those of language-handicapped children: What surface features of linguistic development allow a child who has less use of grammatical morphemes and a less developed semantic notion system to be equated in MLU with a child who has greater use of grammatical morphemes and a more developed semantic notion system? This question points out the possible drawbacks involved in studies that compare various features of language in groups of children who are matched for MLU.

Freedman and Carpenter's (1976) investigation of the semantic notions reflected in the speech of normal and language-handicapped children also involved matching according to MLU. The MLUs of the four normal and four language-handicapped children ranged from 1.40 to 2.10 morphemes. The semantic notion classification scheme of Brown (1973) was utilized as the means by which the children's spontaneous utterances were analyzed. Included also were the notions *introducer + entity* (*nomination*, e.g., "That car"), *recurrence + entity* (e.g., "More juice"), and *negation + entity* (e.g., "No shoe.").

In order to reduce the potential influence of the frequent use of only a few utterance types on the frequency of a given semantic notion, Freedman and Carpenter (1976) employed as data the ratio of the number of different utterance types reflecting a semantic notion to the total number of utterances reflecting the notion. The results indicated that the semantic notions reflected in the language-handicapped children's speech were very similar to those reflected in the speech of the normal children. The only difference observed was the language-handicapped children's greater use of utterances reflecting *introducer + entity*. The normal child language literature reveals that this notion is one of the earliest to emerge. In this regard, the Freedman and Carpenter findings are quite similar to those of Leonard et al. (1978).

Lee (1976) examined the semantic notions reflected in the speech of normal and language-handicapped children from a different perspective. She compared several different groups of children, including: 1) younger language-handicapped children; 2) older language-handicapped children; 3) two groups of mentally retarded children matched according to syntactic development with the younger and older language-handicapped children; 4) two groups of normal children matched according to syntactic development with the younger and older language handicapped-children; and 5) two groups of normal children matched according to chronological age with the younger and older language-handicapped children.

In her method of analysis, Lee modified Fillmore's (1971) case grammar, supplementing it by further inspecting verbs associated with semantic notions. Of particular interest was Lee's analysis of the children's errors with regard to these semantic considerations. An examination of these semantic errors in the four groups of normal children indicated that the nature of the errors changed with increasing syntactic development. One of the most common problems involved the absence of a semantic notion seemingly required in a particular utterance produced by the child. For example, an utterance such as "Doggie get," should have contained the semantic notion *object*. Similarly, "He puts his finger," was used by the child without including the semantic notion *goal*. With increasing development, such errors decreased. A different type of error, however, began to emerge. The children generally began to include obligatory semantic notions in their utterances; however, they sometimes selected a verb, which had lexical characteristics inconsistent with the semantic notions reflected in the utterance, such as "put" in the utterance "Putting shirt up." The appearance of this type of error seemed to be a fairly common occurrence in normal children between the approximate ages of 2.50 to 4.00 years.

Only the oldest group of mentally retarded children had progressed beyond the use of stereotypical utterance types to make a semantic analysis of their errors feasible. Their errors generally involved omissions of obligatory semantic notions. The speech of the younger group of language–handicapped children also consisted primarily of the omission of obligatory semantic notions; although their speech involved considerably more semantic variation than that of the retarded children. The speech of the older group of language-handicapped children displayed a slight reduction in semantic notion omissions and a substantial increase in errors involving the use of the wrong verb for the semantic notions reflected in the utterances.

A close inspection of Lee's data revealed that the speech of the language-handicapped children represented a less mature level of semantic development than that of the normal children with whom they were matched for chronological age. The younger normals committed errors primarily by selecting an inappropriate verb to accompany the semantic notions of an utterance, while the younger language-handicapped children's errors generally involved the omission of obligatory semantic notions. Similarly, the older language-handicapped children made both these types of errors with equal frequency, while the older normals progressed to the point where errors were relatively infrequent and solely in the form of inappropriate verb selection.

The speech of the two groups of language-handicapped children seemed quite similar to their normal counterparts who were matched for syntactic development in terms of distribution of the types of semantic errors. Furthermore, the change in error distribution from semantic notion omission to inappropriate selection of the accompanying verb in the younger to older language-handicapped groups paralleled that of normal children. Taken together, this evidence suggests that the semantic errors of language-handicapped children are of the same nature as those of younger, normal children.

"Language handicapped" has been used as a convenient although imprecise term for children whose difficulties center chiefly around linguistic functioning. Such children, as the term is used here, display linguistic skills seemingly disparate from their general level of intellectual, social, and emotional development. In addition, however, investigations were performed with other groups of children exhibiting linguistic difficulties.

Coggins (1979) collected samples of speech from four Down's syndrome children, two with MLUs below 1.50 morphemes and two with MLUs between 1.60 and 2.00 morphemes. Coggins did not use a normal group of children for comparative purposes; instead, he compared the semantic notion categories represented in the Down's syndrome children's speech with those described by Brown (1973) for normal children. His results indicated that the Down's syndrome children concentrated on the same, rather small number of semantic notions that normal children at the same level of MLU are reported to use.

Down's syndrome children with considerably higher MLUs were studied by Layton et al. (1976). The semantic notions in the spontaneous speech of these nine children, with MLUs averaging 5.37 morphemes, were compared with those in the speech of normal children with lower MLUs (4.63 morphemes) and normal children with higher MLUs (7.66 morphemes). Interestingly, the normal children were matched with the Down's syndrome children according to mental age. The semantic notion classification system of Chafe (1970) was employed for analysis purposes. The results indicated that the normal and Down's syndrome children used the same semantic notions. Differences existed in terms of their frequency of usage. The low MLU normal group was strikingly more different from the high normal group than from the Down's syndrome children. On the whole, the Down's syndrome children seemed more similar to the lower normal group than the higher normal group.

Using the system of Schlesinger (1971), Burns and Webster (1975) compared the semantic notions reflected in the spontaneous utterances of normal and emotionally disturbed children, matched according to MLU. Several differences emerged from this comparison. The *agent + action* (e.g., "Boy go") notion was evidenced more frequently in the speech of the emotionally disturbed children, while *agent + experience* (e.g., "I see") and *dative + object* (e.g., "Ball me") were evidenced more frequently in the speech of the normal children. Interestingly, these results are quite similar to the findings of Leonard et al. (1978). However, Burns and Webster interpreted their results somewhat differently. They pointed out that their results may have been related to difficulties that emotionally disturbed children have with perceptions of experience or, more generally, with self-concept. Some children may steer their perceptions away from relationships pertaining to their own experiences and may instead show an over-attention to overt acts. This interpretation may prove correct; however, it should be pointed out that *agent + action* is an earlier emerging notion, while *agent + experience* and *dative + object* are later developing ones. This raises the possibility that the emotionally disturbed children were instead simply showing a level of semantic notion development similar to that of younger normal children.

In summary, the studies indicate that the semantic notion systems of handicapped children may show certain deficiencies that require intervention. Furthermore, the nature of these semantic notions relative to those of normal children suggests that the intervention strategies adopted might benefit from information about normal semantic notion development. Training considerations represent the next topic.

ISSUES IN THE TRAINING OF SEMANTIC NOTIONS

The nature of semantic notion training is a critical issue. Although semantic notions clearly have cognitive parallels, a distinction must be made between semantic notions and cognitive notions. Semantic notions may properly be viewed as those aspects of cognitive structure that the child may attempt to communicate.

One important reason for this distinction is that semantic notions, being linguistic in nature, are categorized in a manner for communication purposes, which may be quite unlike underlying cognitive structures. Children's conceptual knowledge that they are capable of initiating actions that effect other objects, that objects can be located in space, or that people have territorial rights over certain objects does not necessarily mean that the semantic notions underlying their utterances can be neatly parceled into categories such as *agent, location,* or *possession*. The fact that children may have acquired certain concepts does not require their semantic categories to be specified according to particular types (see Slobin, 1966). For example, the cognitive attainment of causality may enable children to partition the relationship that they express into notions such as *agent* or *action*, but there is no reason why they should form such categories instead of more narrow ones (Bowerman, 1976). For instance, children might view activities expressed in utterances such as "Put box," "Throw ball," or "Give cookie" differently from those expressed in utterances like "Break it," "Open box," or "Cut pie" because the former utterances involve a change in location while the latter involve a change in state. Children may, in fact, mark such distinctions by using different syntactic rules to express each utterance. Similarly, relationships expressed in utterances such as "Daddy face" and "Daddy bed" might *not* be viewed as the same (*possession*) because one involves an animate and his body part and the other an animate and an object to which he has privileged access. Finally, there is no reason to assume that children even need the ability to express or comprehend the linguistic equivalents of the relationships they understand in their nonlinguistic environment (Bloom, 1973).

The distinction between cognitive and semantic notions is necessary in order to place the nature of semantic notion training in focus. The goal of training cognitive prerequisites to semantic notions, as seen in the work of investigators such as Bricker and Bricker (1974), is quite different from that of training semantic notions. Although the latter is clearly dependent upon prerequisite cognitive attainments, it is, nevertheless, primarily a linguistic enterprise.

Determining the Semantic Notions to Train

Typically, semantic notions represent a focus of training during the early period of linguistic development. By the time young normal children's MLU exceeds 2.00 morphemes, between eight and 15 semantic notions are evidenced in their speech (Brown, 1973). Frequently, semantic notion training, in conjunction with lexical training, may represent the beginning point of intervention with nonverbal children. The lower the level of the children's linguistic development, the greater the number of choices regarding which semantic notions to train.

There seem to be several feasible rationales for selecting the semantic notions to train.

Rationale 1: The Selection of Semantic Notions for Training Should Be Based on the Frequency with Which They Are Reflected in the Speech of Young Normal Children   This rationale (adopted by Miller and Yoder, 1974) is sound because frequency of occurrence may reflect the relative importance that children place on the different relationships of objects, people, and events about which they might communicate. Although there seems to be considerable variation among individual children, investigators are now attempting to determine which semantic notions are evidenced most frequently in the speech of large groups of children (e.g., Florance et al., 1976).

Rationale 2: The Selection of Semantic Notions for Training Should Be Based on the Sequence in Which Semantic Notions Emerge in the Speech of Normal Children   Miller and Yoder (1974) viewed this as less useful than the frequency of occurrence rationale because children's two-word utterances simply reflect the semantic notions evidenced during the single-word period in a more specific fashion. Few if any new semantic notions emerge with the onset of two-word utterances.

It is true that a primary distinction between the semantic notions of the single- and two-word utterance periods may be one of semantic specificity (see Greenfield and Smith, 1976; Rodgon et al., 1977). However, this added specificity in two-word utterances has made it easier to examine the order of emergence of particular semantic notions. These investigations of children's two-word utterances are, collectively, beginning to paint a picture quite consistent with Slobin's (1973) position that semantic notions emerge in a fairly consistent order. (A review of the available evidence appears elsewhere. See Leonard, 1976.) The sizes of the language samples utilized by some of these investigations were not sufficiently large to rule out the possible influence of the frequency of occurrence of the semantic notions on the observed order of emergence. This possible factor makes it feasible to present only a general order in which semantic notions emerge. (No ordering is intended within each cluster):

> *notice*
> *nomination*
> *negation*
> *recurrence*

action

object

agent

location

attribution

possession

experience

experiencer

instrument

An order of emergence such as this must be viewed with caution for two reasons. First, the particular semantic notion categories may reflect investigators' views of child language as much as they do the child's own language. Second, this ordering is based on word combinations that, in context, suggested a particular notion. However, these studies did not require the child to possess a productive syntactic coding rule for the semantic notion. Provided that other satisfactory means of identifying semantic notions are available, such a requirement is not essential. (In fact, it might be argued that this requirement confounds the study of semantic notions with syntactic factors.) However, when a productive syntactic coding rule is required, changes in the ordering of semantic notions can be expected (see Braine, 1976). Nonetheless, it is notable that different investigations agreed concerning the order in which semantic notions appear. Since the time of Miller and Yoder's (1974) writing, the order of emergence rationale for the selection of semantic notions for training has become quite realistic.

Rationale 3: The Selection of Semantic Notions for Training Should Be Based on the Child's Available Means of Surface Coding   This rationale is influenced by Slobin's (1973) principle that new semantic functions are first coded in previously acquired linguistic forms. For example, if a child has already acquired *agent* + *object*, coded in a noun + noun form (e.g., "Daddy door"), the semantic notion of *possession* rather than *attribution* may be selected for training because the former can be coded in the same noun + noun form. The availability of an existing coding rule may make the acquisition of the new semantic notion easier for the child.

Rationale 4: The Selection of Semantic Notions for Training Should Be Based on the Relative Frequency of the Nonlinguistic Relationships in Which Children Involve Themselves and Which are Possible to Communicate   The adoption of this rationale, which is perhaps the most individualized, requires observation of children in a setting resembling as closely as possible a natural situation for them. Tabulating the frequency with which they involve themselves in different types of activities is necessary. The semantic notion selected for training would be consistent with the type of nonlinguistic relationship in which the children were most frequently involved.

For example, one child with whom I dealt was observed for two sessions in a playroom setting. His most frequent activity consisted of attempts to perform actions deliberately made difficult for him, such as releasing a jack-in-the-box that had a tight lid, or reaching for a toy car just out of his reach. Often the child turned to me and pointed to the desired object or led me to it, going as far in some instances as moving my hand toward it. The high frequency of these behaviors led to the decision to train the semantic notions of *action, object,* and *agent.* Quite clearly, if the child was to produce an utterance in such circumstances, it would probably reflect one or more of these semantic notions (e.g., "Get," "Open box," "Larry get").

The use of this rationale for selecting semantic notions for training may be beneficial in that it provides children with the means to verbally communicate some perceived meaningful relationship in the environment. The training that follows this type of selection process is linguistic in nature; the children should have already demonstrated attainment of the cognitive notions required in order for the acquisition of the semantic notions to be possible.

Methodological Considerations

Central to the process of training semantic notions is the need for verbal stimuli to be accompanied by nonlinguistic relationships, which could serve as appropriate referents. If children are to learn that required utterances, such as "Ball chair" and "Cup floor," communicate a notion of *location,* they must be exposed during training to objects that share some spatial relationships with other objects. This is consistent with Bloom's (1973) position that children learn a linguistic mapping of environmental relationships that was understood previously. Children should clearly possess knowledge of these types of relationships before semantic notion training; however, unless the nonlinguistic relationships are presented to them during training, it may be quite unclear what types of notions are actually coded by the utterances they are to acquire. Examples of approaches making use of such nonlinguistic relationships are those of MacDonald and Nickols (1974), Willbrand (1977), and McLean and Snyder-McLean (1978).

After the appropriate nonlinguistic relationships during training are provided, other methodological decisions must be made that pertain to the type of verbal stimuli utilized and the manner in which the nonlinguistic events are presented. Such decisions are illustrated in the approach proposed by Miller and Yoder (1974), who suggested that a single, frequently occurring experience can serve as the referent for a particular semantic notion. This experience should be paired with the appropriate linguistic coding. After the child demonstrates mastery of this task, multiple experiences capable of serving as appropriate referents for the semantic notion should be presented. The approach proposed by Miller and Yoder makes use of imitation. The child is required to imitate the stimulus utterance, with subsequent fading of imitative prompts in order to promote spontaneous use of the utterances reflecting the semantic notion is consistent with the presented nonlinguistic relationship.

Table 2 summarizes the early phases of a training program, similar to the Miller and Yoder (1974) approach. This program was utilized to teach *location* to a boy, age 2 years, 3 months. Important information, such as the consequent events and the criteria for completing a given training phase, are excluded only to emphasize the stimulus and response components of the program. The child subsequently produced single-word utterances that reflected the names of the locations of particular objects. Although this observation suggested that the training program was successful, it may not be proper to conclude that the child had acquired the semantic notion of *location*.

Table 2.   The early phases of location training

Words to be taught: *"chair," "bed," "table," "floor"*
Materials to be used: chair, bed, table, floor, cup, ball, car, and doll

		Exemplary stimulus	Exemplary response
1.	a.	Place a familiar object so that the child can see it on something that he or she can identify.	
	b.	"Where's the ball?"	
		"Point to it." (Use gestural and physical prompts if necessary.)	The child points to the ball.
2.	a.	Refer to 1a.	
	b.	"Where's the ball?"	
		"Point to it."	The child points to the ball.
3.	a.	Refer to 1a.	
	b.	"Where's the ball?"	The child points to the ball.
4.	a.	Refer to 1a.	
	b.	"Where's the ball?"	
		"Chair, say chair."	"Chair."
5.	a.	Refer to 1a.	
	b.	"Where's the ball?"	
		"Chair."	"Chair"
6.	a.	Refer to 1a.	
	b.	"Where's the ball?"	"Chair."

Some investigators have been reluctant to elevate the meanings of children's single-word utterances to semantic notion status. For example, Brown (1973) suggested that it may not be safe to credit children with a semantic notion, like *possession*, unless they show the ability to alternate between the name of a present object (e.g., "shoe") and the name of its possessor (e.g., "Mommy"). This kind of caution may be appropriate. Although they convey different types of meanings, single-word utterances lack structural information and cannot specify relationships between words (Bloom, 1973). Furthermore, the specification of relations between words may represent a cognitive attainment beyond that at which many children at the single-word stage are operating. This attainment takes the form of internalized action schemes, which permit the relational aspects of the referent to be represented in the absence of the referent. Single-word utterances, on the other hand, may represent the use of words that are still action-dependent (Morehead and Morehead, 1974).

To explore the feasibility of Brown's more stringent definition of semantic notions to semantic notion training during the single-word stage, my research assistant and I worked with a language-handicapped girl, age 2 years, 11 months, who, at the commencement of training, operated at the single-word utterance stage. At the outset, she showed no evidence of single-word utterances that represented the names of possessors of objects. Our goal was to establish a means of teaching her to describe an object alternately with its name and its possessor. In order to maximize the likelihood that she would perceive the possessive relationship during stimulus presentation, the objects used as training materials belonged to us and were routinely on our person; my watch, ring, comb, and pen and my assistant's watch, ring, keys, and purse. At the beginning of each session, we would place each object on the table in front of the child.

Initially, the use of the lexical items associated with the objects was established. Our names were also included in lexical training because the child would need to know them in order to name the possessor of a given object at a subsequent point in training. Lexical training commenced with an imitative stage; the experimenter pointed to an object and said "What's this? Say _____ ." (When a person served as the stimulus in question, the verbal stimulus was changed to "Who's this? Say _____ .") All correct responses were reinforced on a continuous schedule; redeemable tokens were dispensed automatically by using a foot switch. After the child correctly imitated each lexical item on five consecutive occasions the child's responses were left under the stimulus control of the question: "What/who's this?" When each lexical item was again appropriately produced on five consecutive occasions, the pretest for single-word utterances representing names of possessors was administered.

This pretest involved presenting each object and asking "What's this?" Immediately after the child's response, a further directive was given: "Tell me about this." At no point during the pretest did the child name the possessor of an object, adding weight to earlier observations that she did not use this type of utterance.

The training procedure represented a modification of the Bandura and Harris (1966) modeling procedure. In the training sessions, my research assistant served as experimenter, and I served as a model. The child was told to listen and pay close attention to the model, for the model was going to talk about the objects in a "special way." When the object was presented to the model, in view of the child, the experimenter asked "What's this?" and the model simply provided the name of the object (e.g., "ring"). Immediately after this response, the experimenter said "Tell me about this," and the model responded by providing the name of the possessor of the object (e.g., "Larry"). Reinforcement was provided for every correct name-of-object/name-of-possessor pair of responses.

Only one-half of the objects were employed during this training. The others were withheld until post-testing. After the model had responded to each of the four objects twice, the child was asked to talk about the objects in the same manner that the model had. At this point, the model and child alternated producing appropriate utterances in response to the objects and the experimenter's "What's this?" and "Tell me about this."

After the child correctly produced each of the name-of-object/name-of-possessor pairs of responses on five consecutive occasions, the post-test was administered in the same manner as the pretest. The experimenter presented each object and asked "What's this?" After the child responded, the directive, "Tell me about this," was given. All eight of the original objects were utilized on the post-test. Four of these objects were withheld from the training of name-of-object/name-of-possessor responses. However, the child had many opportunities to associate the objects with their respective possessors because each was removed from the model and experimenter and placed on the table at the commencement of all sessions. It seemed that the child's use of the name-of-object/name-of-possessor responses to the withheld objects provided a look at the degree to which her acquisition of single-word utterances reflected *possession* and could not realistically be attributed to rote memorization effects. This was not deemed too much to expect of a child whose single-word usage is to be credited with a semantic notion such as *possession*.

The post-test results are presented in Table 3. The two errors that occurred may have been attributable to the child's inattentiveness. After administering the post-test, the two objects on which errors were noted were again presented, and the child performed correctly. In any case, the child's performance with the objects withheld from training was encouraging. The possessor of each object was named without error. This suggested that during training, she probably was not simply memorizing a specific name of a person to produce when a particular object was presented, but instead may have been providing the name of the person with whom the object could be logically associated. Nevertheless, our work with this child was primarily for illustrative purposes. Before definitive conclusions can be reached, a greater number of objects and possessors and, of course, children should be used. However, our work with this child suggested the feasibility of this type of training approach for purposes of semantic notion training at the single-word utterance stage.

When young children produce two-word utterances, their increased semantic specificity makes it more appropriate to assume that the semantic notions reflected in their utterances are truly relational. This is not to say that the semantic notions reflected in their speech are precisely the same as our interpretation of them (see Howe, 1976; Duchan and Lund, 1979); however, this increase in specificity does enable us to have a better picture of what children are learning to communicate.

A discussion of two of my investigations involving semantic notion training at the two-word stage will help clarify the role that training may play in a child's acquisition of semantic notions.

First Investigation   Eighteen children whose MLU ranged from 1.75 to 2.25 morphemes served as subjects (Leonard, 1975a). None of

Table 3.   Post-test performance after training designed to establish single-word utterances reflecting possession

Test object	"What's this?"	"Tell me about this."
Included during training		
Larry's ring	"Denise"[a]	"Larry"
Larry's pen	"Pen"	"Larry"
Denise's purse	"Purse"	"Denise"
Denise's watch	"Watch"	"Denise"
Withheld from training		
Larry's watch	"Watch"	"Larry"
Denise's keys	"Keys"	"Denise"
Denise's ring	"Watch"[a]	"Denise"
Larry's comb	"Comb"	"Larry"

[a] This response is deemed incorrect.

the children were diagnosed as mentally retarded, neurologically impaired, or hearing-impaired. Some of the older children possessed an apparent language delay. Through a modeling procedure similar to the one adopted by Bandura and Harris (1966), these children were trained in the use of two-word noun + verb utterances, such as "Larry sit." Such utterances were not previously noted in the speech of these children.

Each child was seen individually, and a third participant (an adult serving as a model) joined in the training procedure. The child was told to listen and pay close attention because the model was going to talk about some events in a "special way." When the visual stimulus was presented, the model was requested to talk about it. Generally, the model talked about the stimulus by using the noun + verb form, which was reinforced. To assist the child in identifying the characteristics shared by all correct utterances, the model intentionally failed to use the noun + verb form in approximately 20% of her utterances. Such utterances were identified as errors and were not reinforced.

After observing 10 utterances, the child was asked to talk about the visual stimuli in the same manner as the model. At this point, the model and child alternated producing appropriate utterances to describe the stimuli. After producing three consecutive correct utterances about the same visual stimuli that were previously presented to the model, the child was required to produce utterances of the noun + verb form in response to novel visual stimuli requiring unmodeled noun + verb utterances. Training was terminated when the child produced 10 consecutive novel and task-appropriate utterances.

One-half of the children were trained in the use of the noun + verb utterance form when describing actual ongoing, enacted events. For example, the child was asked, "What's happening here?" while observing me sit in a chair. These children were assigned to one of three conditions:

1. For one-third of the children, events were exposed which, if described, would require utterances reflecting *agent* (e.g., "Larry jump").
2. For another one-third of the children, four different types of events were randomly exposed: those that linguistically would reflect *agent* + *instrument* (e.g., "Hammer hit"), *experiencer* (e.g., "Larry sneeze"), and *object* (e.g., "Ball roll").
3. For the remaining one-third, only clues to events were exposed which, if described, would require utterances reflecting *agent*, *instrument*, *experiencer*, and *object*. For example, I stood in the middle of the room pointing alternately to myself and a chair next

to me and requested the child to tell me: "What's happening here?" A noun + verb utterance such as "Larry sit" was required in such a circumstance. The actual event that the utterance described was never carried out.

The remaining children were assigned to one of three tasks that were identical to those in which the other children were involved, except that pictures (depicting events or clues) rather than live events or clues were used as visual stimuli. For example, in one condition, a picture of a man driving a car was presented along with the request "What's happening here?" In the depicted clue condition, one picture took the form of a man standing next to a car, suggesting (in response to: "Make up what's happening here") an utterance such as "Man drive."

Notably the children presented with actual events or clues rather than pictures of events or clues showed greater use of the noun + verb form reflecting the semantic notions under investigation. Another important finding was that the children presented with events rather than clues to events during training showed greater use of the noun + verb form reflecting these semantic notions. These two findings together support the point made earlier: During semantic notion training, verbal stimuli should be accompanied by nonlinguistic events that could serve as appropriate referents.

A less expected finding of this study was that the children presented during training only with actual or depicted events requiring utterances reflecting *agent* did not differ in their post-test use of noun + verb utterances reflecting any of the four semantic notions from the children presented with events requiring utterances reflecting each of these four notions. This finding should probably not suggest that through the manipulation of nonlinguistic events requiring utterances reflecting one particular semantic notion (e.g., *agent*), children may in addition acquire several other semantic notions (e.g., *instrument, experiencer,* or *object*). It is true that the children presented only with events requiring utterances reflecting *agent* subsequently showed use of noun + verb utterances that reflected (at least in the adult system) other semantic notions. However, by virtue of the fact that the children applied the same syntactic form to each of these events simultaneously, there is no evidence that the children viewed them as involving distinct semantic notions.

This is not to say that the children had acquired an abstract syntactic form that had no semantic basis. DeVilliers' (1981) discussion of the Leonard (1975a) data probably best illustrates this point. Numerically speaking, the greatest post-test use of the noun + verb form in the Leonard study was associated with nonlinguistic events designed to depict *agent* relationships, regardless of the training condition to which the children were assigned. Applying the framework of the literature on natural concepts (e.g., Rosch, 1975; Rosch and Mervis, 1975), deVilliers concluded that category membership in the children's two-word utterances may not have been "all or none," but best considered analog, where there were some good examples, the prototype of the category (in this case, *agent* in the adult system) and other less good examples that "surrounded" it (e.g., *instrument* or *experience* in the adult system). Thus, what the children may have acquired was a syntactic coding rule for a rather broad, analog-based semantic notion, centering on *agent*-like relationships.

Second Investigation   This was very similar to the first in experimental design and focus (Leonard, 1975b). I was interested in determining whether or not the findings of the first study would apply as well to children representing a more handicapped population. The children, numbering 24, were functioning in the mild range of retardation. All were diagnosed as displaying language difficulties.

Like the first study the children were assigned to one of three training conditions. Unlike the previous study, however, all children were presented with ongoing (rather than depicted) events or clues to such events. Results indicated that the children presented with actual events rather than clues to events showed greater use of noun + verb utterances reflecting the semantic notions under investigation.

Although the children presented during training with events requiring utterances reflecting *agent* subsequently showed substantial use of utterances reflecting *agent*, the children of the group presented only with these events during training did not show much use of noun + verb utterances reflecting the other three semantic notions. This finding can be interpreted to mean that although the children were able to apply the syntactic form to a semantic notion throughout training, they were less apt to include peripheral instances as members of the semantic category. This tendency, of course, is not limited to handicapped children. From Braine's (1976) study it is clear that normally developing children often show evidence of extremely narrow semantic categories.

The nature of the training procedure involved in these two investigations seems to hold promise as a means of determining just what language-handicapped children learn during semantic notion training. Assume that a child is trained to produce noun + noun utterances reflecting *possession* in a manner similar to the manner in which single-word utterances reflecting *possession* were trained in the pilot investigation reported earlier. For example, upon being shown my pen, and given the directive, "Tell me about this," the child consistently produces an utterance such as "Larry pen." During post-testing, assume that the child is also exposed to someone performing some act with the objects. For example, the experimenter might pick up and hold my pen and ask the child, "Tell me about this." If the child responded with "Larry pen," it could be concluded only that the child is capable of indicating a possessive relationship, even in the face of distracting stimuli. However, an utterance such as "Denise pen" requires quite a different interpretation. Provided that we were careful in ensuring that the child had not previously used the noun + noun form to code relations resembling *agent + object*, the child's use of "Denise pen" (if such usage was fairly consistent) could suggest that the child perceived the experimenter's association with the pen as sufficiently similar to my association with the pen to use the same syntactic coding rule to express it. Thus, rather than assuming that the child acquired the semantic notion of *possession* during training, it might be safer to conclude that the child acquired a more general notion, such as *physical association* or the like. The child's usage might have been based on a principle such as: If the object is being manipulated by or is in close proximity to a particular person, use this person's name in the utterance. If not, use the name of the person who usually manipulates or is in close proximity to the object.

This issue was pursued in a preliminary fashion with a young language-handicapped boy, age 3 years, 9 months, whose speech consisted of single- and two-word utterances. Before working with this child, no use of noun + noun, noun + verb, or verb + noun utterances was observed.

Before noun + noun *possession* training commenced with this child, the lexicon was established. The same materials used earlier were employed here, and at the beginning of each session these objects were placed on the table in front of the child. Lexical training was conducted in a manner identical to the pilot investigation reported earlier; first by pairing the question "What/who's this?" with the imitative prompt and subsequently through the use of the question alone.

The pretest involved presenting each object, accompanied by the directive, "Tell me about this." At no point during the pretest did the child produce a two-word utterance reflecting *possession* or name the possessor of the object, confirming previous observations that he had not yet acquired this semantic notion. Also included on the pretest was an enactment with four of the objects, whereby the nonpossessor of the object acted on the object in some obvious manner. These enactments were also accompanied by the directive, "Tell me about this."

No instances of utterances reflecting *agent* + *object, action* + *object*, or *agent* + *action* were observed.

Training involved the use of the modeling procedure. After the experimenter informed the child to observe the manner in which the model responded, the object was presented to the model, in front of the child, and the experimenter said, "Tell me about this." The model responded in each circumstance with an appropriate noun + noun utterance reflecting *possession* (e.g., "Denise purse"). Reinforcement was provided on a continuous schedule.

One-half of the objects were employed during training and the remaining one-half were withheld until post-testing. After the model responded to each of the four objects twice, the child was asked to talk about the objects in the same manner as the model. The child and model then alternated producing appropriate utterances in response to the objects and the experimenter's verbal directive. When the child had produced task-appropriate utterances for each object on five consecutive occasions, the post-test was administered.

The post-test was identical to the pretest. Because all eight objects were used in the post-test, an examination of the child's use of noun + noun utterances reflecting *possession* could be assessed when objects not involved in training were presented. Furthermore, the enactments included in the post-test enabled an examination of the extent to which the child might apply the newly acquired noun + noun form; such an application might be taken to mean that the child's semantic categorizations were actually broader than those illustrated during training.

The results are presented in Table 4. This table shows that the noun + noun form was used as well when describing objects withheld from training. Such usage suggested that the child was acquiring a coding rule rather than merely memorizing a specific utterance for each object. Particularly interesting were the child's utterances used to describe actions performed on objects. Three of the four utterances suggested that the child was continuing to provide the name of the possessor plus the name of the object, despite the change in the manner of visual stimulus presentation. The sole nonpossessive utterance produced also took the noun + noun form. Because he applied the newly acquired noun + noun form to code a nonpossessive relationship, it might be assumed that rather than acquiring *possession* the child had acquired a more general associative notion. Yet, his other three utterances in these situations make it more appropriate to view the exception as an error rather than as evidence of a broader semantic categorization than *possession*. This was, in fact, confirmed through a

Table 4.   Post-test performance after training designed to establish two-word utterances reflecting possession

Test object and situation	"Tell me about this"
Included during training	
Larry's ring is presented.	"Larry ring"
Larry's pen is presented.	"Larry pen"
Denise's purse is presented.	"Denise pocketbook"
Denise's watch is presented.	"Denise watch"
Withheld from training	
Larry's watch is presented.	"Larry watch"
Denise's keys are presented.	"Denise keys"
Denise's ring is presented.	"Denise ring"
Larry's comb is presented.	"Larry comb"
Action on trained object	
Denise drops Larry's pen.	"Larry pen"
Larry pushes Denise's watch.	"Denise watch"
Action on untrained object	
Denise hits Larry's comb.	"Larry comb"
Larry throws Denise's keys.	"Larry keys"[a]

[a] This response is deemed to be incorrect.

re-presentation of this test item upon completion of the post-test, where the child provided the name of the possessor plus the object name. A final point concerning the semantic categorizations that may have been reflected in this child's post-test performance: The only possessive relationships included on the post-test were those involving persons who had participated as possessors during noun + noun training. Had the child been tested on possessive relationships involving other persons (whose names he knew) and objects to which the child knew these persons had privileged access, the scope of his noun + noun rule could have been more adequately assessed. Thus, the possibility remains that the child had acquired not a coding rule for *possession*, but instead a coding for a more narrow semantic categorization, such as the relationship between his "friends" at the clinic and the objects he associated with them.

SUMMARY

This chapter dealt with certain issues pertaining to semantic considerations in early language training. A case was made for studying the semantic notions reflected in the speech of language-handicapped children. Semantic notions are quite central to early language acquisition, and they interact with both syntactic and more general cognitive processes—two processes of questionable status in the language-handicapped child. Comparative studies suggested that relative to normal peers, language-handicapped children seem to possess deficient semantic notion systems reminiscent of those of younger normal children. This finding suggests that semantic notion training could involve the application of normative information, such as the sequence in which semantic notions emerge in the speech of normal children.

This sequence is not the only basis for selecting a semantic notion for training. This chapter has suggested other bases that may be appropriate. Regardless of the means by which a semantic notion is selected, however, certain conventions should probably be involved in the training procedure. The most critical seems to be the presentation of nonlinguistic events that represent the types of relationships to which the semantic notion being trained refers. Without this information, the child may be acquiring little more than a word-ordering rule of little substance and stability.

Semantic notion training at the single-word stage poses certain challenges. Because single-word utterances provide no structural information, it is not clear that their meanings are truly relational. At this level of linguistic development, a more cautious approach to semantic notion training would be to teach more than one type of response to a given object or event. At the two-word stage of linguistic development, relational information is available, and it seems that semantic notions can be trained more readily at this level. However, such training must be highly systematic in assessing what the child is actually learning. It seems to be one thing to train semantic notions and quite another to train semantic notions conforming precisely to those envisioned by the person doing the training.

ACKNOWLEDGMENT

I wish to thank Denise Meyer for her able participation in the pilot work reported in this chapter.

REFERENCES

Bandura, A., and Harris, M. 1966. Modification of syntactic style. J. Exp. Child Psychol. 4:341–352.

Bloom, L. 1970. Language Development: Form and Function in Emerging Grammars. MIT Press, Cambridge, MA.

Bloom, L. 1973. One Word at a Time. Mouton, The Hague.

Bowerman, M. 1973. Early Syntactic Development: A Cross-Linguistic Study with Special Reference to Finnish. Cambridge University Press, New York.

Bowerman, M. 1976. Semantic factors in the acquisition of rules for word use and sentence construction. In: D. Morehead and A. Morehead (eds.), Normal and Deficient Child Language. University Park Press, Baltimore.

Braine, M. 1976. Children's first word combinations. Monogr. Soc. Res. Child Dev. 41, Serial No. 164.

Bricker, W., and Bricker, D. 1974. An early language training strategy. In: R.L. Schiefelbusch and L. Lloyd (eds.), Language Perspectives—Acquisition, Retardation, and Intervention. University Park Press, Baltimore.

Brown, R. 1973. A First Language: The Early Stages. Harvard University Press, Cambridge, MA.

Burns, M., and Webster, B. 1975. A comparison of semantic relations present in the productive systems of normal and emotionally disturbed children. Paper presented to the American Speech and Hearing Association, DC.

Chafe, W. 1970. Meaning and the Structure of Language. University of Chicago Press, Chicago.

Coggins, T. 1979. Relational meaning encoded in the two-word utterances of Stage 1 Down's syndrome children. J. Speech Hear. Res. 22:166–178.

DeVilliers, J. 1981. The process of rule learning in child speech: A new look. In: K.E. Nelson (ed.), Children's Language, Vol. 2. Gardner Press, New York.

Duchan, J., and Lund, N. 1979. Why not semantic relations? J. Child Lang. 6:243–253.

Edwards, D. 1973. Sensory-motor intelligence and semantic relations in early child grammar. Cognition 2:395–434.

Edwards, D. 1978. The source of children's early meanings. In: I. Marková (ed.), The Social Context of Language. John Wiley and Sons, New York.

Fillmore, C. 1968. The case for case. In: E. Bach and R. Harms (eds.), Universals in Linguistic Theory. Holt, Rinehart and Winston, New York.

Fillmore, C. 1971. Some problems for case grammar. Georgetown Univ. Monogr. Lang. Ling. 24:35–56.

Florance, C., Cook, P., and Henry, P. 1976. Designing language intervention strategies. Paper presented to American Speech and Hearing Association, Houston.

Freedman, P., and Carpenter, R. 1976. Semantic relations used by normal and language-impaired children at Stage I. J. Speech Hear. Res. 19:784–795.

Greenfield, P., and Smith, J. 1976. The Structure of Communication in Early Language Development. Academic Press, New York.

Howe, C. 1976. The meanings of two-word utterances in the speech of young children. J. Child Lang. 3:29–47.

Layton, T., Harvey, E., and Sharifi, H. 1976. Semantic usage in Down's syndrome and normal children's language. Paper presented to the American Speech and Hearing Association, Houston.

Lee, L. 1976. A study of normal and atypical semantic development. Unpublished manuscript, Northwestern University, Evanston, IL.

Leonard, L. 1975a. The role of nonlinguistic events and semantic relations in children's acquisition of grammatical utterances. J. Exp. Child Psychol. 19:346–357.

Leonard, L. 1975b. Relational meaning and the facilitation of slow learning children's language. Am. J. Ment. Defic. 80:180–185.

Leonard, L. 1976. Meaning in Child Language. Grune and Stratton, New York.

Leonard, L. 1979. Language impairment in children. Merrill-Palmer Q. 25:205–232.

Leonard, L., Bolders, J., and Miller, J. 1976. An examination of the semantic relations reflected in the language usage of normal and language handicapped children. J. Speech Hear. Res. 19:371–392.

Leonard, L., Steckol. K., and Schwartz, R. 1978. Semantic relations and utterance length in child language. In: F. Peng and W. von Raffler-Engel (eds.), Language Acquisition and Developmental Kinesics. Bunka Hyoron, Tokyo.

MacDonald, J., and Nickols, M. 1974. Environmental Language Inventory. Ohio State University, Columbus.

McLean, J., and Snyder-McLean, R. 1978. A Transactional Approach to Early Language Training. Charles E. Merrill, Columbus, OH.

Miller, J., and Yoder, D. 1974. An ontogenetic language teaching strategy for retarded children. In: R.L. Schiefelbusch and L. Lloyd (eds.), Language Perspectives—Acquisition, Retardation, and Intervention. University Park Press, Baltimore.

Morehead, D., and Ingram, D. 1973. The development of base syntax in normal and linguistically deviant children. J. Speech Hear. Res. 16:330–352.

Morehead, D., and Morehead, A. 1974. From signal to sign: A Piagetian view of thought and language during the first two years. In: R.L. Schiefelbusch and L. Lloyd (eds.), Language Perspectives—Acquisition, Retardation, and Intervention. University Park Press, Baltimore.

Piaget, J. 1954. The Construction of Reality in the Child. Basic Books, New York.

Rodgon, M., Jankowski, W., and Alenskas, L. 1977. A multi-functional approach to single-word usage. J. Child Lang. 4:23–44.

Rosch, E. 1975. Cognitive representations of semantic categories. J. Exp. Psychol. 104:192–233.

Rosch, E., and Mervis, C. 1975. Family resemblances: Studies in the internal structure of categories. Cog. Psychol. 7:573–605.

Schlesinger, I. 1971. Production of utterances and language acquisition. In: D. Slobin (ed.), The Ontogenesis of Grammar. Academic Press, New York.

Slobin, D. 1966. Comments on McNeill's developmental psycholinguistics. In: F. Smith and G. Miller (eds.), The Genesis of Language. MIT Press, Cambridge, MA.

Slobin, D. 1970. Universals of grammatical development in children. In: G. Flores d'Arcais and W. Levelt (eds.), Advances in Psycholinguistics. North-Holland, Amsterdam.

Slobin, D. 1973. Cognitive prerequisites for the development of grammar. In: C. Ferguson and D. Slobin (eds.), Studies of Child Language Development. Holt, Rinehart and Winston, New York.

Steckol, K., and Leonard, L. 1979. The use of grammatical morphemes by normal and language impaired children. J. Commun. Disord. 12:291–302.

Tyler, S. 1969. Cognitive Anthropology. Holt, Rinehart and Winston, New York.

Willbrand, M. 1977. Psycholinguistic theory and therapy for initiating two word utterances. Br. J. Disord. Commun. 12:37–46.

chapter 6

An Empirical/Measured Approach to Language Training

The Use of Past-Tense Morphology

Michael D. Smith

Communication Disorders
Western Carolina University
Cullowhee, North Carolina

Kenneth F. Ruder

Bureau of Child Research
University of Kansas
Lawrence, Kansas

Kathleen Stremel-Campbell

Oregon State System of Higher Education
Teaching Research Division
Monmouth, Oregon

contents

The publication of Chomsky's (1959) review of Skinner's monumental *Verbal Behavior* (1957) triggered considerable debate over fundamental questions concerning factors that control the development and use of language. Skinner articulated a strict behavioral view of language. He placed primary emphasis upon external variables, principally in the form of environmental contingencies that function to determine the substance of emerging verbal behaviors. In contrast, Chomsky supported a strict nativistic view of language, which emphasized internal variables in the form of linguistic predispositions or innate linguistic potentials.

Some 20 years later, the debate continues. Applied behavior analysts maintain that linguistic behavior emerges primarily as a function of environmental contingencies that determine the strength and, hence, the relative status of modeling complexes that constitute much of a person's early linguistic environment (Guess et al., 1974, 1978a; Garcia and DeHaven, 1974; Staats, 1974; Harris, 1975; Guess et al., 1978; Hegde et al., 1979; Hart and Risley, 1980; Hegde, 1980a, 1980b; Baer, 1981; Hegde and McConn, 1981). In essence, this is a general statement of an *independence* hypothesis. As Staats (1974) argued, the unity of what seems inherent in the structure of language is in reality determined on the basis of outside forces (i.e., modeling events and contingencies of reinforcement). These provide the formation of networks of stimulus-response classes that are capable of being verbally mapped. It follows that the concept of linguistic structure per se (structure outside of what is environmentally induced) and the related notion that linguistic forms are by varying degrees interdependent are ill-founded.

Current Chomskyan or neoChomskyan theory contrasts with an independence hypothesis. Numerous linguists, psychologists, and speech-language pathologists have used Chomskyan theory to construct adequate models of language development and intervention, all of which assume the interdependence of linguistic forms. Over the years, the result has been the transformation of Chomskyan theory itself. It has lost much of its nativistic character and seems capable of meshing with present theories of cognitive and linguistic development among normal and abnormal populations (Ruder and Smith, 1974; Cromer, 1981; Keil, 1981; Bruner, 1982; Wanner and Gleitman, 1982).

Despite what has transpired since the 1960s, for those committed to designing efficient language training programs, there exists the very real possibility of establishing a middle ground. The point of view adopted here is that an eclectic or integrated position should be established by combining those aspects of linguistic, psycholinguistic, and operant theory (as practiced by applied behavior analysts) that have the potential to contribute to the development of efficient language intervention strategies (e.g., see Smith, Ruder, and Waryas, Chapter 1). Such a viewpoint represents an outgrowth of the Chula Vista Language Conference (Schiefelbusch and Lloyd, 1974), where a comprehensive effort was made to avoid polemics in favor of synthesizing theories and data of various disciplines. The result of the conference was that the advantage of working toward the formation of a unified theory of language intervention was recognized by specialists with different perspectives but common concerns and goals.

What follows is a set of detailed suggestions to assist the interventionist when designing language training programs. These suggestions represent an integration of various linguistic and psychological theories. More directly, this chapter is concerned with the implications that linguistic, psycholinguistic, and operant theory have for the training of morphology, specifically the production of regular past-tense morphology and, by necessity, the phonological constraints that contribute to its formation.

Why the focus on morphology? Principally because the results of numerous studies using operant procedures to train morphological forms (e.g., past-tense and plural morphology) are very often cited as evidence that the training of linguistic forms in general can be accomplished without consideration of internal linguistic variables or complexity factors (Welch, 1981). The practice has been to demonstrate the potential of an independence hypothesis, wherein the emphasis is placed upon the manipulation of external variables chiefly as they relate to techniques of modeling and the establishment of reinforcement contingencies (Guess et al., 1968; Guess, 1969; Schumaker and Sherman, 1970; Sailor, 1971; Baer et al., 1972; Guess and Baer, 1973a, 1973b; Risley, 1977; Guess et al., 1978; Hegde et al., 1979; Hegde, 1980a, 1980b; Hart and Risley, 1980; Baer, 1981).

No matter what the data indicate concerning complexity factors as they affect the acquisition of morphological forms among normal and abnormal populations (see especially Berko, 1958; Brown, 1973; Lovell and Bradbury, 1967; Newfield and Schlanger, 1968; Johnston and Schery, 1976; Derwing and Baker, 1977, 1979; MacWhinney, 1975, 1978; Bybee and Slobin, 1982), few concerted efforts have been made to determine whether or not the remediation of linguistic deficits might be facilitated by training programs whose designs reflect a consideration of complexity factors and the interdependence of linguistic forms. Witness, for example, that no substantive attention was given to the effects (negative or positive) that complexity factors might have on attempts at language intervention in Connell et al.'s (1977) observations on what constitutes relevant criteria for evaluating the design, effectiveness, and reliability of language intervention programs.

A unified theory of language intervention must recognize the possibility that there are alternatives to an independence hypothesis and that these have not yet been given ample consideration (Miller and Yoder, 1974; Ruder and Smith, 1974; Bloom and Lahey, 1978; Muma, 1978; McLean and Snyder-McLean, 1978; Wiig and Semel, 1980; Cole and Cole, 1980; Aram and Nation, 1982; Schiefelbusch and Bricker, 1981). This chapter first elaborates on the implications that linguistic, psycholinguistic, and operant theories have for the training of past-tense morphology. Next, it focuses on the organization, application, and results of an intervention program designed to train regular past-tense morphology through the use of concurrent training techniques. Finally, a discussion of procedures that may be used in isolating and, subsequently, training interdependent linguistic forms is presented. As becomes evident shortly, underlying much of this study is a deep concern for the relevance and utilization of an applied generative phonology, a form of phonology chiefly developed by Compton (1970, 1976), Ingram (1976, 1981), and Lorentz (1976).

LINGUISTIC THEORY AND PHONOLOGICAL APPLICATIONS

Since its inception as part of modern linguistic theory, generative phonology has been concerned with the adequate characterization of what underlies a native speaker's phonological behavior. Its advantages over traditional taxonomic analysis have been recognized and widely discussed by many linguists (e.g., Postal, 1968; Chomsky and Halle, 1968; Sommerstein, 1977). Since the 1970s, a considerable amount of experimental data have been collected in support of the feature-centered phonological representations as opposed to the more traditional segment-centered representations, where the phoneme is assumed to be an irreducible entity. Jakobson (1941) and, later, Chomsky and Halle (1968), in rejecting the concept of an irreducible phoneme, proposed that the evolution of a phonological system is dependent upon the detection of distinctive feature oppositions, out of which emerge phoneme oppositions (the members of which are realizations of hierarchically arranged feature matrices). In experimental research, many testing procedures have been used to determine the relative saliency and the hierarchical arrangement of distinctive features (e.g., LaRiviere et al., 1974; Liberman, 1974; Singh, 1975, 1976, 1978; Stewart and Singh, 1979). At the very least, it can be argued that the data support the general Jakobsonian notion that distinctive feature or *distinctive fea-*

ture-like oppositions, not phoneme oppositions, are central to a language's phonological system.

Recent attempts have been made to determine whether or not generative phonology has implications for applied research. The combined research of Compton (1970, 1976), McReynolds and Bennett (1972), McReynolds and Engmann (1975), McReynolds (1978), Singh (1975, 1978), Lorentz (1976), Costello and Onstine (1976), Ingram (1976, 1981), Ruder and Bunce (1981), and Elbert and Weismer (1983) indicates that an applied generative phonology has considerable promise. For example, McReynolds and Bennett (1972) demonstrated some time ago that newly trained features appropriately generalize to and subsequently come to underlie nontrained segments (e.g., given a subject with control of the voiceless plosives /p/, /t/, /k/, training a /p/-/b/ voicing contrast resulted in generalization to nontrained /t/-/d/ and /k/-/g/ voicing contrasts). Demonstrations of this sort can be interpreted as provisional support of the reality of distinctive feature-like oppositions and of the potential of an applied generative phonology.

If an applied generative phonology is to be developed to a point where it serves as a practical means of remediation, additional demonstrations of the functional reality of phonological features are necessary. Just as important, the utility of rule structures of the sort found in generative phonology must be demonstrated (Elbert and Weismer, 1983). With the exception of Compton (1970, 1976), Lorentz (1976), and Ingram (1976, 1981), previous applied research has been limited to determining the practical implications that context-free segmental constraints (Chomsky and Halle, 1968) have for the feature compositions of individual sound segments and for feature generalization across classes of sound segments. Because the context-sensitive sequencing constraints of generative phonology (Chomsky and Halle, 1968) also have potential relevance, it seems that the effect of feature compositions of adjacent segments should be assessed with at least as much vigor as context-free segmental constraints.

MORPHOLOGICAL APPLICATIONS

The utility of context-sensitive sequencing constraints may be assessed by studying local assimilatory processes, wherein the feature composition of one segment is altered as a function of the feature composition of an immediately adjacent segment. In particular, the study of the phonological principles governing the formation of past-tense morphology provides a way to determine whether various phonological variations are predictable on the basis of assimilation phenomena. Because much of what is said below about the training of past-tense morphology applies to plural morphology, attention is also given to the characteristics of plural morphology.

The various manifestations of past-tense and plural morphology and the factors that determine their distribution require some discussion at this point. At least since the time of Bloomfield (1933), both past-tense and plural morphology have been characterized for the most part as consisting of three phonologically conditioned variants: the [-t], [-d], and [-əd] past-tense allomorphs and the [-s], [-z], and [-əz] plural allomorphs. Of the phonologically conditioned past-tense markers, [-əd] predictably occurs after stems ending in either voiced /d/ or voiceless /t/; voiced [-d] predictably occurs after all other stem final voiced segments; and voiceless [-t] predictably occurs elsewhere, namely after all other stem final voiceless segments. In plural morphology, which follows a similar pattern, [-əz] predictably occurs after stem final voiceless or voiced sibilants and affricates; voiced [-z] predictably occurs after all other stem final voiced segments; and voiceless [-s] predictably occurs elsewhere. The result of such a characterization is that past-tense morphology and plural morphology are each considered to be a unitary linguistic form with three different, phonologically conditioned manifestations or allomorphs.

Because the only recognized function of the epenthetic vowel in [-əd] and [-əz] is to block the occurrence of nonpermissible sequences (across morpheme boundaries), Martinet (1965) and Akjmanova (1971) suggested that there are but two past-tense and plural allomorphs: [-t], [-d] and [-s], [-z], respectively, with the [-əd] and [-əz] variants being formed by insertion of an epenthetic vowel that belongs neither to the stem nor to the inflection. The allomorphic status of the [-əd] and [-əz] variants is especially questionable when considering that the past-tense and plural formations requiring them are generally the last to be acquired (Berko, 1958; Cazden, 1968; Slobin, 1971; Solomon, 1972; Brown, 1973; Johnson, 1974; Derwing and Baker, 1977, 1979; Gray and Cameron, 1980). A plausible explanation is that such formations are superceded by and, later, alternate with null past-tense forms, where the stem final segments are similar or identical to the [-t], [-d] or [-s], [-z] allomorphs (e.g., /pent/ (paint) ~ /pent + əd/ and /glæs/ (glass) ~ /glæs + əz/). The occurrence of null forms seems, then, to be predictable on the basis of the phonetic nature of the stem final segments involved (Bybee and Slobin, 1982).

The existing data on allomorphic distribution, especially those reported in Berko (1958), Johnson (1974), Gray and Cameron (1980), and Bybee and Slobin (1982), suggest rather strongly that the deletion or insertion of an epenthetic vowel segment is not a productive phonological process. There are data then upon which to argue that for the young child, neither the [-əd] past-tense allomorph nor the [-əz] plural allomorph is a productive linguistic form. Consonant with just such a view, the position adopted in this study is that the past-tense morpheme has two productive allomorphs: [-t] and [-d]. Likewise, the plural allomorph has but two productive allomorphs: [-s] and [-z]. As indicated below, the distribution of each allomorph is determined by a process of voicing assimilation to stem final segments (i.e., left-to-right voicing assimilation):

1. A voiceless allomorph ([-t] or [-s]) marks stems terminating in voiceless segments.
2. A voiced allomorph ([-d] or [-z]) marks stems terminating in voiced segments.

THE QUESTION OF PHONOLOGICAL COMPLEXITY

Assuming that abstract linguistic representations that have *direct* ties to surface representations are learned (rather than given), it can be presumed that the learning process is jointly determined by the amount of exposure to and complexity of the oppositions and contrasts involved. In the case of past-tense and plural allomorphs, we are concerned with how exposure to and complexity of the /t/-/d/ and the /s/-/z/ oppositions affect the acquisition of past-tense and plural morphology. The following question then needs to be considered: Is acquisition a function of: 1) the frequency of exposure; 2) the complexity of the items to which one is exposed; or 3) both frequency of exposure and complexity of the items to which one is exposed?

Brown (1973) answered such a question in his comprehensive set of analyses of developmental data concerned with the acquisition of grammatical morphemes in English (as singularly reported in Berko, 1958; Brown and Fraser, 1963; Miller and Ervin-Tripp, 1964; Cazden, 1968; Anisfeld et al., 1968; Anisfeld and Gordon, 1968; Bryant and Anisfeld, 1969; Menyuk, 1969). He found the acquisition of English grammatical morphemes to be a function of various semantic and phonological complexity factors. He also found that factors such as frequency of exposure alone or combined, frequency of exposure, and complexity of items exposed to do not significantly alter their pattern of acquisition. Because each of the past-tense and plural allomorphs is a variant of a single morpheme, the allomorphs of each set do not contrast semantically. It follows then that the order-of-acquisition within a particular morpheme (i.e., the distribution of its allomorphs) as opposed to the order-of-acquisition across morphemes may, to a large extent, be predicted on the basis of phonological complexity of factors.

Table 1.   Marked/unmarked values for the phonological oppositions /t/, /d/, /s/, and /z/

	Oppositions				
	/t/	−	/d/	/s/	−	/z/
Consonantal	U (+)[a]		U (+)	U (+)		U (+)
Voicing	U (−)		M (+)[b]	U (−)		M (+)
Complexity level	0		1	0		1

[a] U, unmarked.
[b] M, marked.

Because this study is concerned with the order of acquisition within particular morphemes, the question of phonological complexity or what has been referred to as phonological markedness needs to be considered (Chomsky and Halle, 1968). Degrees of markedness are computed on the basis of demands placed upon the perceptual and/or articulatory systems when processing speech stimuli. Feature assignments (whether plus or minus) that do or do not fall within the more natural state of the segments in question are designated as being unmarked and marked, respectively. As illustrated in Table 1, when assessing the relative degrees of markedness of voicing oppositions such as /t/-/d/ and /s/-/z/, the member of each segment pair which deviates least from the more natural state of such consonants (voicelessness) is treated as being the least marked and, hence, the least complex member. Consequently, the voiceless [-t] past-tense allomorph and the voiceless [-s] plural allomorph are the least complex of their respective sets.

As Smith and Ruder (1975) argued, the concept of markedness has considerable relevance. Where possible, training studies of morphological forms might be designed to control and, hence, determine the effect of markedness. To assess the effect of markedness on the training of past-tense and plural morphology, two sequential training conditions are needed: *[-t] > [-d] and [-d] > [-t] training sequence conditions for past-tense morphology and [-s] > [-z] and [-z] > [-s] training sequence conditions for plural morphology.* A comparison of the results obtained under these training conditions (referred to later as *implicit* concurrent training) will yield data bearing on the question of whether or not initial training of an unmarked form facilitates subsequent training of a marked form.

THE QUESTION OF MORPHOLOGICAL COMPLEXITY

Along with considering the question of phonological complexity, the closely related question of morphological complexity must also be considered (Foley and Locke, 1971). When dealing with morphological forms, it is necessary to remember that unlike phonological segments such as /t/ and /d/ or /s/ and /z/, morphological forms such as those that mark past tense and pluralization have a semantic function, rendering them more complex than their phonological counterparts. And perhaps it is attributable to this additional complexity that phonological processes operating within morpheme boundaries may at times fail to apply appropriately across morpheme boundaries. Menyuk and Looney (1972) observed that segments such as /t/ and /d/ or /s/ and /z/ may be treated differently when functioning as markers of past tense or plurality than when functioning simply as stem final segments. When functioning morphologically, the chances are greater that they will be omitted at the surface.

In discussing the acquisition of past-tense and plural morphology, Brown (1973) was concerned with an extension of just such a point. He claimed that the ability to appropriately form past-tense and plural expressions hinges on learning that some sequencing constraints are relaxed within but not across morpheme boundaries. Specifically, he proposed that the selection of past-tense and plural allomorphs occurs on at least two levels of complexity, each of which involves sequencing constraints that define permissible segment combinations:

1. Least complex: allomorphic selections typically constrained by a *general* rule of voicing assimilation
2. Most complex: allomorphic selections constrained by an *inflection-specific* rule of voicing assimilation

Both levels of morphological complexity are in fact governed by the same basic principle of voicing assimilation outlined earlier, namely left-to-right or progressive voicing assimilation. The catch, however, is that when functioning as phonetic segments as opposed to allomorphs, regardless of their voicing status, /t/ and /d/ or /s/ and /z/ may combine with the voiced segments /n/, /m/, /r/, /l/, or any vowel to form legitimate combinations. The phonetic status of these segments leads to voicing neutralization within morpheme boundaries, and unless morpheme boundaries are respected, the tendency to gloss over voicing contrasts may inappropriately extend across morphemes and result in unacceptable past-tense or plural formations (e.g., the past tense of /pɪn/ (pin) being produced as /pɪn + t/ rather than /pɪn + d/ and the plural being produced as /pɪn + s/ rather than /pɪn + z/). The point then of an inflection-specific rule of voicing assimilation is to specify that when /n/, /m/, /r/, /l/, or any vowel is stem final, only voiced segments are permitted to function as past-tense [-d] or plural [-z] allomorphs.

There are now two options to consider when designing programs to train past-tense or plural morphology: 1) *avoid the training of forms that operate at the second level of complexity; or* 2) *train forms that operate at the first and second levels of complexity but under conditions that control for the existing variations in sequencing constraints.* Given their frequency of occurrence, forms that operate at the second level of complexity warrant training. Thus, in addition to the two training conditions proposed at the conclusion of the preceding section, a third training condition is now necessary: *simultaneous training of the past-tense allomorphs and plural allomorphs.* The position taken here is that under simultaneous training (to be referred to later as *explicit* concurrent training), the inducement is to treat the past-tense allomorphs and plural allomorphs as members of affix classes subject to a general rule of voicing assimilation regardless of the status of the stem final segments involved.

The consequence is that this set of three training conditions is sufficient to control for the effects of phonologically and morphologically complexity factors. A comparison of results obtained under each of the three training conditions will provide information that is essential to answering the question underlying this entire chapter: Are there alternatives to an independence hypothesis in language training?

A STEP BEYOND AN INDEPENDENCE HYPOTHESIS

If there are alternatives to an independence hypothesis where the training of morphology is concerned, the alternatives hinge on the argument that the distribution of the past-tense and plural allomorphs is predictable: Their distribution is determined on the basis of phonological conditioning in the form of a voicing assimilation process. As Ruder and Smith (1974) pointed out, when training such morphological forms, we are, at the same time, attempting to train a phonological process or context-sensitive sequencing constraint. *The initial emphasis in training then may be placed on only one of the allomorphs, primarily the least marked (i.e., [-t] for the past-tense and [-s] for pluralization). The remaining allomorph should emerge (with only a minimum of training), provided that generalization of initial training on the least marked allomorph occurs.*

The prevailing view, however, deters alternatives to language training programs based on an independence hypothesis. For example, operant training studies that have focused on past-tense and plural morphology maintain that the past-tense and plural allomorphs are arbitrarily related to preceding verb stems, entailing the claim that phonological constraints on voicing assimilation are inoperative (Guess et al., 1968; Guess, 1969; Schumaker and Sherman, 1970; Sailor, 1971; Baer et al., 1972; Guess and Baer, 1973a, 1973b). Staats (1974) claimed that the term "morphology" is a misnomer in that allomorphs involved are nothing more than independent phonological manifestations that mark particular semantic distinctions. According to Staats (1974), the distribution of the so-called allomorphs is not predictable by any general principle; it is predictable only on the basis of their respective reinforcement histories and, therefore, each allomorph must be trained individually. Schumaker and Sherman's (1970) often cited training study reflects this viewpoint. On the basis of their findings, they claimed that once a particular allomorph of a morpheme is trained, it is likely to overgeneralize and violate phonological constraints on voicing assimilation. As evidence, they cited examples where once the [-t] past-tense allomorph was trained and generalization probes were administered across a class of verb stems requiring the [-d] allomorph, the [-t] rather than [-d] allomorph was used as the past-tense marker.

Similar views are implicit in Palermo and Eberhart (1968), Palermo and House (1970), and Palermo and Parrish (1971), who argued that the principles governing the distribution of a morpheme's allomorphs are either similar or identical to those principles governing paired associate-learning. Along the same lines, Braine (1973) conjectured that the mapping of a set of allomorphs onto specific sets of lexical items is similar to the mapping of a set of responses onto specific sets of stimuli, with the primary variable being the strength of associations established. Predictability was seen as a function of association strength rather than phonological constraints. At least before the developmental onset of differential association strength or reinforcement histories, the basic argument was that the past-tense as well as plural allomorphs are potentially free variants. For example, the past tense of /pap/ (pop) might be produced as either /pap + t/ or /pap + d/.

Now the intent here is not to question the use of operant techniques for training language. Their potential has become increasingly evident since the 1960s. Open to question, however, is the assumption that the occurrence of overgeneralization disproves the functional reality of phonological conditioning factors. Alternatively, we opt to argue that the overgeneralization effects obtained in previous training studies were the result of the immediate effects of training or artifact as linked to superficial analysis of selected probe items.

Concerning the immediate effects of training, a theory of phonological conditioning predicts that data obtained from post-treatment studies would demonstrate that phonological conditioning factors become operative once the immediate effects of training subside.

The question of artifact most importantly concerns complications arising out of Brown's (1973) second level of morphological complexity. In order to demonstrate that a trained allomorph (e.g., [-t]) will overgeneralize to stems that require an untrained (or previously trained) allomorph (e.g., [-d]) and, in the process, argue that phonological conditioning factors have little usefulness in applied settings, the potential interference arising out of contrasting phonological constraints (i.e., a general rule of voicing assimilation as opposed to an inflection-specific rule of voicing assimilation) must be carefully assessed. Potential interference effects, however, were not assessed in previous training studies where massive overgeneralization effects occurred. An independence hypothesis was cited in order to explain the apparent ineffectiveness of phonological conditioning factors. Again, the point was made that the acquisition of so-called allomorphic forms is a singular function of independent reinforcement histories (see especially Guess et al., 1968; Schumaker and Sherman, 1970; Sherman, 1971; Sailor, 1971).

Another possible source of artifact lies in the method used to record reliability (accuracy checks) in Guess et al. (1968), Guess (1969), Schumaker and Sherman (1970), and Sailor (1971). The general practice was to monitor only the phonetic shape of the final segment in a given response. For example, in the case of past-tense responses, there was concern only for whether [-t] or [-d] occurred. No checks were made on the accuracy of stem final segments. Hence, in probes where overgeneralization of [-d] occurred, possibilities were ignored that the past tense of verbs like /klæp/ (clap) might have been produced as /klæb + d/, with the final /p/ being realized as either the voiced member of the /p/ - /b/ contrast or as a neutralized segment. In responses like /klæb + d/, there exists a case of regressive voicing assimilation, where the strength and subsequent overgeneralization of the trained [-d] allomorph creates a permissible phonetic environment as a consequence of reversing the direction in which the phonological conditioning factors normally operate. Similar possibilities exist with pluralization. For example, overgeneralization of the [-z] allomorph might force the plural of nouns such as /kæt/ (cat) to be produced as /kæd + z/ and not /kæt + z/. If such overgeneralizations occurred, they pose a challenge to an independence hypothesis.

A third possible source of artifact involves the method of stimulus presentation. The allomorphs being trained may have been stressed to the point that they were relatively more prominent than their corresponding stems, thus contributing to a situation where the allomorphs and their corresponding stems took on the properties of discrete or independent behaviors. This being a possibility, it might be argued that as a precondition to obtaining massive overgeneralization, the independent status of the behaviors in question must first be induced.

Important to note here is that when strictly defined, an independence hypothesis entails the claim that as a result of training linguistic forms that comprise past-tense or plural morphology, an initial training effect should not be found. That is, in training past-tense or plural morphology, if in one condition the unvoiced allomorph ([-t] or [-s]) is trained to criterion and followed by training of the voiced allomorph ([-d] or [-z]) to criterion and, in a reversed or second condition, the voiced allomorph ([-d] or [-z]) is trained to criterion and followed by training of the unvoiced allomorph ([-t] or [-s]) to criterion, the difference in terms of trials to criterion between or within the two conditions should not be remarkable. In summarizing the effects of initial training of plural morphology, Sailor (1971) pointed out that in a condition like the former, it took the first of his subjects no more than 50 trials to reach criterion with the [-s] allomorph, followed by no more than 18 trials to reach criterion with the [-z] allomorph. And in the reversed condition, it took the second of his subjects 42 trials to reach criterion with the [z] allomorph and 15 trials with the [-s] allomorph. Although the differences in trials to criterion within and between the two conditions were not elaborated on, they seem to be illuminating. First, the difference in trials to criterion within conditions (42 trials versus 15 trials and 50 trials versus 18 trials) is interesting if for no other reason than it indicates a general interdependence among the allomorphs (i.e., no matter which allomorph is trained first, the second allomorph requires considerably fewer trials to criterion). Next, the difference in trials to criterion between conditions (a total of 68 trials for the [-s] > [-z] sequence versus a total of 57 trials for the [-z] > [-s] sequence) suggests that there is a direction to their interdependence, namely one which favors the initial training of the [-z] allomorph.

Schumaker and Sherman's (1970) study of past-tense morphology also yielded signs of an initial training effect. In a [-t] > [-d] training sequence, trials to criterion for the [-d] allomorph were noticeably less in number than the trials to criterion for the [-t] allomorph, and for at least one subject, the degree of overgeneralization (where [-t] generalized to stems requiring the [-d] allomorph) was unexpectedly limited. Unfortunately, a [-t] > [-d] training sequence was not paired against a [-d] > [-t] training sequence, ruling out what could have possibly been a demonstration of their interdependence.

Such differences in trials to criterion are at variance not only with predictions based upon an independence hypothesis; they are also at variance with predictions based upon a theory of association strength, where the acquisition of past-tense and plural morphology is viewed as a function of exposure to a relatively balanced proportion of exemplars of each allomorph (Palermo and Parrish, 1971). Predictions based upon an independence hypothesis or theory of association strength may be more appropriate when dealing with the acquisition of morphological formations where allomorphs are (from a linguistic point of view) arbitrarily related to preceding stems. For example, consider the acquisition of plural formation in German wherein nouns with very similar phonological topographies assume quite different plural formations, as in representative examples like *hand - hande* (hand) versus *land - lander* (land). Park (1971) suggested that the acquisition of plural formation in German involves a rote or association process, where singular and plural formations are learned as paired forms.

Observations like the above are not strictly meant to imply that an independence hypothesis is necessarily deficient. Rather, they are intended to point out that the relevance of an independence hypothesis is an empirical question. In the context of this chapter, therefore, an independence hypothesis is interpreted as being nothing more than an hypothesis and not a refutation of what is, by contrast, an interdependence hypothesis.

At this point, it is quite obvious that this chapter is concerned with the design and structural-linguistic components of efficient language intervention programming. However, because the language training literature has yet to address substantially the question of what, on a *comparative* basis, constitutes efficient language intervention programming, there exists no consistent rationale for determining what procedures are best suited for the training of particular linguistic forms. And, because too few previous efforts have been made to deal with the task of training what may well be interdependent as opposed to independent linguistic forms, little is known about how interdependent linguistic forms should be treated—except that they should be treated much as they have been treated in the past; that is, as independent forms to be trained in a serial manner.

Now, how might we otherwise proceed if our precise goal is to train past-tense morphology? What seem to be interdependent linguistic forms ought to be trained in a concurrent fashion. To elaborate on suggestions made earlier, we can resort to *implicit* concurrent training of the two productive past-tense allomorphs. Given the assumption that the distribution of the past-tense allomorphs is predictable and rule-bound, initial training of one of the allomorphs, the [-t] allomorph for example, may result in the occurrence and, hence, the simultaneous training of the remaining allomorph.

A procedure of implicit concurrent training of past-tense morphology does not necessitate that the [-t] past-tense allomorph be trained initially. It is possible that initial training of the [-d] allomorph may result in the implicit training of the [-t] past-tense allomorph. Consequently, a training condition where the [-t] past-tense allomorph is trained initially should be paired against a condition where the [-d] allomorph is trained initially. The data obtained under the paired implicit concurrent training conditions will bear on the question of whether or not initial training of an unmarked form (i.e., the [-t] allomorph) will facilitate training of a marked form (i.e., the [-d] allomorph). Because order-of-training varies under such paired training conditions, the data obtained will also bear on the issue of reducing overgeneralization effects.

To assess the effects of initially presenting implicit [-t] - [-d] contrasts, *explicit* concurrent training of the allomorphs must be introduced. Explicit concurrent training of two productive past-tense allomorphs does not assume that they are independent linguistic forms. Rather, it assumes that an explicit [-t] - [-d] contrast provides a concrete basis for inducing that, in addition to being tense markers, the two allomorphs constitute a set of affixes that is subject to voicing assimilation at the two levels of morphological complexity discussed above.

The training study described below was specifically designed to assess the relative effectiveness of implicit and explicit concurrent training conditions. Viewing the problems involved in the training of past-tense and plural morphology as being generally representative of various basic problems in attempting to train other potentially interdependent linguistic forms, it is hoped that the results of this training study will clarify some of the critical issues presented thus far in this chapter.

CONCURRENT TRAINING OF PAST-TENSE MORPHOLOGY

At the outset, the training of past-tense morphology under conditions that tap the phonological principle of voicing assimilation seems to be a relatively simple proposition, and it may well prove to be so in the end. As a group, the concurrent training conditions just described represent a case in which the critical stimulus for a subsequent allomorphic response (i.e., the [-t] or [-d] past-tense allomorph) exists in the form of a stem final voiceless or voiced segment. As Cofer (1963) suggested, when training the production of such morphological forms, it is appropriate to invoke the *principle of least effort*. When applied to a study like this one, the principle of least effort asserts that the articulation of a segment that deviates least from the articulation of an immediately prior segment is likely to impose few demands on subjects undergoing the training of past-tense morphology. In effect then, the challenge here perhaps is to operationalize little more than a *morphologically based principle of least effort.*

TRAINING METHOD AND PROCEDURE

Subject Population and Preliminary Considerations

Twelve developmentally disabled, severely impaired persons were the subject population for this study. Their chronological ages ranged from 8 to 14 years, and their mental ages ranged from 3 to 4 years. At the time of this study, each of the subjects was working through a rudimentary-level language training program, resembling those described in Stremel-Campbell and Waryas (1974) and Waryas and Stremel-Campbell (1978).

Before entering production training of past-tense morphology, all of the subjects completed a general training program in verb tense comprehension, encompassing the simple present tenses, the simple past tense, and the simple future tense of both regular and irregular verb forms. Comprehension training of the simple verb tenses preceded production training chiefly on the grounds that prior receptive control of a particular linguistic form is likely to facilitate the acquisition and maintenance of expressive control of the same linguistic form (Stremel-Campbell and Waryas, 1974; Waryas and Stremel-Campbell, 1978). For basically the same reason, production of past-tense morphology was elicited under conditions where training items were presented in context rather than in isolation. An approach of this sort is not common among those training studies carried out under an independence hypothesis, where typically the tactic has been first to obtain echoic or nonreceptive control of the target behaviors.

Production Pretest

Each subject was pretested to determine if he or she could produce any past-tense forms before entering production training. Production was pretested with picture sets (trigrams of line drawings) representing: 1) the simple present progressive tense; 2) the simple past tense; and 3) the simple future tense of a particular verb. The procedure used to elicit verbal responses involved the experimenter's pointing to a particular picture in a picture set while asking the subject comment on the picture. Twenty regular verb forms were tested for production. These same verb forms had served earlier as the stimuli for the pretraining of verb tense conprehension. Ten of the past-tense verb forms represented the verb stem class requiring the [-t] past-tense allomorph, and the remaining 10 past-tense verb forms represented the stem class requiring the [-d] allomorph. Each of the verb forms was tested twice, yielding a total of 40 trials. If a subject correctly produced two or more past-tense forms, he or she was excluded from the study.

Training Stimuli

The training stimuli used under each of three training conditions described below consisted of the following verb sets:

Set A—Verb + [-t]	Set B—Verb + [-d]
watched	spilled
dropped	combed
pushed	climbed
dressed	played
baked	poured

The 10 training items were selected from among the set of 20 verbs that were pretrained for comprehension but were not produced during production pretesting. The remaining 10 verbs were used later strictly as generalization probes administered upon the termination of training.

Training Conditions

Training was carried out under three conditions; the first two served as implicit concurrent training and the last one served as explicit concurrent training. Of the total of 12 subjects, four were randomly assigned to each of the following training conditions:

> Training Condition I (implicit)
> Step 1: Verb + [-t] training (Verb Set A)
> Step 2: Verb + [-d] training (Verb Set B)
>
> Training Condition II (implicit)
> Step 1: Verb + [-d] training (Verb Set B)
> Step 2: Verb + [-t] training (Verb Set A)
>
> Training Condition III (explicit)
> Simultaneous verb + [-t] and verb + [-d] training
> (Verb Sets A and B)

To test for the possible effects of both immediate generalization and overgeneralization of training on the past-tense forms of a particular verb set (e.g., Verb Set A), after the completion of Step 1 within Training Conditions I and II, intermediate generalization probes were administered across the past-tense forms not trained in the immediately preceding step (e.g., Verb Set B). After completion of Training Conditions I, II, and III, final generalization probes were administered across past-tense forms of untrained verbs, the past-tense forms of which were comprehended but not produced during pretesting. Training Conditions I, II, and III were thus arranged as follows:

<u>Training Condition I</u>
1. Step 1: verb + [-t]
2. Intermediate generalization probes: verb + [-d]
3. Step 2: verb + [-d]
4. Intermediate generalization probes: verbs + [-t]
5. Final generalization probes

<u>Training Condition II</u>
1. Step 1: verb + [-d]
2. Intermediate generalization probes: verb + [-t]
3. Step 2: verb + [-t]
4. Intermediate generalization probes: verb + [-d]
5. Final generalization probes

<u>Training Condition III</u>
1. Simultaneous training: verb + [-t] and verb + [-d]
2. Final generalization probes

Training Phases

The two training steps of Training Condition I and Training Condition II and the single step of Training Condition III progressed through the four training phases described below. In Training Conditions I and II, after each step had passed through each of the four training phases, the intermediate generalization probes were administered. In the case of Training Condition III, once the four training phases were completed, the final generalization probes were administered and training was terminated.

Training Phase I   Under Training Phase I, production training of past-tense morphology began with pairing auditory stimuli with the presentation of picture sets (identical to those used in production pretesting). Each subject was required to match auditory stimuli (e.g., "The boy <u>watched</u> TV") with the appropriate visual stimuli by means of a pointing response. Here and throughout the other three training phases, response behavior met with intrinsic reinforcement (verbal praise). The auditory stimuli consisted of past-tense forms representing the target verb set(s) and were arranged into blocks of randomized training items. Under Training Conditions I and II, each training block consisted of two repetitions of the past-tense forms of a single verb set, yielding a total of 10 trials per block. Under Training Condition III, each training block consisted of a single repetition of each past tense form of both verb sets, yielding also a total of 10 trials per block. The same held true for training under the remaining three phases described below.

The individual error rates that occurred during this first phase provided a check on whether or not the levels of comprehension of past-tense verb forms obtained under receptive pretraining were being maintained sufficiently. Once criterion was reached (90% correct response rate for two successive training blocks), the next phase began.

Training Phase II   In an effort to elicit productions of past-tense verb forms, interverbal leads were paired with appropriate visual stimuli (e.g., "You say, the boy watched TV" paired with an appropriate visual stimulus, with the correct response being "watched"). If a subject failed to respond, a verbal stimulus was provided (e.g., "watched"). After a correct response was produced, the appropriate verbal response was again modeled in order to strengthen the tie between the subject's response, the model, and the reinforcement. When criterion was reached (90% correct response rate within a single training block), a subject entered Training Phase III.

Training Phase III   In an effort to elicit productions of past-tense verb forms in an expanded context, combined question-interverbal leads were paired with appropriate picture stimuli (e.g., "What did the boy do? (you say) the boy watched TV"). When criterion was reached (90% correct response rate within a single training block), a subject entered Training Phase IV.

Training Phase IV   The procedure was similar to that used in Training Phase III. However, production of past-tense verb forms was elicited by question stimuli alone (e.g., "What did the boy do?") paired with appropriate visual stimuli. No interverbal leads were used. Upon reaching criterion (90% correct response rate within a single training block), intermediate generalization probes were administered for Training Conditions I and II.

Each past-tense form was tested twice in each of two blocks, yielding a total of 20 intermediate generalization probes per verb set. For instance, under Training Condition I, where the [-t] allomorph was initially trained, the possibilities were that the [-t] allomorph would either properly generalize or overgeneralize to the stems requiring the [-d] allomorph. If training did not properly generalize to stems requiring the [-d] allomorph (as reflected in a probe accuracy of less than 90%), the next training step was taken and, once completed, a second set of intermediate generalization probes was administered. In Training Condition III, because of the simultaneous training of Verb Sets A and B, intermediate generalization probes could not be administered across the [-t] and [-d] past-tense forms.

In general terms, the purpose of the four training phases was to ensure as much as possible that free production of past-tense forms would occur and, beyond that, become incorporated into a subject's functional linguistic repertoire (the main purpose of Training Phase IV). The underlying assumption here is that prior receptive control or comprehension of a particular linguistic form is necessary but not sufficient to obtain expressive control of the same linguistic form (the main purpose of comprehension pretraining and Training Phase I). With this in mind, various prompts were used to elicit bound productions of the past-tense verb forms (the main purpose of Training Phases II and III). Such a procedure was designed to bridge the gap between the receptive and expressive control of the past-tense verb forms. This approach to training is endorsed by Ruder et al. (1974) and Ruder et al. (1977), who demonstrated that an efficient method of training production is one where initial comprehension training is followed by intervals in which bound productions are elicited—the result being that free production is likely to emerge with a minimum of subsequent prompting.

Final Generalization Probes

In order to test for the effects of past-tense training on the production of untrained verbs, final generalization probes were administered across the untrained verbs contained in the verb sets listed below (items which were comprehended but not produced before training):

Regular: [-t]	Regular: [-d]
picked	pulled
touched	hugged
bounced	moved
spanked	tied
brushed	cried

Scoring of Responses

A response was judged as correct or incorrect based on adherence to the principle of voicing assimilation. Specifically, responses obtained under the administration of training trials and intermediate generalization probes were scored on the basis of left-to-right or progressive voicing assimilation, wherein the phonetic status of a stem final segment (voiced or voiceless) controls allomorphic selection. Final generalization probes were scored along the same lines, with the exception that particular attention was given to the occurrence of right-to-left or regressive voicing assimilation, wherein the phonetic status of an inflected allomorph (voiced or voiceless) triggers a shift in the direction of voicing assimilation. The purpose for doing so was to determine the overall pattern of past-tense formation obtained upon the completion of training (keeping in mind that unlike intermediate generalization probes, items presented as final generalization probes were not subject to subsequent training).

Intermittent reliability checks were made by an independent observer during the administration of intermediate and final generalization probes. The responses scored by the independent observer matched those scored by the experimenter at a level of 90% or above.

ANALYSIS OF CONCURRENT TRAINING

The results of this training study are discussed in terms of how they pertain to the following issues: 1) the effectiveness of implicit concurrent [-t] - [-d] training; 2) the effectiveness of explicit concurrent [-t] - [-d] training; and 3) the reduction of overgeneralization effects.

Implicit Concurrent Training

Analysis of the data obtained under Training Conditions I and II provides an answer to the question: Are there signs of an initial training effect where prior training of one of the past-tense allomorphs facilitates the production of the remaining past-tense allomorph? First, as illustrated in Figure 1, each of the two past-tense allomorphs were subject to initial training effects. Second, the [-d] allomorph seems in general to have been sensitive to initial training on [-t] more than [-t] was sensitive to initial training on [-d]. When the training of the [-d] allomorph followed rather than preceded the training of the [-t] allomorph, considerably fewer trials to criterion were required (133 trials versus 185 trials). The data, then, seem to favor the initial training of the [-t] allomorph.

To determine if the above observations are based on significant findings, statistical analyses were performed on the raw data. The results of a series of t-tests indicated that the initial training effect obtained with the [-t] allomorph was not significant (at the 0.05 level) when compared to the initial training effect obtained with the [-d] allomorph. It is important to note, nonetheless, that the initial training effect obtained with the [-t] allomorph approached significance. The lack of a significant difference does not necessarily cast doubt on the interdependence of the two past-tense allomorphs. As Figure 1 illustrates, a proportional sensitivity exists among first-trained allomorphs and their second-trained counterparts (representing initial training effects). The direction of their interdependence is however debatable.

The data specifically relating to the trials to criterion required of each past-tense allomorph across Training Conditions I and II may be relevant when addressing the issue of initial training effects and, consequently, the issue of which of the two past-tense allomorphs should be initially trained. As can be ascertained, the data indicate that the [-t] allomorph imposed less of a demand on subjects than did the [-d] allomorph, regardless of the training sequence employed (i.e., [-t] > [-d] or [-d] > [-t]). A t-test for related measures was used to determine if the difference in trials to criterion was significant. If predictions are based on the data reported in Sailor's (1971) training study of plural morphology, the past-tense allomorph second-trained can be expected

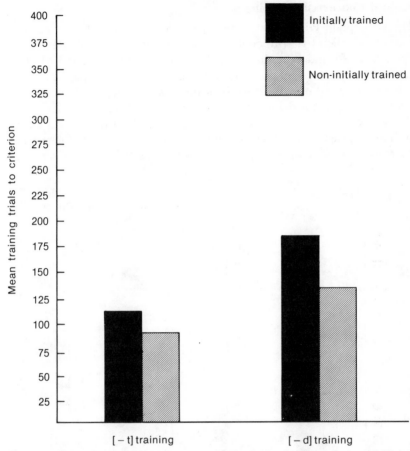

Figure 1.   Proportional sensitivity among first and second trained allomorphs with Training Conditions I and II.

to impose fewer demands and, hence, necessitate fewer training trials than the allomorph first-trained. Contrary to such an expectation, the results of the *t*-test for related measures indicated that the [-t] allomorph required significantly fewer training trials than did the [-d] allomorph (at the 0.05 level). This then is a demonstration of the relevance of markedness. When combined with the magnitude of the initial training effect obtained with the [-t] allomorph, the results suggest that when training past-tense morphology, a training condition where the unmarked [-t] allomorph is first-trained (Training Condition I) imposes fewer demands on subjects and, therefore, is more appropriate than a training condition where the marked [-d] allomorph is first-trained (Training Condition II).

Explicit Concurrent Training

Unlike implicit concurrent training, explicit concurrent training provides an explicit [-t] - [-d] contrast, and, consequently, provides a concrete basis for inducing that, as past-tense markers, [-t] and [-d] function as members of an affix class that is subject to the constraints of voicing assimilation. An analysis of the raw data depicted in Figure 2 provides a basis for determining whether or not there was a significant difference among Training Conditions I, II, and III (through the four training phases) and, at the same time, to determine whether or not there was an advantage to presenting an explicit [-t] - [-d] contrast at

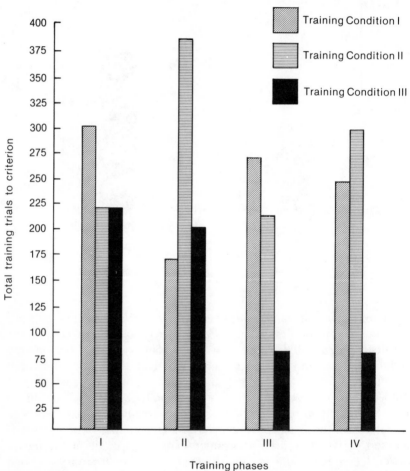

Figure 2.   Total trials to criterion as a function of training phases within Training Conditions I, II, and III.

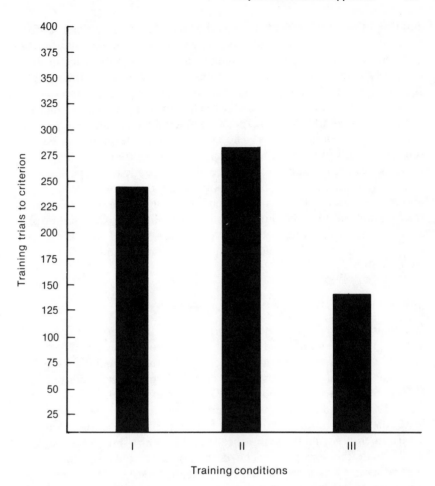

Figure 3.   Total means in trials to criterion as a function of Training Conditions I, II, and III.

the surface. An analysis of variance was performed to determine whether or not there was a significant difference among Training Conditions, I, II, and III. The results indicated that there was a significant difference among the training conditions (at the 0.05 level).

To determine which of the three training conditions contributed to the significant difference among Training Conditions I, II, and III, a Newman-Keuls test of the difference between total means (trials to criterion) was performed. The Newman-Keuls test analyzed the data displayed in Figure 3, where total means in trials to criterion are treated as a function of training conditions. The data suggest that the presentation of an explicit contrast was the basis for the significant difference among the training conditions. The results of the Newman-Keuls test confirmed that explicit concurrent training was more efficient than either of the implicit concurrent training procedures (at the 0.05 level). As illustrated in Figure 3, most notable about explicit as opposed to implicit concurrent training was the decline in trials to criterion (across training phases) after initial responding behavior was obtained through the first two training phases. The effect can be interpreted to be the principal result of utilizing an explicit [-t] - [-d] contrast.

Whatever substance there is to an independence hypothesis is seemingly masked by the results obtained under explicit concurrent training. As stated above, an independence hypothesis operates under the assumption that what linguists and psycholinguists call allomorphs are arbitrarily related to preceding word stems. Little if any difference, then, should have been detected between the implicit and explicit training conditions.

REDUCTION OF OVERGENERALIZATION EFFECTS

The results of the final generalization probes that were administered across Training Conditions I, II, and III were not of the type that might be predicted in lieu of an independence hypothesis. Judging from the position adopted by Guess et al. (1968), Schumaker and Sherman (1970), Sherman (1971), Sailor (1971), Baer et al. (1972), Guess and Baer (1973a), and Staats (1974), the occurrence of overgeneralization (e.g., the inappropriate extension of the [-t] past-tense allomorph to environments normally taking the [-d] allomorph) should be the rule rather than the exception. The data, however, indicate that overgeneralization was more the exception than the rule.

A combined total of 800 generalization probes was administered. Of this total, 320 served as intermediate generalization probes under Training Conditions I and II, and 480 served as final generalization probes across Training Conditions I, II, and III. Less than 8% of the responses qualified as clear instances of overgeneralization. In stark contrast, more than 70% properly qualified as generalization responses. The remainder of less than 20% consisted of mixed responses (i.e., null or present-tense responses). Out of this collection of data, two principal patterns of overgeneralization emerged, one involving a reversal of the expected course of voicing assimilation and a second involving the production of a silent block to voicing assimilation. In the first case, overgeneralizations were distinguished by the intrusion of one past-tense allomorph ([-t] or [-d]) for the other. In turn, signs of regressive voicing assimilation surfaced such that the voicing value of stem final segments shifted, reflecting approximations to the voicing value of the allomorphic intruder. In regard to the latter pattern of overgeneralization, instances of voicing assimilation, like those just described under the first case, were blocked by the introduction of a noticeable and, at times, audible pause, which functioned to effectively isolate the stem final segments from the production of either past-tense allomorph.

In connection with these two patterns of overgeneralization, the relatively weak overgeneralization effects obtained with forms that operate at Brown's (1973) second and most complex level of morphological complexity merit emphasis. Again, according to Brown (1973), proper use of the [-d] past-tense allomorph entails an inflection-specific rule; otherwise, the past-tense forms of verbs, such as those contained in Verb Set B (i.e., spill, play, pour), are just as or more likely to be produced with the [-t] allomorph (i.e., the past tense of /spɪl/(spill) produced as either /spɪl + t/ or /spɪl + d/).

Of the overgeneralizations that occurred during the administration of generalization probes under Training Conditions I and II, very few overgeneralizations occurred during intermediate [-t] probes under Training Conditions I (namely, overgeneralizations on to Verb Set B items, which occurred subsequent to the training of the [t] allomorph and before the training of the [-d] allomorph). If a noninflection-specific rule rather than an inflection-specific rule is more basic, the prediction would be that considerable overgeneralization of the trained [-t] allomorph would occur onto probe items calling for the [-d] allomorph. However, even though the intermediate [-d] probe items were in effect weighted in favor of the application of a noninflection-specific rule and, hence, overgeneralization of the [-t] allomorph, only 10 such overgeneralizations occurred out of a possible total of 48.

If it is assumed that a noninflection–specific rule is less complex and more basic than an inflection-specific rule, the overgeneralization pattern is not the predicted one. A partial explanation may be derived by considering the complexity or markedness of clusters formed by stem final segments and past-tense allomorphs (as determined by either an inflection-specific rule or a noninflection-specific rule). Consider, for example, the final clusters in /spɪl + d/ - /spɪl + t/ (spilled) and /pɔr + d/ - /pɔr + t/ (poured). The implication of Cairns' (1969) and Smith and Ruder's (1975) observations of unmarked and marked consonant clusters is that such final clusters are unmarked when both segments are voiced (e.g., /spɪl + d/ and /pɔr + d/) and are marked when one of the segments is voiceless (e.g., /spɪl + t/ and /pɔr + t/). In the case of past-tense morphology, an inflection-specific rule may be preferred because it represents a reduction in markedness across sequences of segments. The relatively weak pattern of overgeneralization obtained, then, is more in line with predictions based on a reduction in markedness than those based on the assumption that a non-inflection-specific rule is more basic than an inflection-specific rule.

Obviously, the extent and nature of the overgeneralization data obtained in this study differ from those data obtained in previous training studies. In the studies cited thus far, it has been collectively indicated that the allomorphs of past-tense and plural morphology must be trained separately or actually retrained in order to avoid or, more critically, correct the score of overgeneralizations that, in the end, is likely to otherwise surface. For example, overgeneralization percentages seemed to be quite high in Schumaker and Sherman's (1970) and Sailor's (1971) training studies. In their training study of past-tense morphology, Schumaker and Sherman (1970) found that once each of the past-tense allomorphs was trained, the effects of initial training of one allomorph were cancelled out by the effects of subsequent training of the other allomorph, resulting in large percentages of overgeneralization (where the second-trained allomorph overgeneralized to the stems requiring the first-trained allomorph). To correct the situation, they were forced to resort to discrimination training, a procedure designed to retrain or reinstate the effects of initial training. In view of the results of the training program outline above, there exist viable alternatives that bypass retraining and, consequently, impose fewer demands on those undergoing intervention.

The Search for Alternatives

The overall results of this training study of past-tense morphology indicate that versions of an independence hypothesis are of questionable relevance when applied to language intervention. Because our goal is to train language in a manner that avoids as much as possible the imposition of unnecessary demands on individuals who are linguistically impaired, alternatives are needed, some of which can be arrived at by virtue of considering the positive effects that the manipulation of internal linguistic variables has on training linguistic behavior. Consequently, when designing language training programs, the internal structure of target behaviors should be adequately considered. This is important because it provides a means of determining if there exists a basis upon which to expect that the training of one linguistic form will appropriately generalize to and, as a matter of course, result in the training (albeit partial) of a related linguistic form.

Distinguishing between independent and interdependent linguistic forms might assist in the future development of intervention programs that will provide a basis for the induction of more appropriate rules or generalized mapping operations. Such distinctions can be discussed in terms of what Ruder and Smith (1974) called componential content (*CC*) analysis. In a fashion similar to Brown's (1973) analysis of morphological complexity, *CC* analysis consists of reducing linguistic forms to their more salient features or components. In general, a *CC* analysis includes consideration of at least three types of phenomena: 1) semantic or conceptual; 2) syntactic or ordinal; and 3) phonological or distributive. Specifically, a *CC* analysis of productive past-tense morphology would take on the following form:

1. Semantic phenomenon: same (past tense)
2. Syntactic phenomenon: same (suffixation)
3. Phonological phenomenon: different (voicing contrast: /t/ - /d/)

The design and results of our training study of past-tense morphology can be recast in the form of *CC* analysis. As pointed out earlier, the difference between the two past-tense allomorphs is phonologically based and, in particular, tied to a rule of differential voicing assimilation. Under the two implicit concurrent training conditions, the major task was to determine whether or not the training of one of the past-tense allomorphs would facilitate the acquisition of the second allomorph. First, the procedure involved a training condition where the [-t] past-tense allomorph was initially trained to criterion, with generalization probes of the [-d] allomorph following (Training Condition I). If the probe accuracy of the [-d] allomorph did not meet criterion, it was subsequently trained to criterion. Second, as a form of replication, under another training condition, the [-d] past-tense allomorph was initially trained to criterion, with generalization probes of the [-t] allomorph following (Training Condition II). As with the former training condition, if the probe accuracy of the nontrained allomorph did not meet criterion, it was subsequently trained to criterion. Under *CC* analysis, the goal is to test for initial training effects. For each allomorph, the critical information involves the number of trials required to meet criterion when it was second-trained (T_s) as opposed to first-trained (T_f). When computed, the ratio of (T_s) over (T_f) for each past-tense allomorph forms a *sensitivity quotient*. A sensitivity quotient of (1.0) or greater indicates that no initial training effect has occurred. On the other hand, a sensitivity quotient of less than (1.0) indicates that an initial training effect has occurred and that a certain degree of interdependence thus exists across the linguistic forms targeted for training. *When two sensitivity quotients that yield signs of an initial training effect are compared (e.g., the sensitivity quotient of [-d] as compared to that of [-t]) and one is found to be noticeably smaller than the other, their interdependence is considered to have a direction, principally one favoring the initial training of the linguistic form that is characterized by the larger of the two sensitivity quotients.*

The data obtained under Training Conditions I and II and the computed sensitivity quotients:

$$\frac{T_s}{T_f} = \frac{90}{115} = 0.78 \text{ for } [\text{-t}]; \frac{T_s}{T_f} = \frac{133}{188} = 0.72 \text{ for } [\text{-d}]$$

indicate that [-t] and [-d] are sensitive to training on each other, and, hence, are interdependent linguistic forms. However, the difference between the sensitivity quotients for [-t] and [-d] are not drastic (0.78 versus 0.72). This lack of a drastic difference between sensitivity quotients need not reflect on their systematic interdependence. Rather, it stands as a sign that their direction of interdependence is indeterminate. When they are the object of training, [-t] and [-d] seem to be reciprocally sensitive linguistic forms.

Under *CC* analysis, the training of reciprocally sensitive linguistic forms should be accomplished best under a condition where they are trained simultaneously. If trials to criterion under an explicit concurrent or simultaneous training condition (Training Condition III) are significantly less than (T_s) and (T_f) summed for each of the individual linguistic forms (Training Conditions I and II), this assumption is verified. The results of this training study provide such verification.

The above reinterpretation of the design and results of our training study supports the claim that when working with impaired populations, it is possible to tap internal structural variables in a way that provides for the establishment of appropriate rules or generalized linguistic operations. Where linguistic forms such as those studied here are concerned, the establishment of non-overgeneralized patterns of response presupposes the ability of impaired individuals to perform rudimentary phonetic analyses. As surprising as it might at first seem, there is evidence that even severely impaired individuals are capable of phonetically analyzing linguistic forms. On occasion, we have observed impaired individuals who have completed training programs in past-tense formation or pluralization produce *back formations*. These formations occur under conditions where stem final segments and morphological units are characterized by complementary sound properties. For instance, when probing for the generalized production of the [-t] and [-d] past-tense allomorphs among individuals who had previously undergone past-tense training, verb forms such as /pent/ (paint) were on occasion analyzed as having: 1) the present tense form /pen/ instead of /pent/, and 2) the apparent null past tense form /pent/ rather than /pent + əd/. Responses that follow or resemble this pattern of back formation were observed to occur among normal children (Berko, 1958;

Slobin, 1971; Brown, 1973) and were interpreted to be the curious result of a process of regularization or rule formation. The principle here is that if a stem final segment is identical or very similar to the phonetic structure of a particular inflection, then the stem final segment suffices as a marker for a particular semantic contrast. Otherwise, redundant marking of a contrast may result. Under back formation, the effect is that a stem final segment takes on the function of an inflection and, at the same time, the word stem itself undergoes at least a momentary change in form.

The Status of an Independence Hypothesis

Unlike the data obtained in previous training studies, the data obtained in this study provide a revealing test of an independence hypothesis. For instance, consider the possible argument that the sensitivity quotients derived from the data obtained under Training Conditions I and II do not indicate an interdependent relationship but rather a general order-of-training effect among trained linguistic behaviors. Such an argument, if literally interpreted, assumes that order-of-training effects are additive. The implication for studies such as the one reported here is that the difference between the total number of trials to criterion necessary under implicit concurrent training (Training Conditions I and II) as opposed to explicit concurrent training (Training Condition III) should be negligible. However, the data indicate quite the opposite; namely, there is a significant difference between trials to criterion required under implicit and explicit concurrent training. Order-of-training effects, therefore, are not additive, and they may well be properly treated as a function of the substantive properties of linguistic behaviors themselves.

CONCLUSION

At this juncture, it seems that there are data-based grounds for arguing that linguistic complexity factors are indeed significant and, therefore, merit our consideration when designing language training programs. In essence, most of what has been said here supports a developmental logic of language intervention, especially as it regards order-of-training effects. In an attempt to move toward an increasingly more adequate logic of language intervention, our efforts should be directed toward quantifying the relative levels of interdependence that exist among linguistic forms that collectively constitute rudimentary functional language.

   As a final note, adaptations of *CC* analysis promise to bring to language intervention technology the potential for greater degrees of stimulus control. In turn, they may well enhance the potential of operant procedures to replace linguistic deficits, with integrated components of functional language. Unlike what is implied in a number of recent intervention studies, such as those carried out by Hegde et al. (1979), Hegde (1980b), and Hart and Risley (1980), when attempting to train enduring linguistic behavior, we might opt to attend specifically to the substance of those forms targeted for training rather than orienting exclusively on training procedures. What is advocated here is nothing more than a focus on the stimulus side of language (see Smith, Ruder and Waryas, Chapter 1 of this volume). Such a focus diverts attention from the isolated issue of training a sufficient number of exemplars (independent of what forms are being trained) to the multifaceted issue of how, or in what specific fashion, a set of exemplars should be treated so that generalization effects within language, itself, are best promoted. Herein, the data indicate a need to inject significant doses of linguistic substance into our efforts to remediate linguistic deficits. At the same time, we do not mean to deny that the *use* of linguistic behavior is critical to the process of language training (see Smith, Ruder and Waryas, Chapter 1 of this volume). We simply assert the need of a deep concern for linguistic substance; namely, what underlies the *use* of language. To preoccupy ourselves too much with issues related to *use* as opposed to substance is to ignore the pivotal role of linguistic structure as it affects the training of functional language. Sympathetic to this very point, Siegel and Spradlin (1978) and Wilbur (1983) underscored the need to orient intervention programming on a *working definition of language.* Synonymous with such a call should be a rejuvenated concern for the structure of language—the structure of what is targeted for training.

REFERENCES

Akjmanova, O. 1971. Phonology, Morphophonology, and Morphology. Mouton, The Hague.
Anisfeld, M., Barlow, S., and Frail, C.M. 1968. Distinctive features in the pluralization rules of English speakers. Lang. Speech. 11:31–37.
Anisfeld, M., and Gordon, M. 1968. On the psychophonological structure of English inflectional rules. J. Verb. Learn. Verb. Behav. 7:973–979.
Anisfeld, M., and Tucker, G. 1967. English pluralization rules of six-year-old children. Child Dev. 38:1201–1217.
Aram, D.M., and Nation, J.E. 1982. Child Language Disorders. C.V. Mosby, St. Louis.
Baer, D. 1981. The nature of intervention research. In: R.L. Schiefelbusch and D. Bricker (eds.), Early Language: Acquisition and Intervention. University Park Press, Baltimore.

Baer, D., and Guess, D. 1973. Teaching productive noun suffixes to severely retarded children. Am. J. Ment. Defic. 2:301–312.

Baer, D., Guess, D., and Sherman, J. 1972. Adventures in simplistic grammar. In: R.L. Schiefelbusch (ed.), Language of the Mentally Retarded. University Park Press, Baltimore.

Baer, D., and Wright, J. 1974. Developmental psychology. In: P. Mussen and M. Rosenzweig (eds.), Annual Review of Psychology. Annual Reviews, Palo Alto, CA.

Bell, A., and Hooper, J. (eds.). 1978. Syllables and Segments. North Holland, Amsterdam.

Berko, J. 1958. The child's learning of English morphology. Word 14:150–177.

Blache, S. 1978. The Acquisition of Distinctive Features. University Park Press, Baltimore.

Bloom, L., and Lahey, M. 1978. Language Development and Language Disorders. John Wiley & Sons, New York.

Bloomfield, L. 1933. Language. Holt, Rinehart and Winston, New York.

Braine, M. 1973. The acquisition of language in infant and child. In: C. Reed (ed.), The Learning of Language. Appleton-Century, New York.

Brown, R. 1973. A First Language: The Early Stages. Harvard University Press, Cambridge, MA.

Brown, R., and Fraser, C. 1963. The acquisition of syntax. In: C. Cofer and B. Musgrave (eds.), Verbal Behavior and Learning. McGraw-Hill, New York.

Bruner, J. 1982. The formats of language acquisition. Am. J. Semiot. 1:1–17.

Bryant, B., and Anisfeld, M. 1969. Feedback versus no-feedback in testing children's knowledge of English pluralization rules. J. Exp. Child Psychol. 8:250–255.

Bybee, J.L., and Slobin, D. 1982. Rules and schemas in the development and use of the English past. Language 58:265–290.

Cairns, C.E. 1969. Markedness, neutralization, and universal redundancy rules. Language 45:863–885.

Cairns, H., and Williams, F. 1972. An analysis of the substitution errors of a group of standard English-speaking children. J. Speech Hear. Res. 15:811–820.

Cazden, C.B. 1968. The acquisition of noun and verb inflections. Child Dev. 39:433–438.

Chomsky, N. 1959. Review of B.F. Skinner's Verbal Behavior. Language 35:26–58.

Chomsky, N., and Halle, M. 1968. The Sound Pattern of English. Harper & Row, New York.

Cofer, C. 1963. Comments on Brown and Fraser. In: C. Cofer and B. Musgrave (eds.), Verbal Behavior and Learning: Problems and Processes. McGraw-Hill, New York.

Cole, M.E., and Cole, J.T. 1980. Effective Intervention with the Language Impaired Child. Aspen, Rockville, MD.

Compton, A.J. 1970. Generative studies of children's phonological disorders. J. Speech Hear. Disord. 35:315–339.

Compton, A. 1976. Generative studies of children's phonological disorders. In: D. Morehead and A. Morehead (eds.), Normal and Deficient Child Language. University Park Press, Baltimore.

Connell, P., Spradlin, J., and McReynolds, L. 1977. Some suggested criteria for the evaluation of language programs. J. Speech Hear. Disord. 42:563–577.

Costello, J., and Onstine, J. 1976. The modification of multiple articulation errors based on distinctive feature analysis. J. Speech Hear. Disord. 41:199–715.

Cromer, R. 1981. Reconceptualizing language acquisition and cognitive development. In: R.L. Schiefelbusch and D. Bricker (eds.), Early Language: Acquisition and Intervention. University Park Press, Baltimore.

Derwing, B., and Baker, W. 1977. The psychological basis for morphological rules. In: Macnamara, J. (ed.), Language Learning and Thought in Children. Academic Press, New York.

Derwing, B., and Baker, W. 1979. Recent research on the acquisition of English morphology. In: P. Fletcher and M. Garman (eds.), Language Acquisition: Studies in First Language Development. Cambridge University Press, London.

deVilliers, J., and deVilliers, P. 1973. A cross-sectional study of the acquisition of grammatical morphemes in child speech. J. Psycholing. Res. 2:267–279.

Elbert, M., and Weismer, G. 1983. Phonological Theory and the Misarticulating Child. American Speech-Language-Hearing Association, DC.

Foley, H.M., and Locke, J.L. 1971. Young children's knowledge of morphological and phonological rules. J. Commun. Disord. 4:259–262.

Garcia, E., and DeHaven, E. 1974. Use of operant techniques in the establishment and generalization of language. Am. J. Ment. Defic. 79:169–178.

Guess, D. 1969. A functional analysis of receptive language and productive speech: Acquisition of the plural morpheme. J. Appl. Behav. Anal. 2:55–64.

Guess, D., and Baer, D. 1973a. Some experimental analyses of linguistic development in institutionalized retarded childrens. In: B.B. Lahey (ed.), The Modification of Language Behavior. Charles C. Thomas, Springfield, IL.

Guess, D., and Baer, D. 1973b. An analysis of individual differences in generalization between receptive and productive language in retarded children. J. Appl. Behav. Anal. 6:311–331.

Guess, D., Keogh, W., and Sailor, W. 1978. Generalization of speech and language behavior. In: R.L. Schiefelbusch (ed.), Bases of Language Intervention. University Park Press, Baltimore.

Guess, D., Sailor, W., and Baer, D. 1974. To teach language to retarded children. In: R.L. Schiefelbusch and L.L. Lloyd (eds.), Language Perspectives—Acquisition, Retardation, and Intervention. University Park Press, Baltimore.

Guess, D., Sailor, W., and Baer, D. 1978. Children with limited language. In: R.L. Schiefelbusch (ed.), Language Intervention Strategies. University Park Press, Baltimore.

Guess, D., Sailor, N., Rutherford, G., and Baer, D. 1968. An experimental analysis of linguistic development: The productive use of plural morpheme. J. Appl. Behav. Anal. 1:297–306.

Harris, S. 1975. Teaching language to nonverbal children. Psychol. Bull. 82:565–580.

Hart, B., and Risley, T.R. 1980. In vivo language intervention: Unanticipated general effects. J. Appl. Behav. Anal. 13:407–432.

Hegde, M. 1980a. An experimental-clinical analysis of grammatical and behavioral distinctions. J. Speech Hear. Res. 23:864–876.

Hegde, M. 1980b. Issues in the study and explanation of language behavior. J. Psycholing. Res. 9:1–22.

Hedge, M., and McConn, J. 1981. Language training: Some data on response classes and generalization. J. Speech Hear. Disord. 46:352–358.

Hegde, M., Noll, M., and Pecora, R. 1979. A study of some factors affecting generalization of language. J. Speech Hear. Disord. 44:301–320.

Ingram, D. 1976. Phonological Disability in Children. Elsevier, New York.

Ingram, D. 1981. Procedures for the Phonological Analysis of Children's Language. University Park Press, Baltimore.

Jakobson R. 1968 (1941). Child Language Aphasia and Phonological Universals. The Hague: Mouton.

Johnson, H. 1974. Zombies and other problems: Theory and method in research on bilingualism. Lang. Learn. 24:105–135.

Johnston, J.R., and Schery, J.K. 1976. The use of grammatical morphemes by children with communication disorders. In: D. Morehead and A. Morehead (eds.), Normal and Deficient Child Language. University Park Press, Baltimore.

Keil, F. 1981. Constraints on knowledge and cognitive development. Psychol. Rev. 88:197–227.

LaRiviere, P., Winitz, H., Reeds, J., and Harriman, E. 1974. The conceptual reality of selected distinctive features. J. Speech Hear. Res. 17:122–133.

Leopold, W. 1949. Speech Development of a Bilingual Child, Vol. II. Northwestern University Press, Evanston, IL.

Liberman, A. 1974. The ordering of rules in phonology and the reality of distinctive features. Ling.: Internat. Rev. 126:45–63.

Lorentz, J. 1976. An analysis of some deviant phonological rules of English. In: D. Morehead and A. Morehead (eds.), Normal and Deviant Child Language. University Park Press, Baltimore.

Lovell, K., and Bradbury, B. 1967. The learning of English morphology in educationally subnormal special school children. Am. J. Ment. Defic. 71:609–615.

MacWhinney, B. 1975. Rules rote and analogy in morphological formations by Hungarian children. J. Child Lang. 2:65–77.

MacWhinney, B. 1978. The Acquisition of Morphophonology. Monogr. Soc. Res. Child Dev. Vol. 40:1–2 (No. 174) University of Chicago Press, Chicago.

Martinet, A. 1965. De la morphonologie. La Linguistique 1:15–30.

McLean, J., and Synder-McLean, L. 1978. A Transactional Approach to Early Language Training. Charles E. Merrill, Columbus, OH.

McReynolds, L. (ed.). 1974. Developing Systematic Procedures for Training Children's Language (ASHA Monograph, No. 18). American Speech and Hearing Association, DC.

McReynolds, L. 1978. Behavioral and linguistic considerations in children's speech production. In: J. Kavanagh and W. Strange (eds.), Speech and Language in the Laboratory School and Clinic. MIT Press, Cambridge, MA.

McReynolds, L., Engmann, D., and Dimmitt, K. 1974. Markedness theory and articulation errors. J. Speech Hear. Disord. 39:93–100.

McReynolds, L., and Engmann, D. 1975. Distinctive Feature Analysis of Misarticulations. University Park Press, Baltimore.

McReynolds, L., and Bennett, S. 1972. Distinctive feature generalization in articulatory testing. J. Speech Hear. Disord. 37:462–470.
McReynolds, L., and Huston, K.A. 1971. Distinctive feature analysis of children's misarticulations. J. Speech Hear. Disord. 36:155–166.
Menyuk, P. 1968. The role of distinctive features in children's acquisition of phonology. J. Speech Hear. 11:128–146.
Menyuk, P. 1969. Sentences Children Use. MIT Press, Cambridge, MA.
Menyuk, P. 1971. The Acquisition and Development of Language. Prentice-Hall, Englewood Cliffs, NJ.
Menyuk, P., and Looney, P. 1972. Relationships among components of the grammar in language disorder. J. Speech Hear. Res. 15:395–406.
Miller, J., and Yoder, D. 1974. Ontogenetic language teaching strategy for retarded children. In: R.L. Schiefelbusch and L. Lloyd (eds.), Language Perspectives—Acquisition, Retardation, and Intervention. University Park Press, Baltimore.
Miller, W., and Ervin-Tripp, S. 1964. The development of grammar in children. In: U. Bellugi and R. Brown (eds.), The Acquisition of Language. Child Dev. Monogr. 29:9–43 (No. 29). University of Chicago Press, Chicago.
Morehead, D., and Morehead, A. (eds.). 1976. Normal and Deficient Child Language. University Park Press, Baltimore.
Muma, J. 1978. Language Handbook. Prentice-Hall, Englewood Cliffs, NJ.
Newfield, M., and Schlanger, B. 1968. The acquisition of English morphology by normal and educably mentally retarded children. J. Speech Hear. Res. 11:693–706.
Palermo, D., and Eberhart, V. 1968. On the learning of morphological rules: An experimental analogy. J. Verb. Learn. Verb. Behav. 1:337–344.
Palermo, D., and House, H. 1970. An experimental analogy to the learning of past tense inflection rules. J. Verb. Learn. Verb. Behav. 9:410–416.
Palermo, D., and Parrish, M. 1971. Rule acquisition as a function of number and frequency of exemplar presentation. J. Verb. Learn. Verb. Behav. 10:44–51.
Park, T.Z. 1971. The acquisition of German morphology. Unpublished working paper, Psychological Institute, University of Berne, Berne, Switzerland.
Piaget, J. 1968. Le Structuralisme. Presses Universitaries de France, Paris.
Postal, P.M. 1968. Aspects of Phonological Theory. Harper & Row, New York.
Risley, T. 1977. The development and maintenance of language: An operant model. In: B. Etzel, J. LeBlanc, and D. Baer (eds.), New Developments in Behavioral Research. Lawrence Erlbaum Associates, Hillsdale, NJ.
Ruder, K.F., and Bunce, B. 1981. A distinctive feature approach to articulation training. J. Speech Hear. Disord. 46:59–66.
Ruder, K.F., Hermann, P., and Schiefelbusch, R. 1977. Effects of verbal imitation and comprehension training on verbal production. J. Psycholing. Res. 6:59–72.
Ruder, K., Smith, M.D., and Hermann, P. 1974. Effect of verbal imitation and comprehension on verbal production of lexical items. In: L. McReynolds (ed.), Developing Systematic Procedures for Training Children's Language, No. 18. American Speech and Hearing Association, DC.
Ruder, K.F., and Smith, M.D. 1974. Issues in language training. In: R.L. Schiefelbusch and L.L. Lloyd (eds.), Language Perspectives—Acquisition, Retardation, and Intervention. University Park Press, Baltimore.

Sailor, W. 1971. Reinforcement and generalization of productive plural allomorphs in two retarded children. J. Appl. Behav. Anal. 4:305–310.

Scandora, J. 1970. The role of rules in behavior. Psychol. Bull. 77:516–533.

Schiefelbusch, R.L., and Lloyd, L. (eds.). 1974. Language Perspectives—Acquisition, Retardation, and Intervention. University Park Press, Baltimore.

Schiefelbusch, R.L., and D. Bricker. 1981. Early Language: Acquisition and Intervention. University Park Press, Baltimore.

Schlesinger, I.M. 1974. Relational concepts underlying language. In: R.L. Schiefelbusch and L. Lloyd (eds.), Language Perspectives—Acquisition, Retardation, and Intervention. University Park Press, Baltimore.

Schroeder, G., and Baer, D. 1972. Effects of concurrent and serial training on generalized vocal imitation in retarded children. Dev. Psychol. 6:293–301.

Schumaker, J., and Sherman, J. 1970. Training generative verb usage by imitation and reinforcement procedures. J. Appl. Behav. Anal. 3:273–287.

Segal, E. 1975. Psycholinguistics discover the operant. J. Exp. Anal. Behav. 23:149–158.

Semel, E., and Wiig, E. 1980. Language Assessment and Intervention for the Learning Disabled. Charles E. Merrill, Columbus, OH.

Shane, S.A. 1973. Generative Phonology. Prentice-Hall, Englewood Cliffs, NJ.

Sherman, J. 1971. Imitation and language development. In: H.W. Reese and L.P. Lipsitt (eds.), Advances in Child Development and Behavior. Academic Press, New York.

Siegel, G., and Spradlin, J. 1978. Programming for communication and language therapy. In: R.L. Schiefelbusch (ed.), Language Intervention Strategies. University Park Press, Baltimore.

Singh, S., and Polen, S. 1972. Use of a distinctive feature model in speech pathology. Acta Symbolica 3:17–25.

Singh, S. 1975. Distinctive Feature Theory Therapy. University Park Press, Baltimore.

Singh, S. 1976. Distinctive Features: Theory and Validation. University Park Press, Baltimore.

Singh, S. (ed.). 1978. Diagnostic procedures in hearing, language, and speech. University Park Press, Baltimore.

Skinner, B.F. 1957. Verbal Behavior. Appleton-Century-Croft, New York.

Slobin, D.I. 1971. On the learning of morphological rules: A reply to Palermo and Eberhard. In: D.I. Slobin (ed.), The Ontogenesis of Grammar: A Theoretical Symposium. Academic Press, New York.

Smith, M.D., and Ruder, K.F. 1975. The relevance of markedness. J. Speech Hear. Disord. 40:545–549.

Solomon, M. 1972. Stem endings and the acquisition of inflections. Lang. Learn. 22:43–51.

Sommerstein, A. 1977. Modern Phonology. University Park Press, Baltimore.

Staats, A. 1974. Behaviorism and cognitive theory in the study of language: A neopsycholinguistics. In: R.L. Schiefelbusch and L.L. Lloyd (eds.), Language Perspectives—Acquisition, Retardation, and Intervention. University Park Press, Baltimore.

Stewart, J., and Singh, S. 1979. Distinctive feature use in speech perception of children. Lang. Speech 22:69–79.

Stokes, T., and Baer, D. 1977. An implicit technology of generalization. J. Appl. Behav. Anal. 10:349–367.

Stremel-Campbell, K., and Waryas, C. 1974. A behavioral-psycholinguistic approach to language training. In: L. McReynolds (eds.), Developing Systematic Procedures for Training Children's Language (ASHA Monogr., No. 18). American Speech and Hearing Association, DC.

Wanner, E., and Gleitman, L.R. 1982. Language Acquisition: The State of the Art. Cambridge University Press, Cambridge, MA.

Waryas, C., and Stremel-Campbell, K. 1978. Grammatical training for the language delayed child. In: R.L. Schiefelbusch (ed.), Language Intervention Strategies. University Park Press, Baltimore.

Welch, S.J. 1981. Teaching generative grammar to mentally retarded children: A review and analysis of a decade of research. Ment. Retard. 19:277–284.

Wiig, E., and Semel, E. 1980. Language assessment and intervention. Charles E. Merrill, Columbus, OH.

Wilbur, R. 1983. Where do we go from here? (A discussion of Part III: Deciding how to carry out language intervention). In: J. Miller, D. Yoder, and R.L. Schiefelbusch (eds.), Contemporary Issues in Language Intervention (ASHA Reports 12). American Speech-Language-Hearing Assoc., Rockville, MD.

chapter 7

Metacognition, Metalinguistics, and Intervention

Robert E. Kretschmer

Teachers College
Columbia University
New York, New York

contents

The goal of language instruction with respect to children who demonstrate communication problems[1] is to help those students become competent speaker-listeners of the language and to be knowledgeable problem-solvers within any given number of subject domains. The process involved in obtaining this goal includes the use of both metacognitive and metalinguistic skills. It, minimally, involves metacognitive and metalinguistic awareness on the part of the instructor, and it may involve establishing or calling upon the meta-abilities of the child, him- or herself. This is because each of these metaprocesses involve making explicit the inherent organization of a particular domain or the person's implicit knowledge of it.

To promote further understanding of the relationship between these abilities and academic and language learning, this chapter is organized as follows: first, certain general notions regarding the relationship between metacognition and metalinguistics are explored, followed by brief discussions concerning the development of metacognitive skills, the parameters affecting metacognitive performance, and the development of metalinguistics skills. Finally, a discussion of meta-abilities and the instructional process is presented.

THE RELATIONSHIP BETWEEN METACOGNITION AND METALINGUISTICS

By definition, there are two aspects of **metacognition**:

Aspect *1*: *A person's knowledge about cognition and cognitive processes* According to Flavell and Wellman (1977), this aspect refers to the relatively stable, stateable, often fallible, and late-developing information that human thinkers have about their own cognitive processes and those of others. In other words, it is the ability of a person to reflect upon his or her own knowledge and thinking abilities.

Aspect *2*: *A cluster of activities that serve to regulate and oversee cognitive operations* Metacognition as a regulatory function refers to those not necessarily stable, somewhat unstateable and relatively age- (although not task- and situation-) independent planning, monitoring and checking activities that an individual might undergo with regard to various cognitive operations. Functionally, these metacognitive skills can either be of a predictive, concurrent or retrospective nature (Kreutzer et al., 1975) and are deemed to be among the highest form of mature human intelligence

---

[1] This term, as used, is generic and includes any and all children who demonstrate language, communication, or language-related academic problems.

(Brown et al., 1982, citing Rozin, 1976; Pylyshyn, 1978; and Gardner, 1978).

In like fashion, **metalinguistics** refers to those aspects of language functioning concerned with: 1) a person's knowledge about language and language operations; and 2) the planning, monitoring, and checking activities that an individual might undergo during language comprehension and production.

One major difference between these two metaprocesses, i.e., metacognition and metalinguistics, is that with the latter, the individual can "step back" and reflect upon the nature of the domain, itself, as an object of thought; with the former, the domain is somewhat more elusive and transparent.

The actual relationship between the two metaprocesses and/or the manner in which an instructor-clinician utilizes the child's awareness of these two domains, undoubtedly, is a function of the actual or, at least, perceived relationship between thought and language. The three basic orientations pertaining to the hypothesized relationship between thought and language and the manner in which each is believed to develop are:

1. *The cognitive dominant approach*   Thought (cognitive processes and nonverbal world knowledge) undergirds all basic language abilities and precedes language in its acquisition. Such an orientation points out that language merely serves to map out that which is already known.

2. *The language dominant approach*   Language dictates (the strong Whorfian hypothesis) or, at least, constrains (the weak Whorfian hypothesis) thought, and language is learned through exposure to it.

3. *The communicative interactional approach*   Thought and language are highly interdependent systems and spawn from a common root, i.e., the symbolic communicative act, itself (Bates, 1976; Bruner, 1978).

With regard to metalinguistics, these positions translate into the following relationships and hypotheses:

1. Metalinguistics skills are but a subset of metacognition.
2. Metalinguistic knowledge, skills, and terminology serve to highlight and bring metacognitive awareness into full fruition.
3. The two processes are semi-autonomous, inextricably related, and mutually reinforcing.

Operating on the assumption that the two metaprocesses exist as semi-autonomous operations, Ericsson and Simon (1980) pointed out that the act of verbalization in reporting on various cognitive operations may be either facilitative, debilitating, or neutral. For example, neutral effects were said to occur when a subject is asked to describe, for example, information that is already available in short-term memory. Ericsson and Simon noted, however, that if a subject was asked to report on available information, but not in verbal or propositional form, the translation process slowed down performance and, as such, represented a debilitating effect. If the material does not exist or exists in a very unclear or unorganized manner, conscious verbalization may or may not prove to be of benefit.

Although metaprocesses are said to be reflective and regulatory acts, such reflections and regulation may not exist in an all or "nothing fashion." Rather, they may exist upon a continuum.[2] Although Piaget (1976) basically accepted this notion, he spoke in fairly categorical terms and, as a result, identified three levels of such abilities:

1. *Autonomous regulation*   The on-line fine-tuning and modulations of various actions and behaviors
2. *Active regulation*   Similar to active trial-and-error learning
3. *Conscious regulation*   The mental formulation of hypotheses with regard to various problems

Although the first level of self-regulation does not seem to involve any form of metaprocessing, the latter two obviously do.

THE DEVELOPMENT OF METACOGNITIVE SKILLS

For any skill, there are two circumstances where conscious reflection or decision making occurs (Brown et al., 1982): 1) during skill acquisition; and 2) during times when cognitive (or linguistic) failure occurs. As a result, metacognitive (or metalinguistic) awareness would seem to stem from the child's active struggle during the learning process and during times of cognitive (or linguistic) dissonance. This notion, however, should not be foreign to those familiar with Piagetian and neo-Piagetian theory, because it is consistent with the notions of equilibration, assimilation, and accommodation.

---

[2] Alternatively, Marshall and Morton (1978) suggested that, at least with respect to metalinguistic regulation, a monitoring apparatus (separate from the normal language processing unit, NLP, entitled EMMA—an Even More Mysterious Apparatus) works in an "all or nothing" fashion. However, the extent and type of information about NLP, to which EMMA has access, varies, giving the illusion of a continuum.

It has been well-documented that children are capable of reflective thought extremely early in their lives, seemingly in the absence of formal conventional language. Piaget (1952), for example, noted that infants during Substage 5 of the sensorimotor period are capable of object permanence, object recall, and the coordinated use of tools to solve simple obstacle problems; at Substage 6, they are capable of object displacement recognition, the generation of presumed covert solutions to problems, and deferred imitation, each of which involves some form of mental representations and rudimentary reflection. According to Piagetian theory, the origins of this reflective, representational thought are rooted much earlier in the child's life. For example, as early as Substage 3, the infant demonstrates the ability to visually search for objects recently presented in his or her field of vision. To accomplish this, it seems reasonable to presume that the child has some mental representation of the object's existence, although not necessarily its permanence. By Piaget's own definition, however, this behavior is not, nor could it be, considered true reflective thought because it exists in the absence of symbolic representation. Within this framework, the relative contribution of formal conventional symbolic systems (language) in the continuation and maintenance of these abilities is downgraded; however, their actual contribution, by other accounts, is still largely unknown.

Because a full account of the behavioral parameters of cognition has yet to be devised and the mechanisms governing such operations are not readily accessible as objects of introspection for most individuals, it is difficult to conceive a specific outline of developmental metacognitive milestones. Despite this, Brown and DeLoache (1978) developed a partial taxonomy of such skills. The list included the following items:

1. Predicting the consequences of an action or event
2. Checking the results of a person's own actions
3. Monitoring a person's ongoing activities
4. Testing for reality
5. Coordinating or controlling deliberate attempts to learn and to solve problems

PARAMETERS AFFECTING METACOGNITIVE PERFORMANCE

As an alternative to discussing the yet unclear developmental outline of metacognitive skills, the various parameters influencing the acquisition and demonstration of such abilities are discussed because it is clear that their development is not simply a function of age. The known parameters are: 1) the characteristics of the learner, which include all of the individual's knowledge, attitudes, and capabilities; 2) the nature of the materials, setting, and previous organizers (e.g., the stimulus' physical structure, conceptual difficulty, and sequence of organization); 3) the criterial tasks (e.g., the use of recognition, recall versus problem solving, etc., in dealing with stimuli); 4) the learning activities or strategies used (e.g., rehearsal and elaboration); and 5) the quality of the interaction between the learner and significant others in the environment.[3]

Parameter 1: Learner Characteristics

With regard to the relationship between learner characteristics, memory, and the acquisition or conscious use of knowledge, three aspects seem to be particularly important: 1) the individual's current fund of factual information; 2) the child's current intellectual capacity level; and 3) the child's "cognitive style," which involves certain aspects of personality.

Current Fund of Factual Information   At first blush, this may seem to be a tautology with respect to the previous statement; however, it merely serves to point out the fact that the closer the match between that which is being learned, studied, or remembered and that which is already known, the more efficient and accurate the process will be. This, in fact, is the basic premise of schema theory accounts of semantic memory (Pearson, 1982). Obviously, the two cannot be identical or no learning could occur. Conscious reflectivity (possibly without additional comprehension or insight), however, would be maximized in this situation. The issues surrounding the importance of a person's factual fund of information or content knowledge have been approached from two complementary perspectives: 1) a static perspective, which emphasizes the extent to which the current state of knowledge effects performance; and 2) the perspective of dynamic knowledge, which is concerned with how the individual's knowledge base comes to be, and how it changes with experience (Brown et al., 1982).

Intellectual Capacity Level   Current approaches to the study of metacognitive abilities have appealed to information-processing accounts. Such accounts emphasize the finite on-line capacity, or central computing space, of any individual (in this case, the child) to deal with information. According to Pascual-Leone (1970), this central computing space was said to be equivalent to the number of schemes or discrete units (or chunks) of information that would be operated upon simultaneously at any given moment. This phenomenon was said to bear a

---

[3] This list of parameters is based in part upon the works of Jenkins (1979) and Brown et al. (1982).

linear relationship with age and to interact with those units of information described above in that their size and nature might increase and differ with age as well.

Cognitive Style   It has been suggested, and reasonably so, that the greater the individual is motivated to perform and is willing to expend both cognitive and attentional energy, the greater the probability of success in any given conscious, cognitive task. In personality theory, this orientation has been associated with a great many constructs, including the need for achievement, reflectivity/impulsivity, and internal/external locus of control. Although motivation is a necessary prerequisite to metacognitive thought, it is not sufficient. It must interact with other variables, some already mentioned and others yet to be, in order for the metacognitive act to occur.

Parameter 2: Nature of Materials, Setting, and Previous Organizers

Obviously, this parameter was alluded to previously with respect to the notion of learner/material correspondence. Not only should there be a correspondence with regard to subject content and lexical items, but there should also be a correspondence at higher levels of organization, such as syntax and discourse. Other aspects of the materials, however, may also influence the learning task, e.g., passage length and organization on the page (in the case of print).

Parameter 3: Criterial Tasks

The manner in which the individual is asked to deal with the material is obviously an integral part of how that material is processed. For example, if an individual is asked to skim printed material in order to locate certain information, he or she might consciously approach the material one way; whereas, if committing the material to memory as in a stage play, the material would be approached differently. Similar examples can be imagined for verbal language, e.g., "skimming" an audiotape for a particular segment or concentrating on a lecture. These criterial demands must be considered not only in terms of the child's ability to employ them but also in terms of the child's ability to properly select their propitious use.

Parameter 4: Learning Activity or Strategy

This includes rehearsing, overtly verbalizing a plan; underlining; note taking; developing macrorules for comprehension, retention, and synopsis writing; self-questioning; and concentrating on previously missed or difficult items (Brown et al., 1982).

Parameter 5: Interaction in Environment

The parent, teacher, or other significant individual in the child's environment is significant in that they stand between the child and the environment and attempt to interpret it to him or her (Feurestein, 1979). The manner in which this is done may be facilitative, debilitative, or neutral with regard to task performance.

None of these parameters operate in isolation; rather, they function interactively to determine eventually cognitive and metacognitive performance. For example, the ability to monitor a child's comprehension of texts is not only a function of age, but also the blatancy of the inconsistencies, the degree to which the inconsistencies are central to the reading-listening task, the relevant background of information of the reader-listener, the criterial demands for information processing, the strategies that the child chooses to monitor the comprehension task, and the degree to which the parent or teacher assists in this process. Similarly, each of the parameters comes into play with regard to such metacognitive operations as study effort-allocation and error-detection and correction.

Not only do each of these significant parameters affect the manner in which children come to acquire and utilize knowledge actively and consciously, but they can be objects of metacognitive thought in their own right. As a result, the following ability should be added to the Brown and DeLoache's taxonomy list: the ability to reflect consciously upon the parameters affecting performance on any metacognitive task, including elaborated versions of each of those cited above.

DEVELOPMENT OF METALINGUISTIC SKILLS

As a subject domain or explicit body of knowledge, language seems to exist as a relatively well-defined set of finite rules and behaviors subject to overt inspection; interestingly, however, the acts of production and comprehension may not be so inspected.

Clark (1978) developed a partial taxonomy of metalinguistic skills that parallels the taxonomy of Brown and DeLoache's metacognitive skills (see p. 214 of this volume). Clark's list included the following:

1. Monitoring ongoing utterances—repairing a person's own speech spontaneously; practicing various speech and language units; and adjusting his or her speech to the age and status of the listener

2. Checking the results of an utterance—seeing whether or not communication has been affected and repairing the conversation when necessary; commenting on the utterances of others; and correcting the utterances of others

3. Testing for reality—making decisions as to whether or not a word or description will or will not work
4. Deliberately trying to learn language units, either by practicing them or role playing
5. Predicting the consequences of language units and rules, such as applying inflections to new words or nonsense words and making judgments of grammaticality
6. Reflecting on the product of an utterance—identifying linguistic units, providing definitions, and constructing puns and riddles

Actually, with reference to item 6, all aspects of linguistic organization can be subjected to metalinguistic or metacognitive inspection, and thus the description of language provided by Bloom and Lahey (1978) is very helpful. In their description of language, Bloom and Lahey identified three general dimensions of organization: 1) the form of the language, i.e., the phono-morphological and syntactic rules of the language; 2) the semantics of the language, involving both general and specific object knowledge as well as semantic and event relationships; and 3) the use of the language, including both its functions and its exophoric and endophoric contexts. Each of these is open to reflective thought.

The following skills and objects of reflection were not mentioned by Clark or Bloom and Lahey but should be included within any taxonomy of metalinguistic abilities: 1) the ability to note synonyms, antonyms, hyponyms, entailments, and presuppositions; and 2) the ability to generate paraphrases.

The taxonomy that was provided by Clark and is presented here was based upon a body of research (which is reviewed briefly below) and was said to be hierarchical in nature. Within this hierarchy, regulatory aspects of metalinguistics were generally said to precede reflective aspects.

Research in the area of developmental metalinguistics has found that even very young children are capable of rudimentary monitoring of comprehension and judgments of grammaticality. For example, it has been noted that around 2 years of age, children are capable of spontaneously correcting errors involving their own pronunciations, word forms, and word order (Clark, 1978); remarking on their speech abilities (Limber 1973); commenting on the superior speech abilities of others and making judgments regarding their own speech (Smith, 1973); and commenting on and playing with different linguistic units, segmenting words into syllables and sounds, and making puns and rhymes (Weir, 1962). It has also been noted that children this young are capable of making simple judgments of grammaticality (Gleitman et al., 1972; deVilliers and deVilliers, 1972; Carr, 1979).

Semantically, children this young make queries about the right meanings of words (Clark, 1978). Pragmatically, they engage in spontaneous self-corrections (Clark, 1978). They attempt to cope with failures of speech acts in that they will restate utterances if their communication attempts are ignored (Kagermann as reported by Foppa, 1978), and they will repeat or change words until they make themselves understood when communication fails (Scollon, 1976).

With regard to these findings, it should be pointed out that although instances of metalinguistic awareness have been reported, the frequency of occurrence of many of these behaviors is quite low and, thus, cannot be considered a characteristic behavior. This is particularly true in the case of judgments of grammaticality and other reflective forms of metalinguistics. In many cases, there is also the question of reliability. As for making judgments of acceptability, Carr (1979) suggested that very young children do not perform on grammatical grounds but, rather, on the basis of their experience with the world. Thus, they may judge sentences unacceptable, if they do not correspond to that which is known about the world. This notion of semantic acquisition and mastery preceding the ability to deal with or acquire syntactic forms is a common finding, which repeats itself even into the middle elementary school years (Hakes et al., 1980) and adolescence (Kretschmer, 1976). To some degree, the above findings are also consistent with Bates' (1976) description of language development, which states basically that the acquisition of perlocutionary aspects of language (the effects produced by particular language usage) precedes that of the illocutionary (loosely defined as semantic) aspects of the language, which in turn precedes the development of locutionary (syntactic) forms. In terms of metalinguistics, this means that control over regulatory aspects may precede reflective aspects.

When children are 3- and 4-years-old, a great deal is learned, or at least manifested, with respect to metalinguistic awareness. In terms of form, for example, children this age have been noted to ask questions about the pronunciations of words (Gleitman et al., 1972), to correct the speech and language of others (Maccoby and Bee, 1965), to segment utterances into words and syllables (Fox and Routh, 1975), and to discriminate anomalous versus well-formed sentences on the basis of selectional restriction rules (Howe and Hillman, 1973). In terms of semantics, Andersen (1975) found that children at this age defined words in terms of overextensions of other words, e.g., "A glass is a cup." As for the definition of the word, "word," Berthoud-Papandropoulou

(1978) noted that 3- and 4-year-old children often equated "word" with the act of speaking, itself, and when asked how many words there were in a sentence, the response was often "two," based upon segmenting the utterance into two parts—a topic and a comment. Finally, with respect to knowledge about lexical words, themselves, children at this age, when asked what a "long word" was, equated the physical length of the word with the size of the referent, e.g., the word *train* was considered a long word (Berthoud-Papandropoulou, 1978). At this age, children have also been found to demonstrate formal recognition of case grammar roles and relationships (Braine and Wells, 1978).

As for pragmatics, children this age have been noted to comment on what they cannot do (Markman, 1977); to make judgments of politeness (Bates, 1976); and to adjust their speech patterns and styles according to: 1) various family and public roles (Andersen, 1977); 2) the age of the individual (Sachs and Devin, 1976); 3) the presumed knowledge of the individual (Menig-Peterson, 1975); and 4) the presence or absence of perceptual supports (Maratsos, 1973). At least with respect to making speech adjustments for age, the behavior of 3- to 4-year-old children does not seem to be a function of communication pressure but rather the adoption of an actual "speech style" (Sachs and Devin, 1976). Finally, children this age demonstrate a rudimentary awareness of the effects of message length and environmental noise on communication. They also demonstrate a similar, but slightly poorer, awareness of the effects of age and time constraints (Yussen and Bird, 1979).

Research has indicated that at approximately five years of age, children can comment on how others (usually younger children) speak, are capable of applying phono-morphological rules to unfamiliar or nonsense words (Berko, 1958), and are sensitive to puns and certain ambiguities (Hirsh-Pasek et al., 1978). Semantically, 5-year-old children were found to understand and use metaphors in a primitive manner (Gardner, 1974; Gardner and Lohman, 1975). Word definitions were noted to be simple collocative phrases, such as a "hole" meant, "You dig a hole" and the word "word" was often identified as a group of letters (Berthoud-Papandropoulou, 1978). Pragmatically, Scholl and Ryan (1975) noted that children at this age were aware of the appropriateness of speech acts and were able to assign the production of simple sentences to younger children and more complex language to adults.

At ages 6 and 7, with the advent of formal schooling, a wide array of academic and metalinguistic skills are taught and learned, including the reading readiness skills of segmentation, identity, and sound/symbol association (Mason, in press). Definitions of words at this age center on salient physical properties of the referent, and the concept of a word becomes identified with parts of larger, meaningful expressions (Berthoud-Papandropoulou, 1978). At approximately 7 years of age, the notions of lexical or semantic synonymy (Sack and Beilin, 1971) and phonological and lexical ambiguity are developing, whereas syntactical ambiguity is not (Shultz and Pilon, 1973).

At age 8, the definition of a word becomes equated with the grammatical parts of speech, and the child is able to define other words, taking into account the interdependence of perceptual and functional features (Berthoud-Papandropoulou, 1978). This late development seems reasonable because in order to generate an adequate definition, it must first be determined what constitutes a good definition. The skill to resolve adequately phonological and semantic ambiguities (Hirsh-Pasek et al., 1978) is usually mastered by the time the child is 10 or 11 years of age, although difficulty with respect to syntactic ambiguities persists until ages 13 to 15 (Shultz and Pilon, 1973). In like fashion, Kretschmer (1976) found that 11- to 14-year-old normally hearing children scaled the acceptability of semantically and syntactically anomalous sentences on the basis of esoteric strategies or semantic integrity, whereas 17-year-old normally hearing individuals preferred a syntactic solution to the scaling procedure. Lastly, Markham (1977) noted that youngsters aged 13 and older still had difficulty monitoring their reading comprehension and were not always aware of inconsistencies in a text.

Certain metalinguistic (and metacognitive) skills are still developing into the adult years. In fact, it could be argued that by definition, a person does not acquire metalinguistic (or metacognitive) competency until adulthood. It should also be pointed out, however, that there is some evidence, contrary to Chomsky's (1965) position, that not all adults have equal intuitive linguistic abilities; rather, variation exists as a function of educational level (Mills and Hemsley, 1976).

META-ABILITIES AND THE INSTRUCTIONAL PROCESS

The intervention teaching process is interactive and involves, at some level, a form of metacognitive and/or metalinguistic awareness. This awareness, as stated before, may manifest itself with respect to either the child or the teacher. In either event, it exists as a part of the deliberate act of teaching and learning. There are at least two interrelated questions with respect to metacognition and the intervention process: 1) What are the extent and nature of the metacognitive and metalinguistic skills that are used in various (re)habilitation programs?; and 2) Can these abilities be directly taught?

Essentially, there are three approaches to the teaching of language and other subject matter, each differing from the other as to the extent to which metacognitive and metalinguistic skills are typically and explicitly demanded of the youngster: 1) a "formal" (or structural) approach; 2) a semi-formal approach; and 3) language learning *in situ*.

Formal or Structural Approach

This approach frequently attempts to explicitly teach children from a very early age metalinguistic terms such as "noun" and "verb," with heavy reliance on the use of external mnemonics (e.g., the Fitzgerald Key, N + V + N). Such approaches demand active reflection on the part of the child, and in practice, they often result in a specifically designed "language lesson," wherein semantically unrelated sentences are presented to hearing- and language-impaired children for analysis, manipulation, or scrutiny. Such decontextualized language instruction can also be observed in use with very young children, such as preschoolers, when sentences are categorized according to various syntactic or case grammar patterns and lexical items are categorized according to what types of wh-questions the items answer, etc. The use of special symbols (e.g., the Wing Symbols), color codes, etc., that denote "parts of speech" also fall within this category. Such approaches emphasize a language-dominant approach to instruction. The apparent logic of this approach is that if the child is explicitly made to practice or be aware of these forms early and often enough, he or she will internalize it.

Potential Problems   Unfortunately, there are a number of potential problems with such an approach, particularly when applied to very young children or when used indiscriminately.

Problem 1   A direct (rather than collateral) relationship between overt and covert behavior is assumed. Such, however, may not be the case, as discussed above. Even if a direct relationship does exist, individuals who utilize this approach often leave the matter of generalization or the transfer from overt instruction to covert performance to chance. (This is not to criticize what is inherent to the approach, itself, but rather the often made assumption regarding its use; that is, if the material is overtly dealt with and practiced, transfer will automatically occur.) The logic of overt practice being a prerequisite to covert use seems to be reasonable to some degree and has been employed as the first step in many studies by Meichenbaum and Asarnow (1978) regarding certain academic skills and covert conditioning. The major difference between the approach advocated by Meichenbaum and Asarnow and the approach described above, however, is that the former systematically links overt and covert behaviors rather than leaving them to chance.

Problem 2   Often, youngsters are taught in a heuristic or mnemonic fashion primarily to deal with only the topography (form) of the language rather than its content or functional use.

Problem 3   Such an approach tends to ignore developmental trends with regard to metalinguistic matters. Illogically (at least with respect to severely language-impaired children), it also asks the children to apply certain metacognitive and metalinguistic behavior and terms to a base that may not yet exist. It should be remembered that meta-activities performed on an operation manifest themselves developmentally after, not before, the object of reflection has been established, and regulatory abilities seem to precede reflective abilities. Developmentally, then, reflective meta-activity is typically the last link in the chain, not the first. Despite this, the formal (structural) approach makes a conscious effort to teach new and formerly unknown concepts via some metaprocessing insights.

Problem 4   Such an approach tends to be highly directive and controlling in nature, making this type of approach potentially counterproductive by fostering an external locus of control and an attitude of learned helplessness. The reason that this might be so is that by making knowledge or information so explicit and linked to mnemonics, the total process is externalized with subject to teacher dominance. As a result, the individual may be absolved from taking responsibility for his or her learning. (The relationship between communication interaction and the development of certain personality variables with regard to hearing-impaired youngsters is discussed in Kretschmer and Quigley, 1981 and Quigley and Kretschmer, 1982.)

Because very little empirical data exists with respect to these notions as applied to language acquisition, very few categorical statements can be made, and, consequently, the statements that have been made so far are based upon guided speculation. It is not known empirically, for example, whether the hierarchy proposed by Clark is inviolate with respect to training or whether lower order abilities are prerequisite to higher order ones.

In Defense of This Approach   It has been pointed out by many individuals working with lower academically functioning and learning-/language-impaired individuals that: 1) the manifest problems presented by these children can and have been addressed by active meta-intervention; and 2) with respect to academic failures, the problem may not be attributable to reduced cognitive or linguistic abilities per se, but rather to the absence or inefficient use of various metaskills. In fact, this issue, with respect to metacognition, was the basis of three recent monographs—*Controversy: Strategy or Capacity Deficit* (Swanson, 1982), *Teaching Exceptional Children to Use Cognitive Strategies* (Hallahan, 1980), and *Metacognition and Learning Disabilities* (Wong, 1982).

How, then, can this position be reconciled with that presented previously? The answer may lie in carefully attending to the interrelationship between these variables affecting learning, metaperformance, and the individual's history. Based upon the previous discussion of these variables, there seem to be times during the course of development that are situationally opportune and propitious for employing certain strategies and not others; performance heightens when the content of the program is consonant with the actual organization and use of the language domain and is fine-tuned to the prior knowledge of the individual child.

Semi-Formal Approach

Although this approach does not require children to develop initially a repertoire of metalinguistic terms, it does treat language instruction in a structured fashion with lessons or therapy sessions being devoted to specific constructions or linguistic principles. Such lessons often require some degree of meta-awareness and comprehension or production monitoring in that they emphasize the prompted and deliberate conscious or semi-conscious choice of one linguistic form over another. Such practices may even require children to make judgments of acceptability. To this extent, then, metaprocesses are practiced and taught. Examples of such an approach include lessons devoted to developing receptive or expressive abilities by lexically or sententially labeling pictures. Sessions involving work at the sentential level may involve a series of unrelated sentences or a cluster of sentences that, based upon some principle, systematically differ from each other. Often a language-dominant orientation is adopted or assumed, although it need not be.

One problem with this approach, at least with respect to young language- and hearing-impaired children, is that the lessons tend to be form-oriented and taught out of context, like the formal or structural approach. They also tend to emphasize the reflective as opposed to regulatory aspect of metalinguistics. Such an approach might be reasonable for the older children who have, presumably, already established some sense of communication and where the material being covered is essentially implicit knowledge being made explicit (emphasizing a cognitive-dominant approach to language instruction); if such is not the case, however, the task demands may be so great or the stimuli so decontextualized as to preclude easy or efficient learning.

Language Learning *In Situ*

In this approach, only the teacher is explicitly aware of the nature of the language learning situation and that which is being learned. This approach presumes that learning is best affected when language is presented contextually and explicitly dealt with only by means of certain prosodic, textual, and conversational features, e.g., intonation and the natural querying and probing techniques involved in normal caretaker-child relationships. Although the natural approach does not employ formal metalinguistic techniques per se, it should not be construed to mean that it is not organized and that specific, goal-oriented activities cannot and are not engineered.

When used with young children, such natural methods employ a number of "now coding"—interactive and question-structuring techniques within the normal play and exploratory activities of children. For older children, such an approach involves carefully constructing experientially based, interactive, conceptual units with planned follow-up, sometimes in the form of discussions. Adequate linguistic progress through this approach, however, is contingent upon the quality of the interaction that is maintained, which in turn is dependent upon the instructor's formal knowledge and awareness of language processes, the dynamic learning abilities of individuals (Feurestein, 1979; Keane, 1982), and the variables affecting learning and memory performance. (For a review of some of these interactional techniques, see Kretschmer and Kretschmer (1978), Bloom and Lahey (1978), Muma (1978), McLean and Snyder-McLean (1978), and Feuerstein (1979).)

Given the above discussion, then, what is the optimal approach with language- and hearing-impaired youngsters? Without specifically attaching age indexes to the hierarchy of instructional methodology, the teacher-therapist might begin ideally with a natural approach that takes full advantage of natural contexts and "normal" child-caregiver interactions. Once some base of communication and regulatory functioning has developed, a combination of a natural and semi-formal approach to language instruction might be used, taking into account the parameters effecting metaperformance, as cited above. At this point, these youngsters might be exposed to certain reflective aspects of metalinguistics in a naturalistic setting, e.g., probing for judgments of pragmatic and semantic acceptability without being held fully accountable for them. Finally, formal structural approaches to language instruction, stressing form and didactic teaching, might be instituted only after a firm base in communication and regulatory functioning has been established and the child has given some evidence of productive and/or prerequisite (precursor) linguistic and/or cognitive knowledge of the forms to be taught.

Conscious efforts to engineer programs that teach the regulatory aspects of metaprocessing can also be devised throughout the course of language instruction. Specific activities (ranging from puppet play to formal discussions and analyses, for example) could be devised to address various regulatory metalinguistic processes, e.g., monitoring speech register, correcting the speech and language of others, or noting such differences. Obviously, the research cited above should be used as a sequence guide when considering this particular scope within a language arts curriculum and when preparing for instruction in this area.

Under certain conditions, such as in the case of cognitively low functioning children and youth, greater emphasis on a semi-formal approach may be necessary in order to establish some initial level of appropriate respondent behavior. If such an approach is needed, however, it is imperative for the instructor to engineer a remedial program recontextualizing the material being taught in order to establish its communicative function and to permit the on-line regulatory aspect of metalinguistics to develop.

SUMMARY

This chapter attempts to define the notions of metacognition and metalinguistics and to discuss their relationship to language/academic learning. Various hypotheses were presented and discussed. Certain developmental findings regarding these constructs were presented, and some of the variables affecting performance in these areas were outlined. Based upon this information, various approaches to teaching were discussed. It was concluded that formal structured approaches emphasizing metaprocesses should be reserved for older children because developmentally, there are a number of prerequisites to adequate performance and, naturally, these abilities are late-developing phenomena.

REFERENCES

Andersen, E.S. 1975. Cups and glasses: Learning that boundaries are vague. J. Child Lang. 2:79–103.
Andersen, E.S. 1977. Learning to speak with style. Unpublished doctoral dissertation. Stanford University, Stanford, CA.
Bates, E. 1976. Language and Context. Academic Press, New York.

Berko, J. 1958. The child's learning of English morphology. Word. 14:150–177.

Berthoud-Papandropoulou, I. 1978. An experimental study of children's ideas about language. In: A. Sinclair, R.J. Jarvella, and W.H.M. Levelt. The Child's Conception of Language. Springer-Verlag, Berlin, Germany.

Bloom, L., and Lahey, M. 1978. Language Development and Language Disorders. John Wiley and Sons, New York.

Braine, M., and Wells, R. 1978. Case-like categories in children. The actor and some related categories. Cog. Psychol. 10:100–122.

Brown, A.L., and DeLoache, J.S. 1978. Skills, plans and self regulations. In: R.S. Siegler (ed.), Children's Thinking: What Develops? Lawrence Erlbaum Associates, Hillsdale, NJ.

Brown, A.L., Bransford, J.D., Ferrara, R.A., and Campione, J.C. 1982. Learning, Remembering, and Understanding: Technical Report No. 244. Center for the Study of Reading, University of Illinois, Champaign, IL.

Bruner, J. 1978. The role of dialogue in language acquisition. In: A. Sinclair, R.J. Jarvella, and W.J.M. Levelt, The Child's Conception of Language. Springer-Verlag, Berlin, Germany.

Carr, D.B. 1979. The development of young children's capacity to judge anomalous sentences. J. Child Lang. 6:227–242.

Chomsky, N. 1965. Aspects of a Theory of Syntax. MIT Press, Cambridge, MA.

Clark, E. 1978. Awareness of language: Some evidence from what children say and do. In: A. Sinclair, R.J. Jarvella, and W.J.M. Levelt, The Child's Conception of Language. Springer-Verlag, Berlin, Germany.

Ericsson, K.A., and Simon, H.A. 1980. Verbal reports as data. Psychol. Rev. 87:215–251.

Feuerstein, R. 1979. The Dynamic Assessment of Retarded Performers. University Park Press, Baltimore.

Flavell, J.H., and Wellman, H.M. 1977. Metamemory. In: R.V. Kail, Jr., and J.W. Hagen (eds.), Perspectives on the Development of Memory and Cognition, Lawrence Erlbaum Associates, Hillsdale, NJ.

Foppa, K. 1978. Language acquisition—A human ethological problem? Soc. Sci. Inf. 17:93–105.

Fox, B., and Routh, D.K. 1975. Analyzing spoken language into words, syllables, and phonemes: A developmental study. J. Psycholing. Res. 4:331–342.

Gardner, H. 1974. Metaphors and modalities: How children project polar adjectives onto diverse domains. Child Dev. 45:84–91.

Gardner, H. 1978. Commentary on animal awareness papers. Behav. Brain Sci. 4:572.

Gardner, H., and Lohman, W. 1975. Children's sensitivity to literary styles. Merrill-Palmer Q. 21:113–126.

Gleitman, L.R., Gleitman, H., and Shipley, E.F. 1972. The emergence of the child as grammarian. Cognition 1:137–164.

Hakes, D.T., Evans, J.S., and Tunmer, W. 1980. The Development of Metalinguistic Abilities in Children. Springer-Verlag, Berlin, West Germany.

Hallahan, D.P. (ed.). 1980. Teaching exceptional children to use cognitive strategies. Exc. Educ. Q. Aspen, Rockville, MD.

Hirsh-Pasek, K. Gleitman, L.R., and Gleitman, H. 1978. What did the brain say to the mind? A study of the detection and report of ambiguity by young children. In: A. Sinclair, R.J. Jarvella, W.J.M. Levelt, The Child's Conception of Language. Springer-Verlag, Berlin, West Germany.

Howe, H.E., Jr., and Hillman, D. 1973. The acquisition of semantic restrictions in children. J. Verb. Learn. Verb. Behav. 12:132–139.

Jenkins, J.J. 1979. Four points to remember: A tetrahedral model and memory experiments. In: L.S. Cermak and F.I.M. Craik (eds.), Levels of Processing in Human Memory. Lawrence Erlbaum Associates, Hillsdale, NJ.

Keane, J.K. 1982. Application of mediated learning theory to a deaf population: a study in cognitive modifiability. Unpublished doctoral dissertation, Teachers College, Columbia University, Columbia, NY.

Kretschmer, R.E. 1976. Judgments of grammaticality by 11, 14, and 17 hearing and hearing impaired subjects. Unpublished doctoral dissertation, University of Kansas, Lawrence.

Kretschmer, R.E., and Quigley, S.P. 1981. Psychoeducational assessment of hearing impaired children. In: R.J. Roeser and M.P. Downs (eds.), Auditory Disorders in School Disorders. Thieme-Stratton, New York.

Kreutzer, M.A., Leonard, C., and Flavell, J.H. 1975. An interview study of children's knowledge about memory. Monogr. Soc. Res. Child Dev. 49:1–60.

Limber, J. 1973. The genesis of a complex sentence. In: T.E. Moore (ed.), Cognitive Development and the Acquisition of Language. Academic Press, New York.

Maccoby, E.E., Bee, H.L. 1965. Some speculations concerning the lag between perceiving and performing. Child Dev. 36:367–377.

Maratsos, M. 1973. Nonegocentric communication abilities in preschool children. Child Dev. 44:697–700.

Markman, E.M. 1977. Realizing that you don't understand: A preliminary investigation. Child Dev. 48:986–992.

Marshall, J.C., and Morton, J. 1978. Grammar as an underground process. In: A. Sinclair, R.J. Jarvella, W.J.M. Levelt, The Child's Conception of Language, Springer-Verlag, Berlin, Germany.

Mason, J.M. Prereading: A developmental perspective. In: P.D. Pearson (ed.), Handbook of Reading Research. Longman Press, New York. In press.

McLean, J., and Snyder-McLean, L. 1978. A Transactional Approach to Early Language Training. Charles E. Merrill, Columbus, OH.

Menig-Peterson, C.L. 1975. The modification of communicative behavior in preschool-aged children as a function of listener's perspective. Child Dev. 46:1,015–1,018.

Meichenbaum, D., and Asarnow, J. 1978. Cognitive behavior modification and metacognitive development: Implication for the classroom. In: P. Kendall and S. Hollon (eds.), Cognitive Behavior Intervention: Theory Research and Procedure. Academic Press, New York.

Mills, J.A., and Hemsley, G.D. 1976. The effects of level of education on judgment of grammatical acceptability. Lang. Speech 19:324–342.

Muma, J. 1978. Language Handbook. Prentice-Hall, Englewood Cliffs, NJ.

Pascual-Leone, J. 1970. A mathematical model for the transition rule in Piaget's developmental stages. Acta Psychologica 63:301–345.

Pearson, P.D. 1982. A primer for schema theory. Volta Rev. 84:25–33.

Piaget, J. 1952. The Origins of Intelligence in Children. International Universities Press, New York.

Piaget, J. 1976. The Grasp of Consciousness: Action and Concept in the Young Child. Harvard University Press, Cambridge, MA.

Pylyshyn, Z.W. 1978. When is attribution of beliefs justified? Behav. Brain Sci. 1:592–593.

Quigley, S.P., and Kretschmer, R.E. 1982. The Education of Deaf Children. University Park Press, Baltimore.

Rozin, P. 1976. The evolution of intelligence and access to the cognitive unconscious. Progr. Psychobiol. Physiol. Psychol. 6:245–280.

Sachs, J., and Devin, J. 1976. Young children's use of age-appropriate speech style in social interaction and role-playing. J. Child Lang. 3:81–98.

Sack, H.G., and Beilin, H. 1971. Meaning equivalence of active-passive and subject-object first cleft sentences. Paper presented at the Developmental Psycholinguistics Conference, State University of New York, Buffalo, NY.

Scholl, D.M., and Ryan, E.B. 1975. Child judgments of sentences varying in grammatical complexity. J. Exp. Child Psychol. 20:274–285.

Scollon, R. 1976. Conversations with a One Year Old: A Case Study of the Developmental Foundation of Syntax. University Press of Hawaii, Honolulu.

Shultz, T.R., and Pilon, R. 1973. Development of the ability to detect linguistic ambiguity. Child Dev. 44:728–733.

Smith, N.V. 1973. The Acquisition of Phonology: A Case Study. Cambridge University Press, Cambridge, MA.

Swanson, H.L. 1982. Controversy: strategy or capacity deficit. Top. Learn. Learn. Disabil. Aspen, Rockville, MD.

Weir, R.H. 1962. Language in the Crib. Mouton, The Hague.

Wong, B.Y.L. (ed.). 1982. Metacognition and learning disabilities. Top. Learn. Learn. Disabil. Aspen, Rockville, MD.

Yussen, S.R., and Bird, J.E. 1979. The development of metacognitive awareness in memory, communication, and attention. J. Exp. Child Psychol. 28:300–313.

chapter

8

Applications of Developmental and Remedial Logic to Language Intervention

Marcia Weber-Olsen

Speech and Hearing Sciences
Texas Tech University
Lubbock, Texas

Kenneth F. Ruder

Bureau of Child Research
University of Kansas
Lawrence, Kansas

contents

The practical value of psycholinguistic and behavioral explanations of language acquisition has been carefully examined by professionals interested in the remediation of child language disorders. Although both disciplines have contributed to an understanding of normal child language acquisition, there are many unresolved clinical issues for those deciding on the best way to teach language to the communicatively impaired child. The efforts of language interventionists to coordinate programs for language-handicapped individuals have become more and more difficult. Bricker and Bricker (1974), Ruder and Smith (1974), Bloom and Lahey (1978), and Muma (1978) detailed many of the disputes and pseudo-issues that curtail consolidated approaches to language training. Bricker and Bricker (1974) referred to this enigmatic set of circumstances as the "language game":

> . . . a yearly sequence of events notable for lack of well defined leagues, established rules, a regular season, or a method for determining a winner (p. 431).

More recently, the language game has evolved into a "communication game," with concerns directed at training the functional use of language more effectively in social contexts and in the child's natural environment. The recent focus on pragmatics and the emergence of social competence in psycholinguistic research exemplifies this new trend toward studying communicative, not just linguistic, development per se. Pragmatics, however, constitutes only part of the communication game; other critical decisions face the language interventionist. Briefly, these include: 1) whether to base a strategy for training on remedial logic or, instead, adhere to normal developmental data for making decisions about what to train and when; 2) whether more emphasis should be placed on how the child acquires language (i.e., processes) rather than what the products of this acquisition process are; and finally, 3) whether language should be trained in conjunction with other domains of the child's developmental functioning, for instance, perceptual, cognitive, and socioaffective skills.

This chapter addresses these issues as they relate to recent psycholinguistic and operant research in child language. Discussion relevant to each of these topics is followed by a more comprehensive description of several language intervention programs. The chapter concludes with a summary and brief discussion of some current theoretical issues that are germane to future strategies for language intervention programming.

PERSPECTIVES ON A DEVELOPMENTAL LOGIC

Psycholinguistic orientations to language training have maintained that the lawful nature of developmental data counters the view that child language is some random approximation of the adult form (Ruder and Smith, 1974; Ruder et al., 1975; Bloom and Lahey, 1978; Waryas and Stremel-Campbell, 1978). The early errors that occur in the normal acquisition process not only validate the nature of a systematic rule-bound linguistic system but also are a useful source of information for language intervention strategies. By programming discrete training steps according to the normal developmental sequence, similar error patterns might be anticipated in, or possibly predicted for, the language-impaired child. The emergence of developmental errors subsequently provides valuable feedback as to whether the impaired child has begun to make higher level abstractions and inferences about linguistic rules and features that he or she previously mastered in the language training sequence.

Consequently, it has been argued that normal language acquisition data can provide a best guess not only of what the content of a language training program should include but also what training sequence a program should take. It is felt that the normal developmental sequence can provide a series of discrete training goals, resulting in a broadly based language structure for the language-impaired child. Moreover, knowledge about alternative linguistic strategies displayed by normal children (see Nelson, 1981 for a review) should also guide interventionists to develop procedures for teaching the language-impaired child that are compatible with the child's own strategies.

Data documenting the advantages of a developmental training approach in contrast to other nondevelopmentally based language programs are, nevertheless, lacking. Most training studies have focused on the efficacy of a specific procedure (for example, Ruder et al., 1975; Courtwright and Courtwright, 1979) as opposed to a comparison of the overall effectiveness of one intervention program or another. Rees (1972) and Ruder and Smith (1974) commented that the normal developmental sequence as the one best approach to establish with the language-impaired child has not been empirically proven or denied. Behaviorists have argued that if empirical data demonstrate that language can be taught out of the normal sequence, then the validity of the developmental approach to language training becomes far less compelling. Guess et al. (1978) proposed that a remedial logic based on operant technology is a more satisfactory approach a retarded population, assuming that these children:

> . . . being taught language relatively late in their lives . . . no longer possess the same collection of abilities and deficits that normal children have when they begin to acquire language (p. 105).

In addition, behaviorists are skeptical of relying on sparse developmental data for formulating a comprehensive intervention strategy (see Guess et al., 1974), particularly because such data have been widely interpreted and, in many cases, challenged by opposing research in developmental psychology and linguistics. Other arguments dismiss the notion that normal development is the same for all children, at least as far as specific acquisition orders are concerned.

It is unlikely that proponents of developmental logic have concluded that children follow a uniform sequence in acquiring similar aspects of their language. Commonalities displayed in the language acquisition process have been underscored (Slobin, 1970; Bloom, 1970; Brown, 1973; deVilliers and deVilliers, 1973; Bowerman, 1975) more so than the differences, but alternative strategies to imitation (Bloom et al., 1974; Ramer, 1976), alternative lexico-grammatical strategies (Bloom et al., 1975; Braine, 1976; Bowerman, 1978), and alternative learning approaches to early word use (Nelson, 1973; Bowerman, 1977; Smith, 1978) also appear in the normal acquisition literature. Likewise, similarities and differences in acquisition of linguistic structures by normal and language-impaired children with comparable linguistic status were reported (see Johnston and Schery, 1976; Leonard et al., 1976; Morehead and Ingram, 1976).

Individual Differences and Intervention Strategies

Most developmentalists would agree that: 1) although individual differences exist in the way children learn language, similarities in this process can still guide clinicians in making principled decisions for facilitating linguistic skills in the language-impaired child; and 2) children's linguistic strategies undergo rapid change from simple hypotheses to complex abstractions about their language (see Bowerman, 1977, for examples) and that cognitive and communicative skills coalesce with the child's linguistic system in vastly different ways (Prutting, 1979, 1982; Bates, 1976b, 1979; Bruner, 1982) so that uniform description of language strategies and acquisition orders is far more the exception than the rule. Recent literature focusing on the child's individual cognitive-linguistic functioning (Bates, 1979; Bruner, 1982) and the influence of parental speech input in shaping the child's linguistic career (Nelson, 1973; Snow and Ferguson, 1977; Waterson and Snow, 1978; Dale and Ingram, 1981) suggests that many of these differences are attributable to differences in the child's initial communicative interactions with his or her speech environment.

Consequently, developmentalists are not in a position to advocate that training for the language-impaired child reiterate the normal developmental sequence under identical learning conditions as some operant training approaches have advocated in the past (see Gray and Ryan, 1973; Carrier, 1976). Instead, it is necessary to identify the language-impaired child's individual linguistic strategies, compare these to normal developmental data in order to ascertain what variability exists in the child's own system, and finally, to exploit these strategies in language training. In this respect, a developmental approach ideally is oriented toward augmenting the child's own strategies and, where appropriate, expanding his or her linguistic repertoire to include structures that are vital to the next developmental stage in linguistic and communicative development. Prutting (1979) referred to this type of language programming as "vertical" and to training that advances the child to developmentally more complex stages as "horizontal," with the goal of language intervention ultimately being child-centered. Halliday (1975) commented on the advantages of a child-oriented as opposed to adult-oriented approach to describing child speech:

> The first approach (adult oriented) . . . involved treating many of the child's utterances, perhaps all of them at a certain stage, as ill formed; they are analyzed as the product of distortions of various kinds, particularly the deletion of elements. This brings out their relationship to the adult forms, but it blocks the way to recognition and interpretation of the child's own system. In the second approach, the child's earliest structures are analyzed as combinations of elements forming a system in their own right (p. 241).

The Products versus the Processes of Language

To accurately describe a child's linguistic system, the processes as well as the products of this system must be thoroughly examined by those delivering clinical services. Several shortcomings have been identified with traditional language assessment and intervention approaches that are aimed solely at quantifying or labeling the products of language (see Muma, 1978, 1981, Chapter 3 of this volume). One major oversight is that the child's rationale for making a response is not adequately examined or described by such approaches. Rather, the *a priori* linguistic categories that are selected and imposed on the child may have little if any relevance to the way in which he or she linguistically processes information.

Past emphasis on the products as opposed to processes of language acquisition can be traced to the decades of taxonomic and generative linguistics. Transformational theories of grammar in the 1960s formalized adult linguistic knowledge by accounting for differences in linguistic competence, or tacit rule knowledge, as opposed to linguistic performance, or actual use of the language (Chomsky, 1965). Although this perspective offered major improvements over past taxonomic approaches to cataloguing adult languages by their parts of speech, Chomsky's generative model, nevertheless, culminated in a rather short-sighted explanation of the language acquisition process. Because language was viewed as basically innate (Chomsky, 1965; McNeill, 1966; Lenneberg, 1967), the child was considered to enter the world equipped with a set of biologically predetermined linguistic universals, which were thought to guide him or her in "discovering" a grammar that was consistent with his or her native adult language. Unfortunately, "nativist" explanations left little to be said for the language-impaired child who might be operating with a biologically deficient system from the very start of his or her linguistic career but who, nevertheless, had the capacity to comprehend and use language.

Nativists' assertions that basic grammatical categories and the phrase structure rules that ordered these constituents were also innate were challenged by those who doubted whether such constructs had any psychological reality for the child learning language (Schlesinger, 1971; Brown, 1973; Bowerman, 1973a, Braine, 1976; and Dore, 1975). Linguists at that time (Fillmore, 1968; Chafe, 1970; Lakoff, 1970) suggested that a generative grammar logically had its origins in the semantic, and not the structural or syntactic, organization of an utterance.

Although the focus on grammatical form and structure evidenced some value in analyzing the syntax of children's early utterances, Bloom (1970) and Schlesinger (1971) faulted the transformational grammar perspective for overlooking children's actual communicative intentions. Thus, models of adult transformational grammar were criticized for not adequately accounting for the role that context and meaning played in interpreting children's first word combinations (Bloom, 1970; Bowerman, 1973b).

Finally, transformational grammar overlooked the potential influence of cognitive and communicative processes that predated and possibly were prerequisites to linguistic development. Chomsky's generative analog, LAD, did not adequately account for the significant roles of caregiver, social environment, and experience in children's early communicative interactions. Consequently, the decade of syntax in the 1960s was replaced by an emphasis on semantic development and, more recently, by a focus on emerging conversational skills in children. Both approaches were comprehensive and carried with them far-reaching implications about not only *what* children learned as they acquired language, but also *how* they universally acquired this knowledge.

Language as an Interrelated Behavioral System

Can language be successfully taught apart from other domains of the child's development? This question is still largely unresolved. Although developmentalists and behaviorists might agree that linguistic, social, and cognitive functions form an interrelated system, there is some question as to whether these domains are mutually dependent, independent, or causally related in any way in the child's acquisition of language (see Bates, 1979). Nevertheless, a number of cognitive psychologists and psycholinguists have emphasized not only the significance of these associated domains in normal communicative development, but have also maintained that certain cognitive and primitive socioaffective developments set the stage for the language acquisition process. Language is thought to map already existing perceptual-conceptual distinctions that the organism is capable of making (Premack and Premack, 1974).

Language and Cognition   It has been argued that sensorimotor schemes described earlier by Piaget (1952) (object permanence, deferred imitation, cognitive awareness of action, time, space, and causality) are instrumental in explaining the nonlinguistic underpinnings of language (Sinclair, 1971; Sinclair-deZwart, 1973). In the early 1970s, many cognitive behaviors were proposed to be actual prerequisites to language acquisition (Slobin, 1970; Greenfield et al., 1972; Bloom, 1973; Sinclair-deZwart, 1973). Following this lead, numerous developmental programs adopted hierarchical training sequences in which a number of cognitive skills were taught as a prelinguistic basis for the subsequent training of linguistic forms.

Behaviorists, on the other hand, disagree that cognitive skill instruction before formal language training is necessary for the language-impaired child. They argue that psychological notions of "concepts" or precepts are vague because they do not correspond to any observable or predictable class of behaviors. Instead, skills like motor and vocal imitation, visual and auditory discrimination, and other attending behaviors are taught as entry skills to a language training program. These skills are similar in that they all have directly observable behavioral concomitants and are in some way manipulable. The remaining sections of this chapter will briefly discuss some of the different perspectives on cognitive abilities in relation to language training.

Language and Pragmatics   The decade of the 1970s brought with it the evolution of semantic development and the need for uncovering context in order to clarify intended meaning in children's early utterances. This was a productive period in the study of child language because semantics paved the way for systematic investigation of cognitive and prelinguistic skills that preceded or accompanied the child's development of a linguistic system. However, only recently have various situational contexts and dyadic interactions been studied as a means of formalizing the child's social or communicative competence (see Prutting, 1982, for a review). Presumably, the child's early interactions with mother, caregiver, and others are vital to his or her later linguistic career even though communication is successful long before the linguistic code is broken (see Bruner, 1982). Nevertheless, research in this area (Dore, 1975; Halliday, 1975; Bates, 1976a, 1979; Greenfield and Smith, 1976; Sugarman-Bell, 1978) has not concurred on any one theoretical model for explaining how language comes to function communicatively for the child. Some of the recent findings in pragmatics research with normal and language-impaired children were examined by Prutting (1979, 1982). Although the implications of this research are not immediately apparent for language intervention programming, it is obvious that these data confirmed interventionists' longstanding intuitions about the centrality of context and interpersonal exchange in the language teaching process. Although communication evolves prelinguistically and may, in some ways, be causally related to the child's own cognitive and social growth, the emergence of language earmarks the first opportunity for all three of these components (cognitive, socioaffective, and linguistic) to consolidate as part of an interrelated system.

APPLICATIONS OF PSYCHOLINGUISTIC AND
BEHAVIORAL MODELS TO LANGUAGE PROGRAMMING

Certainly, many issues other than those mentioned above compel the interventionist to critically examine the appropriateness of clinical services delivered to the language-impaired child. A few of these issues surface in this section, which highlights similarities and differences among several developmental and nondevelopmental programs for language-impaired children. Figure 1 imposes an organizational structure for the remainder of the section; a brief overview of the components to this model follows.

Traditionally, speech and language clinicians initiate their services by collecting useful background and diagnostic information by administering a number of formal and/or informal language tests and measurements. An *assessment* of the child's level of functioning, as such, helps to determine the most appropriate program curriculum and teaching strategy for meeting the child's remedial needs.

Although initial evaluations precede therapeutic steps, the importance of maintaining an ongoing means of assessment cannot be overstated (see Longhurst, Chapter 2 of this volume; Muma, Chapter 3 of this volume). Such a procedure provides for the continual reevaluation of program effectiveness and allows for modification of program *content* and/or *teaching strategies* in order to expedite the training process. For this reason, Figure 1 assigns the latter two components equal hierarchical status with assessment.

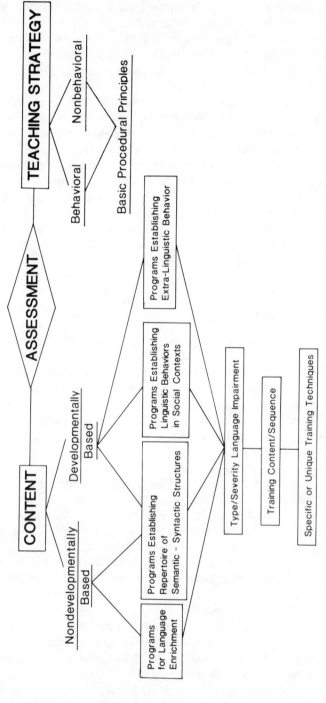

Figure 1.   An organizational structure for this section.

Teaching strategies are categorized into either behavioral or non-behavioral paradigms.

Behavioral Teaching Strategies   These strategies do not exclude psycholinguistically oriented intervention programs because the majority of them integrate behaviorally guided principles, such as modeling, imitation, successive approximations, and reinforcement with normal language acquisition data in order to produce a series of discrete language training goals (Miller and Yoder, 1974; Ruder and Smith, 1974). Graham (1976) described these programs as a synthesis of psycholinguistic and behavioral paradigms; data from the psycholinguistic model "determines what will be taught," while principles derived from the behavioral model "determine what instructional procedures will be used to teach the program content" (p. 383). Examples of several behaviorally oriented language training programs include those designed by Stremel and Waryas (1974), Miller and Yoder (1974), Bricker and Bricker (1974), MacDonald (1975), McLean and Snyder-McLean (1978), Carrier (1974), Gray and Ryan (1973) and Guess et al. (1974, 1978). The first five of these programs are psycholinguistically based, while the latter three derive primarily from nondevelopmental operant models of language acquisition.

Nonbehavioral Teaching Strategies   These strategies (Bereiter and Englemann, 1966; Lee et al., 1975; Miller, 1978) incorporate some behavioral principles but in a more general, less systematic way. Adherence to behavior modification as the recognized procedural model, in general, does not characterize these programs.

Figure 1 also illustrates the diversity of many language intervention programs in terms of their general content. This chapter describes various programs on the basis of how their language curriculum aligns with a normal developmental sequence. Further subdivisions are made according to specific program goals; for example, establishing prelinguistic and extralinguistic behaviors, using parents as agents of change, establishing syntactic repertoires, and so forth.

In programs designed for the populations of language-impaired children, specific program goals, sequences, and training techniques are all descriptions that are subsumed under the broad category *program content*. The remainder of this chapter involves the categorization and description of several intervention programs that are based on the classification system represented in Figure 1.

The Structure and Content for Language Training

Several intervention programs for the young language-impaired child (Bricker and Bricker, 1974; Miller and Yoder, 1974; Stremel and Waryas, 1974; MacDonald, 1975) are constructed on the premise that the forms of language code basic semantic intentions. Such programs intend to augment the language-impaired child's communicative competence by identifying and training early-emerging semantic functions and relationships. Most of these programs, therefore, have attempted to update outmoded training approaches that have previously taught syntactic structures in a semantically empty context. However, as Graham (1976) pointed out, the degree to which various intervention strategies consider these semantic constructs as "directly programmable events" differs.

Miller and Yoder (1974) outlined a developmental progression of early semantic functions and relations that coincide with a number of grammatical classes and relationships. *Adjective + noun* and *noun + verb + object* combinations, for example, have the *attributive* function and *agent + action + object* relations as their respective semantic correlates. The objective of the *Miller and Yoder Intervention Program* is to train children to use grammatical forms appropriately in order to express certain meanings or communicative events. Communicative events, in turn, are composed of many environmental situations and rule-governed features that must be simulated in the therapeutic setting.

Early relational functions, for example, *recurrence, rejection,* and *nonexistence,* are trained by pairing lexical markers with situational events so that the child can begin to anticipate the appropriate verbal utterance(s) that will communicate his or her intentions in the linguistic environment. As an example, a trainer might begin the sequence by requiring the child to verbalize "more" as a request for additional sips of orange juice or milk (*recurrence*).

Other programs (Bricker and Bricker, 1974; Stremel and Waryas, 1974; MacDonald, 1975) set up similarly constructed environmental situations for eliciting a target verbal response. In this way, linguistic structures being taught are congruent with contextual cues encoding the communicative intent of a particular utterance.

Although syntax and semantics have been highlighted as the two basic components of developmentally based programs, recent research has also stimulated interest in training cognitive skills as prerequisite structures to language. Many of these programs share Premack and Premack's (1974) premise that language can be viewed as the mapping of already existing conceptual and perceptual distinctions. Some developmental programs have been oriented in the direction of training many of the sensorimotor and perceptual skills corresponding to Piagetian stages of development (for example, Bricker and Bricker, 1974).

Remedial Logic Perspectives Perhaps the major differentiation between developmental and nondevelopmental approaches to language training is reflected in the nature of their operating models. Most operant programs (Gray and Ryan, 1973; Carrier, 1974; Guess et al., 1974, 1978; Hollis and Carrier, 1978), for example, are products of logistical and behavioral analysis systems. Training sequences are specified and arranged on the basis of previous experimental data or binary systems of logic (e.g., Carrier, 1974). The field-tested success of language-delayed children in learning linguistic structure determines the final, most effective training procedures (e.g., Guess et al., 1978). Program content rests ultimately on its teaching value; linguistic structures are trained from short, simple responses and are successively built into more complex constructions. A functional analysis of behavior also uses measures of error rate, trials to criterion, maintenance of learned responses, and generalization as direct feedback sources in determining the effectiveness of a particular training program.

Not all nondevelopmentally based language programs, however, are derived from an operant- or logistically based model. Lee et al. (1975) and Bereiter and Englemann (1966), for example, constructed teaching systems from an entirely different perspective. Their programs are compared and contrasted later in this chapter.

A second differentiation between most developmental and nondevelopmental programs is the former's emphasis on cognitive skill acquisition. Although prelinguistic and/or cognitive skills have been viewed as prerequisite or concomitant structures to language acquisition by the developmentalists, many nondevelopmentalists contend that only certain entry skills must precede formal language training. In general, these include: attending behavior, gross and fine motor imitative skills, visual and auditory discrimination skills, and some receptive labeling skills. For the most part, nondevelopmental programs attempt to indirectly stimulate nonverbal or conceptual skills by manipulating overt responses at the very onset of training. Hence, the outcomes of training may be much the same for developmental and nondevelopmental intervention approaches, but there is a difference of opinion as to whether certain cognitive skills must be trained before formal linguistic structures or whether these skills eventually are manifested as part of the language training process without any direct intervention. The following section examines the current focus on how such content (prelinguistic skills, cognitive prerequisites, semantics, and so forth) is structured for inclusion in syntax-training programs from both developmental and remedial logic perspectives. Subsequent comparisons focus on pragmatics and language training, parent involvement, and environmentally based programs.

Training Semantic-Syntactic Structures

Developmentally Based Programs   Developmentally based programs, for the most part, are directed at remediation for the young, moderate to severely language-impaired child. Bricker and Bricker (1974) developed a program for developmentally delayed children from numerous etiological backgrounds, e.g., retarded, cerebral palsied, and other neurophysiologically and/or emotionally disturbed children. Their program is primarily preventive in nature; remediation is begun early in infancy and advances to school-age. Populations of normal and developmentally delayed children from 6 months to 6 years are integrated into various therapeutic settings. The *Preschool and Intervention Project* (Bricker and Bricker, 1971, 1972, 1974) shares features with behavioral, cognitive, and psycholinguistic approaches to language acquisition. The program model assumes that mastery of prelinguistic forms of behavior is a prerequisite to later language skills. Following the Piagetian influence of cognitive learning, this program emphasizes the child's conceptual development as it progresses according to a sensorimotor lattice of skill acquisition.

The formal language training program is sequentially arranged to include the following features: 1) simple response learning; 2) gross motor imitation; 3) categorization and functional use of objects; 4) establishment of receptive vocabulary; 5) verbal imitation of sounds and words; 6) object and event naming; and 7) syntactic comprehension and production of words, phrases, and simple sentences of the *actor + action + object* construction. Training curriculum consists of 20 subprogram steps designed to achieve these program objectives. An extensive assessment battery, consisting of an adaptive screening instrument and test-teach system for evaluating reflexive, sensorimotor, preoperational, and later developmental cognitive skills in relation to the child's linguistic abilities, determines the child's placement within the program.

A number of specific training procedures are used. A two-choice discrimination paradigm, for example, is used for training receptive vocabulary items. This method works to minimize any of the child's inappropriate response-selection strategies, like position or object preferences and avoidances.

Based on previous research findings (Bricker, 1972), manual signs are employed as a training technique for facilitating word-object associations during vocabulary training. Gross motor imitation training precedes fine motor and verbal imitation. The rationale for this sequence is based on research suggesting that large motor movements may be prerequisite skills for finer articulatory movements required for speech (Baer et al., 1967; Bricker and Bricker, 1971). The child's generalization of trained language responses is maximally stimulated by employing parents and teachers as secondary trainers in external therapeutic settings.

Bricker et al. (1976) elaborated the specific hierarchical phases for training the pivotal *agent* + *action* + *object* structure in an updated version of the Bricker and Bricker (1974) project. The purpose of this program is to move the child from a functional classification of objects and comprehension of labels to the production of three-word (*agent* + *action* + *object*) utterances. More advanced training involves operations made on the entire *agent* + *action* + *object* construction or on elements within this structure, such as negative or tense demarcation, question transformations, and noun or verb modifications, so that basic propositional statements increase in grammatical and semantic complexity.

Not only is the functional use of forms advocated in this intervention program but also training that provides for maximum generalization to novel stimuli, settings, or activities. Specific suggestions are provided for incorporating newly trained structures into group language activities, snack time, outdoor play, music, and story time or free-play settings. A series of probe checks are advised at the start of each training phase and at regular intervals throughout the training period in order to objectively determine when criterion performance has been met by the child and if generalization to similar or more advanced linguistic structures has occurred.

Miller and Yoder (1974) developed a language intervention program similar in many respects to the Bricker et al. (1976) training model. Emphasis was again given to cognitive-perceptual development as prerequisite to linguistic learning; early cognitive skills (object permanence and behaviors related to time, space, and causality) were viewed as instrumental in mapping linguistically based, semantic functions for the child. In this program, semantic and syntactic features culminate and emerge productively as the child learns language. The program, however, is not directed at the delayed infant population as was the initial Bricker and Bricker (1974) project. In general, the Miller and Yoder (1974) language training program deals with a preschool (and older) population of mentally impaired children.

Minimal entry requirements specified for the program include an intact speech mechanism, cognitive awareness of one or more semantic functions, and imitative or spontaneous approximations of single words.

Miller and Yoder (1974) summarized the developmental sequence of early acquired semantic functions from several child language studies (Bloom, 1970, 1973; Brown, 1970; 1973; Schlesinger, 1971). The content of the language program is based on this research and begins with early one-word relational functions encoding *recurrence, nonexistence,* and *nomination* and later advances to two- and three-word utterances expressing functional and/or semantic relations. Functional relations include expansions of five basic functions: 1) *existence*; 2) *recurrence*; 3) *nonexistence*; 4) *rejection*; and 5) *denial*. Semantic relations deal with the pivotal *agent* + *action* + *object* construction and other numerous relations expressing *attribution, location, possession,* and so forth, all of which can operate upon the basic pivotal structure.

The training sequence of this program coincides with a normal developmental sequence and, therefore, is based upon frequency of occurrence and orders of emergence in normal children; otherwise it is not programmatically specified. Like the Bricker et al. (1976) program, objects, events, and nonlinguistic experiences relevant to the child's cognitive awareness are suggested as the place to start training. A single, frequently occurring experience that represents a particular semantic function is paired with its appropriate lexical marker. Once the child has reached criterion at this labeling task, multiple experiences expressing the same function are introduced. Initial training of a single function is recommended until the child demonstrates mastery; then, additional functions are introduced concurrently in the training sequence.

After the child has acquired a repertoire of single words, expansions to longer utterances are advised; these should include relational functions previously expressed. For example, "more" (a relational function expressing *recurrence*) is expanded to "more milk," "more cookie," and "more juice," etc. Expansions and modeling procedures are characteristically one step more advanced than the child's productive language level. Comprehension, imitation, and spontaneous production techniques are advocated as the most efficient means of establishing and stabilizing learned language responses. Like the initial Bricker and Bricker (1974) program, reinforcement contingencies are extended to the natural environment when possible so that the child is rewarded or praised only when his or her responses are emitted within an appropriate context.

Remedially Based Programs   A few language programs have developed non-oral teaching systems, involving manual sign training for severely speech- and/or hearing-handicapped children.

Nonspeech Language Initiation Program (Non-SLIP)   Developed by Carrier (1974), Non-SLIP uses a plastic chip symbol system similar to the symbol system designed by Premack (1970, 1971) in teaching rudimentary linguistic rules to chimpanzees. The program was designed primarily for children with a diagnosis of severe to profound mental retardation who do not use speech for communication or who are not viable candidates for learning through more conventional speech and language programs. Non-SLIP has also been applied with some success to deaf, deaf-blind, and multiply handicapped children (Hollis and Carrier, 1978). Carrier (1976) emphasized that this program is not intended as a total language training program; rather, it was developed as a means of *initiating* severely language-impaired children into the communicative process so that the transition to programs requiring speech as the primary response mode would be less difficult.

Some aspects of this program for the severely handicapped are to be commended because a complex response topography for learning language is eliminated. The child is taught to match specific symbol arrangements to a number of environmental events; although these events are varied, they are represented only by picture stimuli. This feature of the program obviously delimits the teaching of language in more functional communicative situations.

Program content and sequence are oriented around training a seven-unit simple, active, declarative sentence of the form, *article + noun + auxiliary + verb + preposition + article + object of preposition.* Earlier research in training additional structures (like interrogative statements, plurals, verb tense markers, and compound and conjoined structures) was discontinued because a majority of children were capable of making the transition to spoken responses once training on the declarative sentence structure was completed.

A behavioral training paradigm serves as the principal teaching strategy for the Non-SLIP program. The specific training sequence begins with rote sequencing and advances to labeling, subject noun, verb, object of preposition, and preposition training (in that order); in all, 12 subprograms implement these training phases.

The first of these subprograms introduces the child to a number of masonite forms that are color-coded. Once color and number discriminations are learned, the child is taught to use these cues by rotely sequencing the masonite pieces on a wooden response tray.

When the child advances to the labeling phase of the program, he or she is then trained to match the color-cued forms to their appropriate picture referents. Subsequent subject-noun training teaches the child to combine his or her previous rote sequencing responses with more recent labeling responses. On a given trial, the child is shown a picture of one of the subject nouns engaged in an action. The child's first response is to place a color-coded symbol for "the" in the first slot on the response tray (learned previously during rote-sequencing training) and then to select one out of 10 subject noun symbols that matches the subject in the stimulus picture. After placing this symbol in the second slot on the tray, the child completes the sequence with the remaining five symbols, all of which differ on color/number dimensions.

This procedure continues in the same fashion for verb, object of preposition, and preposition training. Terminal behavior is reached when the child can sequence a mixed array of symbols in response to several sets of pictures so that a grammatical seven-word declarative "utterance" appears on the response tray. Generalization tests conducted throughout the training period determine whether the child can respond to novel pictures by manipulating symbols appropriately and whether the child has transferred his or her skills to the verbal level. A speech training phase of the program has also been designed for children who are initially capable of giving verbal responses. After children have mastered this stage of communicative skill, they are usually advanced to other speech- or manual-mode language programs, where they receive training on additional linguistic rules and syntactic constructions.

An obvious drawback to this program is that sequencing is a rote response, taught before any referential or relational meanings are provided for the masonite forms; hence, the forms do not take on symbolic significance until the labeling phase of the program is begun. Although the logistics of this program are such that this procedure is necessitated, it might be well to consider that acquisition of linguistic symbols and rules is facilitated sooner in some children when these elements are taught concomitantly with their differential semantic functions. It was Schlesinger's observation that

> It is not very plausible that the child should learn to produce empty structures which he subsequently stuffs with meaning (1971, p. 85).

Despite its differences from developmentally based programs, however, the Non-SLIP intervention model has obvious advantages in getting children who have previously failed to learn language through conventional speech modes started in the communicative process.

Guess et al. (1974, 1978) developed a language program similar in some respects to Non-SLIP. Although this program was originally designed to teach language in a speech response mode, it has also been successfully adapted to exact English signing and to communication boards for nonspeech children. The program is most appropriate for severe to profoundly retarded or developmentally delayed children who are nonimitative and do not use speech for communication. Teaching strategies are designed around an operant model for modifying behavior.

Assessment and pretraining evaluation of communicative abilities precede the child's placement into the 60-step program for training functional language skills. Assessment procedures involve the collection of descriptive and audiological background information, neurological findings, receptive and imitative language test performance, vocal diversity and frequency data, and data on attending behaviors as well as selection of appropriate reinforcers for later training purposes.

The child's performance on tests of vocal and motor imitation determine whether he or she will require vocal imitation training before formal language training. Procedures for imitation training, however, are not specified and still are being empirically tested to determine if motor imitation training precludes the need for teaching vocal and verbal imitation skills. Once the child is reliably imitating at a vocal level, he or she is placed in the functional speech and language training program.

A training manual compiled for field-testing purposes provides programmed instructions for administering each training step specifying training goals, stimulus materials, setting, trainer instructions, and instructions for generalization training. Provisions outlined in the manual have to some extent controlled for standard program administration across a variety of remedial sites.

Training content is categorized according to the following sequence: 1) persons and things; 2) action with persons and things; 3) possession and color; and 4) size, relation, and location. Each one of these content areas has been organized along five broader dimensions:

Reference—trains the child that labels or linguistic events symbolize certain events or referents in the environment

Control—teaches "request" forms of the language so that the child learns to manipulate or manage his environment through labels

Self-extended control—expands the child's knowledge and control of his or her environment by teaching how to request additional information (through questions)

Integration—establishes ongoing integration of previously taught skills with newly acquired skills for dialoguing with another person

Reception—requires the child to comprehend previously taught verbal responses

Emphasis is placed on production in training to make the communicative elements of language immediately available and useful to the child. Once the child has completed expressive training at a particular program level, a number of comprehension post-tests determine whether receptive training on the same structure is necessary. Comprehension training, when necessitated, is administered in a yes-no response paradigm. To some extent, this particular feature may restrict the program's success with children who possess severe receptive language deficits and, therefore, demonstrate little understanding or appropriate use of the differential functions for the linguistic structures taught in production. Conversely, the child with fewer receptive then expressive deficits should benefit from a program that concentrates, as this one does, on production training.

As the child advances in production training, his or her single-word responses are expanded to progressively longer utterances, which are primarily declarative and interrogative statements. The former constructions are taught as labeling (reference) and request (control) forms in response to trainer questions. For example, trainer questions of the form, "What want?" or "What want do?" require the child to request some desired object or activity in the form, "I want [verb label]." Objects and activities that are used as eliciting stimuli are adapted to the needs and events that surround the child and typify his or her daily environment.

Interrogative constructions are taught as wh-questions ("What that?" or "Where's candy?") and yes-no question transformations ("Is that big?"). The child learns to ask questions as a means of achieving self-extended control of his or her environment. Integration of these responses is achieved by presenting the child with a mixture of old and new stimuli and requiring appropriately worded questions to each item.

A unique two-trainer method has been experimentally adapted to teach a particular content area of the program: first and second person pronominal usage. The usefulness of this technique is illustrated in the way it lessens the possible "I/you," and "your/my" confusions. In one method, the child observes as the first trainer presents the eliciting stimuli to the second trainer, who models the correct response and is reinforced; the child then imitates the target response. A second "stimulus-chaining" method engages the two trainers in some verbal interaction (which consists of previously learned responses) while leading into the next-to-be trained behavior.

Attempts are made early within training to program the child's generalization of trained linguistic behaviors to other stimuli and settings. Probes designed to evoke language, for instance, have been employed as a means of measuring transfer in structured and spontaneous situations. These features of the program make it especially attractive to clinicians and trainers, who must account for the effectiveness and long-range usefulness of their therapeutic services to the severely language-handicapped child.

Language Intervention Approach   Like previous nondevelopmental programs, the language intervention approach elaborated by Gray and Ryan (1973) works from an operating model based on logistics and an experimental analysis of behavior. The delivery system of this model follows programmed operant-conditioning techniques discussed earlier; that is, language responses from the child are initially elicited through imitation procedures with gradual fading to spontaneous speech levels. Responses are built from short to increasingly longer spontaneous utterances up to an eight-word limit; this feature of the program compares to the Non-SLIP model (Carrier, 1974).

The program basically was designed for the mild to moderate language-impaired child with expressive language deficits. Viable candidates for this program are primarily those children with intact comprehension abilities but delayed grammatical skills. Pilot research indicated some success in applying this program to dysphasic, autistic, bilingual, trainably retarded, and deaf children.

The overall curriculum of the program is based on several linguistic selection criteria: 1) a cross-sectional representation of language forms necessary for speaking; 2) inclusion of high frequency and common linguistic forms; and 3) inclusion of basic forms that lead to more complex grammatical constructions. The program content was designed around a phrase structure grammar, which conceptually leads up to a "mini-language system." A mini-language, in turn, equips the child with the basic linguistic rules for advancing to an adult language system. In actualizing this end product, the mini-language system integrates previously taught grammatical constructions into two final propositional forms: the declarative and interrogative sentence. A total of 40 individualized language programs (a separate program for each grammatical form to be taught) and one articulation program are available to train grammatical skills in a logistically programmed order, for example, noun identification, *is* + verb + -ing, *are* + interrogative, and so forth. Elementary programs precede programs requiring more advanced grammatical constructions.

The child's existing language skills are assessed by a 34-item test administered on an imitative basis. Based on response complexity and the nature of his syntactical errors on the test, the child is subsequently placed at a program level that allows him or her to initially succeed in training. Further comprehension and spontaneous production testing is not administered, but once the child has successfully completed each training program, a criterion post-test is given that consists of a number of stimulus questions designed to elicit a correct grammatical response.

When the child fails the criterion test or does not show improved performance in training, he or she is placed on one of the branching index steps of the program. Each branch index consists of a number of additional procedures that program smaller discrete steps to the desired final response.

A few modeling techniques are unique to the Gray and Ryan (1973) program and warrant further discussion. There are basically four different echoic models that the trainer differentially employs throughout the training sequence: 1) *immediate complete*, in which the entire response is modeled; 2) *delayed complete*, which models all of the response but on a delayed basis; 3) *immediate truncated*, which cues part of the response; and 4) *delayed truncated*, which models part of the response on a delayed basis. These techniques are used in a specified sequence until the child learns the acceptable protocol for each and is reliably responding. In final training stages, echoic prompts are removed, and the child is expected to respond spontaneously to an eliciting question or stimulus.

In conclusion, there are both advantages and disadvantages of this program over other intervention models. On the positive side, the relative ease of administering each training program frees professionally trained clinicians from clinical activities and allows other trained paraprofessionals to work directly with the child. However, this program feature may not extend to severely language deficient children, who may require more extensive remediation. One limitation of this program is that its use is restricted to a population of children with primarily oral or expressive language deficits.

The assessment procedures for this program also seem to be less than comprehensive for determining precisely what the child knows or does not know about his or her language. Because comprehension and spontaneous production measures are not available, the child's actual understanding and use of syntactic constructions cannot be directly evaluated. However, attention to home carry-over, to some extent, encourages generalization of trained constructions in natural conversational contexts while also getting parents directly involved in the remediation process.

Interactive Language Development Teaching System   Developed by Lee et al. (1975), this system was formulated from previous research with normal and language-impaired children (Lee, 1966, 1974; Lee and Canter, 1971). Although this program acknowledges the contributions of psycholinguistic research in accounting for normal language acquisition, it does not conform to all aspects of the normal developmental sequence. Therefore, we have classified this intervention model as a nondevelopmentally based program, because it conforms principally with models based on remedial logic.

Developmental Sentence Types (DST) (Lee, 1966 and 1974) and Developmental Sentence Scoring (DSS) (Lee and Canter, 1971; Lee, 1974) represent a clinical adaptation of normal language acquisition data for the purpose of assessing the grammatical status of language-impaired children. The DST classifies spontaneous pre-sentence utterances into one of the following: 1) noun phrases; 2) designative sentences, which mention topic but do not comment (such as "that dog" or "this bike"; 3) predicative sentences, which mention both topic and comment (such as "dog dirty"); 4) subject-verb sentences, in which the sentence topic, a noun, bears some grammatical relationship to any noncopular verb (for example, "the boy is eating"); and 5) utterance fragments, including adverbials, prepositional phrases, and adjectivals.

Lee (1974) concluded that many of the grammatical forms outlined by the DST chart roughly coincide with Brown's (1973) semantic classification system; predicative sentences, for example, parallel the semantic function designated by *entity* + *locative* and/or *entity* + *attribute* while subject-verb sentence types correspond to *agent* + *action*, *action* + *object*, and *action* + *locative* constructions. Lee (1974) however, noted that the DST chart imposes an adult grammar on children's single-word utterances because single words do not reveal actual grammatical relations or their corresponding parts of speech.

The DSS technique outlines a developmental sequence of grammatical forms in each of eight categories for classifying children's complete sentences. These include: 1) indefinite pronouns or noun modifiers; 2) personal pronouns; 3) main verbs; 4) secondary verbs; 5) negatives; 6) conjunctions; 7) interrogative reversals; and 8) wh-questions. DSS analyzes a corpus of 50 of the child's spontaneous sentences, assigning a weighted score for each grammatical structure that appears later in the developmental sequence. The child is credited with a particular structure only when it meets syntactic, morphological, and semantic requirements of adult standard English; that is, when a grammatically complete sentence has been uttered.

Once overall scores on the DST or DSS are obtained for a child, they are compared with normative charts (Lee, 1974) to determine the child's percentile level of performance and to assess relative amounts of language delay in chronological months. This information permits a prescriptive remedial package to be developed for the child based on the nature and extent of his or her grammatical deficits.

Although the *Interactive Language Development Teaching System* was not designed specifically for any one language-impaired population, it seems to be best suited for children with mild to moderate language deficits. Because mastery of grammatical forms receives the greatest emphasis in the training program, children with minimal or no verbal abilities are not likely candidates for this program. Hence, the features of this program make it more amenable to a language-delayed child who has successfully completed training at a more basic level but who requires further language remediation to improve his or her productive grammatical skills.

In this program, a nonbehavioral approach is used as an overall teaching strategy with a storytelling format advocated as the best way to present target grammatical structures. Behavioral events are not systematically programmed, as they are in the Guess et al., (1974, 1978) or Gray and Ryan (1973) approaches, but specific trainer questions and interchange procedures are used as a means to elicit responses and provide the child with feedback about the grammatical completeness of his or her responses. Program content and sequence are determined by the child's grammatical deficits so that lesson goals are usually one step more advanced than the child's language level.

If the child's original constructions are not grammatically complete, the clinician uses a hierarchy of interchange techniques for eliciting a more accurate or elaborated response. These include respectively: 1) direct imitation from the child; 2) a reduced model, in which part of the desired target response is modeled; 3) expansion requests, which cue the child (without verbal models) that his or her original response was incomplete, for example, "Tell me the whole thing" or "Tell me some more"; 4) repetition request, in which the child is simply told to repeat his or her response to the question (used as a cue to assist reformulation of an incorrect response); 5) repetition-of-error as a cue for correcting a response; 6) self-correction request, in which the clinician asks the child to judge whether his or her response was correct or incorrect; and 7) rephrased question, that is, a restatement of the question by the clinician to elicit the target grammatical structure.

Evaluation of children's progress in training is made on a quantitative basis over quarterly intervals by tape-recording a spontaneous language sample and submitting it to DST or DSS analysis. Overall grammatical growth can be compared with other children within the same language group and against normative percentiles at varying chronological ages.

Two limitations of the program are evident in the structure of each teaching lesson. First, a large number of responses from the children are imitatively cued by the repetitive nature of the storytelling and also by the format of the trainer questions. Second, although the program specifies that receptive tasks precede production responses in training, direct comprehension instruction is not detailed. Apparently, receptive tasks refer to the child's exposure to previously modeled target constructions. These features of the program seem somewhat incongruent with Lee et al.'s (1975) observation that a language training approach must recreate a spontaneous, nonimitative, and meaningful setting, where both receptive and expressive skills can be practical.

If the storytelling procedure reduced redundant grammatical cues and relied more on self-directive questions ("Tell me about the story" or "Tell me what happened?"), more accurate assessment of the child's spontaneous grammatical productions could be made. Nevertheless, the advantages of this program in identifying and treating the child with mild to moderate expressive grammatical deficits are to be commended.

LANGUAGE IN CONTEXT

The language training programs discussed thus far, whether developmental or remedial have one thing in common: an emphasis on training structure. This emphasis on syntactic and/or semantic structure can likely be attributed to psycholinguistic and behavioral research prominent in the late 1960s and early 1970s. However, in the late 1970s, research emphasis began to shift from the study of the acquisition of grammatical forms and structures to the study of the uses of language in social contexts. The developmental data that began to emerge demonstrated that the social use of language was determined by conversational rules and restrictions (see Grice, 1968; Lakoff, 1970) just as specifically as were rules governing syntactic, semantic, or phonological forms. Conversational rules specify how language is to be used in particular social contexts to accomplish specific goals and form the bases for communicative competence.

Language intervention programs based on pragmatic theory and data are, as yet, very limited in number. In the few programs that generally claim to focus on the pragmatic features of communication, a dichotomy between a developmental and remedial logic is less apparent than between programs designed to train syntactic and/or semantic structures. Perhaps the focus on pragmatic features of communication will serve as a common meeting ground for behavioral and developmental approaches to language training. In the following discussion, it is difficult to categorize intervention approaches according to developmental or remedial logic because lines of demarcation are exceedingly fine. Hence, discussion of these programs is categorized by program goals rather than underlying program logic.

Pragmatics and Language Programming

The pragmatic features of language have only recently been highlighted in intervention programs for language-impaired individuals. Although many of these programs emphasize functional communication, very few intervention strategies have operationalized pragmatic components for specific training purposes. One exception is a recently modified language program developed previously by Stremel and Waryas (1974). Their updated interactive model (Waryas and Stremel-Campbell, 1978) embodies the how, what, and why of language so that language is established early as a social communicative system for the child.

Although this program was originally piloted on moderate to severe mentally retarded and language-impaired children who were equipped to learn language primarily through a speech response mode, a non-oral analog of the training model has been developed to accommodate severely speech-impaired or nonverbal children.

Regardless of the attention given to semantic and pragmatic components, grammatical aspects of language (that is, syntactic and morphophonological) are considered to be of central importance. Waryas and Stremel-Campbell viewed their model as an interactive system incorporating semantics (meaning), syntax (structure), and pragmatics (function).

Like many programs, a series of assessment procedures determines the child's initial performance levels and the point at which training should begin. Four components of an extensive assessment battery (a behavioral checklist, general tests, specific tests, and spontaneous language samples) collectively determine how well the child displays knowledge and use of language. The child's spontaneous utterances are categorized according to the four pragmatic functions specified in Halliday's (1975) research (instrumental, regulatory, interactional, and personal functions). Semantic relations encoded by the child's utterances coincide with those elaborated by Miller and Yoder (1974); these same utterances are, in turn, submitted to a grammatical analysis to determine their syntactic complexity.

The child's initial performance is the basis for placement in either an early conceptual training program or an oral language/non-oral language training program. Program content for early conceptual training consists of attending behaviors, object perception, object permanence, functional use of objects, matching, object discrimination, and direction following. These are requisite prelinguistic skills that the child must have mastered before advancing to the oral/non-oral language training programs.

Content for the oral and nonoral language programs consists of three subprograms (*early*, *early intermediate*, and *late intermediate* training), each of which specifies structures, semantic relations, and communicative functions to be taught:

1. *The Early Language Training Program*   This subprogram parallels the program content of the Bricker et al. (1976) and Miller and Yoder (1974) models. Grammatical constituents (nouns, verbs, and adjectives) are initially trained separately and are incorporated later into the basic grammatical structure (*noun* + *verb* + *noun*),

which encodes two possible semantic relationships—*agent* + *action* + *object* ("Boy throw ball") and *person affected* + *state* + *object* ("I want milk"). By expanding and refining additional lexical items in terms of their semantic functions, the child can be taught many combinatorial possibilities for producing the basic grammatical structure. An early social communication system between clinician and child is also introduced in this program.

2. *The Early Intermediate Program*   This subprogram continues to expand the child's utterances by introducing additional lexical items and markers (internal questions and negation) that will transform the child's sentences from their simple declarative form. At this point in the intervention period, the child is placed in group training sessions. Grammatical structures including prepositions, pronouns, and verb tense markers are trained for the purpose of increasing the variety and complexity of the child's utterances. Unstructured activities employed in the group training sessions are one means for establishing peer and adult social communication.

3. *The Late Intermediate Program*   This subprogram focuses on more advanced language functions and structures. The child learns to transform existing structures to others; he or she learns to syntactically refine his or her own utterances and learns the utility of language for acquiring new information.

Concurrent and serial training steps are important components to the training sequence. The child, for example, may receive simultaneous training on a number of two-word constructions; for example, noun + noun (*agent* + *object*), adjective + noun (*attributive* + *entity*), and noun + verb (*agent* + *action*) relations. Once criterion on target structures has been met; the child is advanced to the next training step, where he or she learns to combine previously learned constructions. For instance, *noun* + *noun and noun* + *verb forms* are combined as *noun* + *verb* + *noun* (*agent* + *action* + *object*) constructions.

A stimulus-response-reinforcement paradigm is used, which incorporates a comprehension, referential imitation, and production format, as do previously discussed intervention models. However, the child is initially pretested in comprehension and production to determine whether instruction time can be shortened by bypassing the reception component of training. In addition to ongoing assessment and branching steps, other techniques contribute to the flexibility and organization of this program.

Ongoing assessment and a continuous data base are recognized here as being critical to evaluating progress and overall program effectiveness. Periodic probes, for example, are used to determine when training steps should be deleted or, alternatively, when additional branching steps are necessary. Success at one level of the program and failure at another indicate the need for smaller, more discrete training steps, more logically sequenced program steps, or more stringent criterion levels at earlier program levels.

Social Use and the Communication Environment

Environmental concerns recently influenced the technology of many language intervention programs, transforming them from restricted training systems to comprehensive communication programs. The *Environmental Intervention Program* developed by MacDonald (1975) and his colleagues is a case in point. This program is directed primarily at the mentally retarded child from 2 to 6 years of age. Like the initial Bricker and Bricker (1974) project, MacDonald developed a parent-assisted language program for training functional language skills, which incorporates tasks for achieving immediate generalization to free-play and conversation. Determining the most appropriate managers and settings for language intervention is the keynote of this program. Previous experimental manipulation of trainer and environmental variables, with the use of programmed training steps resulted in more successful language gains in a number of language-impaired subjects when compared to their controls (see MacDonald et al., 1974).

MacDonald (1975) delineated three diagnostic training batteries for assessing the child's communicative skills at various levels: the Parent-Child Communication Inventory, the Environmental Pre-Communication Battery, and the Environmental Language Inventory.

The Parent-Child Communication Inventory   This battery is an informal questionnaire, identifying the range of the child's linguistic and nonlinguistic skills as evidenced in the home. It also serves a useful purpose in alerting parents to their role in the child's communicative development.

The Environmental Pre-Communication Battery (EPB)   This battery (Horstmeier and MacDonald, 1978) determines prelinguistic skills and communicative intents of children with minimal vocal repertoires. It assesses a range of skills, including attending and responding behaviors, meaningful play, receptive language, motor and verbal imitation, and cued verbal production, in response to commands or questions. A series of prescriptive training packages are available for children who require training at these early prelinguistic and linguistic levels.

The Environmental Language Inventory (ELI)   This is the most advanced assessment battery, (MacDonald and Nickols, 1974), designed for those children with some prelinguistic skills but minimal expressive language. The assessment procedure not only evaluates the child's language deficient skills, but determines where training should start. It has three components.

Component 1   Although training objectives are primarily concerned with increasing utterance length and grammatical complexity, the goals of the ELI are also directed at establishing early semantic functions underlying syntactic structures of the language. The training sequence begins with three frequent semantic-grammatical rules and progresses to remaining rules on the basis of their frequency of occurrence, much like the Miller and Yoder (1974) strategy.

Component 2   Context is operationalized by pairing specific nonlinguistic cues with the linguistic structure being taught. Throwing a ball into the air and requesting the child to say "throw ball" is one way of linguistically marking a contextual event for the child. When clinicians or parents set up these situations, priority is given to those experiences that occur regularly in the child's daily environment.

Component 3   Generalization is implemented at the initiation of training. Unlike previous approaches, the authors contend that establishing an extensive imitative repertoire before advancing to spontaneous verbal production is unnecessary and unwarranted. Instead, verbal production of an utterance is trained in conversation or free-play as soon as the child has learned to imitate the target response. This procedure is a unique means for integrating language within a social interaction system as soon as remedial services are initiated.

The teaching strategies incorporate behavioral principles so that each training session, whether held in a clinical setting or in the home, is structured according to specified antecedent and consequent events. Parents participate in writing training steps and administering lessons while their children are still enrolled in the clinic. Once parents have learned to administer training steps and reinforcement schedules appropriately to their child, the therapeutic environment is shifted from the clinic to a home setting. In this way, parents become immediate agents of change; they are an integral part of their child's communicative development in an environment where language ultimately has its greatest social utility.

Miller (1978) outlined an assessment and intervention model for augmenting a range of pragmatic skills in the language-impaired child in a natural communicative setting. The intervention environment is structured, according to Miller (1978), so that the child is free to choose from a number of activities that embellish social contexts for communication. In this way, the child, not the clinician, constructs appropriate meanings for the various social contexts underlying language. Consequently this approach, unlike MacDonald's (1975), views the clinician or parent as a facilitator or modeler of socially appropriate communicative behavior but not as one who intervenes directly to structure communicative events according to a predetermined protocol of antecedent and consequent behaviors. Hence, this program calls for a physical environment arranged into several work, play, or activity centers in which the child is free to participate with peers and clinicians.

Once assessment has uncovered the range and variety of linguistic and nonlinguistic devices available to the child for conveying his or her communicative intentions, the clinician's intervention objective is to model progressively more complex communicative behaviors for the child. The child, in turn, is expected to acquire more sophisticated skills through observation and/or imitation of the clinician, peers, or the social contexts that call for specific communicative skills. These behaviors include a variety of nonlinguistic and linguistic devices that assist in the social use of language. Once these skills are ascertained as part of or missing from the child's repertoire, the child's skill as a conversational participant is determined. This objective is accomplished by quantifying the child's relative dominance as a speaker, turn-taking and topic maintenance skills as well as skills for repairing communicative breakdowns. Suggestions are made for increasing the number and type of communicative skills displayed by the child in each of these communicative endeavors.

The major philosophical difference between Miller's (1978) approach and previous developmental approaches for programming social competence is that the child is allowed to construct his or her own interpretation of the social contexts that motivate language. In this regard, behavioral principles for implementing intervention objectives are not advocated. Rather, the clinician is regarded as one who fulfills an indirect role as a communicative facilitator or modeler but not as one who predetermines the exact linguistic structure of social events that are to unfold in therapy.

Establishing Extralinguistic Behaviors   Whether the child has the early representational means for matching his precepts with language serves as a point of departure for several developmentally based training programs. The Muma *Dump and Play* model for communication (Muma, 1975), as an example, does not lend itself to establishing a set of prelinguistic or early linguistic behaviors in the language-impaired child. Rather, the model involves a series of conversational operations (for children who are either mildly language-delayed or marginal communicators), that vary according to speaker-listener roles. Dumping is an operation involving the issuance of a coded message presumed to be the "message of best fit." Play operations, on the other hand, pertain to the realization of communicative license (acceptability). As the child becomes more sophisticated in his or her use of a language, he or she is able to rely on a greater number of linguistic, nonlinguistic, and extralinguistic devices (for example, pausing, speech rate, or inflection) to actualize these operations.

Clinical applications of the *Dump and Play* model were detailed by Schewan (1975) and Longhurst and Reichle (1975). One general application is exemplified in a number of interpersonal communication tasks devised earlier by Glucksberg et al. (1966) and Longhurst (1972), in which two individuals assigned either speaker or listener roles must attempt to communicate across a visual barrier. Both individuals have an identical array of stimulus objects in front of them; the speaker's task is to effectively describe a target stimulus so that the listener is able to identify it from the entire set of stimuli. Stimulus objects may vary from geometric forms to nonsense line drawings, functional objects, action pictures, and so forth.

Longhurst and Reichle (1975) discussed ways to measure speaker effectiveness and listener accuracy of the communicative episodes established through these interpersonal tasks. The clinical import of these structured communicative activities for the language-impaired individual is overwhelmingly positive. Initially, a child can be taught effective speaker communication skills by describing an array of simple objects to a familiar listener (parent, peer, or clinician). As his or her communicative effectiveness improves to a specified criterion level, the child can be advanced to more complex stimuli and/or more unfamiliar or difficult listeners. Visual screens can be varied in size to evoke additional nonlinguistic cues (e.g., gestures or facial feedback) between listener and speaker (Longhurst and Reichle, 1975). Speaker and listener roles can be exchanged and topic/comment cues introduced in order to facilitate improved production and comprehension of target language constructions. Any number of variations can be improvised in various settings (therapy, home, or school) to assess and teach the *Dump and Play* communication skills to the language-delayed child (refer to Glucksberg et al. (1966), Longhurst (1972), and Stout (1973) for specific methodological considerations).

Programs for Language Enrichment   The acquisition and mastery of language has been regarded as essential for communication within as well as outside of a person's own community. Yet, many communicative barriers have persisted between standard English-speaking and dialectical groups in the United States. Such barriers have left many schoolbound children at a significant disadvantage when these children are confronted with cultural and linguistic norms that deviate from their own community's standards. Recent educational efforts have, to some extent, ameliorated this problem by providing early preschool enrichment. The basic plan has been directed at enhancing the ethnic child's conceptual experience through language and providing alternative linguistic styles and codes for the child so that he or she can make educational and social adjustments to a predominantly Anglo society. Bereiter and Englemann (1966) pioneered efforts to accomplish these goals with disadvantaged preschool children by developing a series of programs for language instruction and other academic subjects (such as reading and math).

The child's experience with conceptual processes is highlighted in the DISTAR language program by training two basic statement forms that express simple identity and modifying relationships. Curriculum or content is divided into beginning and advanced language programs, with training concentrated on the acquisition of two basic constructions: 1) *identity first-order statements* of the form, "This is a X"; and 2) *modifying or second-order statements* of the form, "This X is Y." Unlike other programs discussed, the sequence for training sentence patterns is not based on their frequency of occurrence in normal child language, grammatical similarity, or complexity but, instead, on the rules of inference that apply to them. For example, sentences like, "The book is green" and "The book is not heavy" appear in a different training order in the program because different deductive hypotheses can be made about these sentences.

The first-order identity statement is taught much like a labeling statement in the affirmative or negative form. The second-order sentence construction introduces the child to polar attributes (for instance, short/long, fat/thin) that modify the subject noun in a sentence. Once mastery for constructing the second-order sentence has been demonstrated, nonpolar attributes occurring in a set of more than two, such as color or food categories, are introduced. Training advances further on multiple polar discriminations ("This rock is hot and this rock is big"), polar deductions ("This rock is not hot; this rock is cold"), and special polars dealing with marked and unmarked adverbs and prepositions (in/on, before/after discriminations).

The advanced language program progresses through the following training sequence:

1. *Compound sentences*—require the conjunctions "and," "or," and "but"
2. *Verb expansions*—tense demarcation, noun-verb agreement, and interrogative reversals
3. *Pronouns* "I"/"you"/"me," "he"/"she"/"it"/"they," and possessives "our"/"his"/"her"/"my"
4. *Expanded polar concepts*—comparative and superlative adjectives
5. *Polar changes*—incorporate sentence constructions for "if"/"then," "and"/"or," "all"/"some," "only" and "because" statements

The DISTAR advanced language program is, in essence, taught as a refined classification system. Numerous causal, conditional, and hypothetical constructs are linguistically introduced to the child through qualifiers, such as "and"/"or" and "if"/"then." In this way, the child's conceptual and deductive processes are focused on through the medium of language.

The actual techniques for training do not vary remarkably from other program procedures; however, a behavioral modification paradigm is not employed. Training is carried out in groups of five to six children. The basic instructional technique is pattern drill, in which children respond in unison or individually to a number of questions designed to elicit a complete grammatical sentence. All training is carried out at expressive levels, thus indicating one major drawback of this program for disadvantaged children who show additional signs of receptive language deficits.

As with many developmental programs, some attempt is made to demonstrate concepts by pairing them with their associated linguistic structures. A yes/no procedure is utilized; the teacher attempts to elicit a delayed imitative response from the children. This is followed by a wh-question, designed to elicit the same response. It is advised that a complete sentence be elicited at all times. If certain children continue to delete morphemes or certain syntactical forms in a sentence, these structures are vocally exaggerated by the teacher to auditorally emphasize the target structure.

Assessment procedures for this program are not elaborate, nor do they seem to be part of the ongoing training procedures. Such shortcomings limit this intervention model for children who have minimal expressive and receptive language deficits and who are in need of broadening their linguistic repertoire in order to succeed academically and socially in a normal school environment. Nonetheless, many of the concepts focused on in this program are behaviors that receive very little direct instruction in the school and yet are important precursory skills to the child's later academic success. This program attempts to enrich the child's existing linguistic repertoire rather than reconstruct it. There is little direct language instruction involved with this program; however, the child's conceptual experience is indirectly enhanced through the medium of language.

SUMMARY

The various language programs discussed in this chapter can be summarized by recalling the basic features that differentiate developmental and nondevelopmental intervention approaches. *Developmental inter-*

vention approaches are characterized by adhering to normal language acquisition data, permitting critical grammatical forms and their usual orders of emergence to guide program content and sequence. An important factor regulating program content is that certain behaviors or sets of behaviors are prerequisite to succeeding stages of language development. Hence, developmental models emphasize the training of cognitive or nonlinguistic behaviors as prerequisites, or at least as accompanying skills, to linguistic development. Once the child has mastered a set of prelinguistic skills as well as a minimal expressive labeling repertoire, the *agent + action + object* construction may be introduced as the pivotal structure for combining single-word utterances. This structure may be subsequently modified and embellished so that the grammatical and semantic complexity of the child's responses is systematically increased throughout training.

Although the degree to which certain prelinguistic and linguistic skills are considered directly programmable differs for each language program, developmental approaches work from similar orientations in deciding what and in what order linguistic behaviors should be trained. Teaching strategies involve behavioral programming principles to effectively teach a language curriculum. Concurrent and serial training procedures are used in conjunction with grammatically progressive expansion to expedite the training process. The usual training format consists of comprehension, imitation, and production components. Mastery at the first two levels is typically requisite before production training is initiated. Generally, the saliency of grammatical construction is enhanced for the child by pairing each trained linguistic form with nonlinguistic cues and semantic events, which, in turn, facilitate the interpretation of the intent of an utterance. In this respect, various meanings as well as communicative functions may be taught in association with target grammatical expressions.

Nondevelopmental programs also stress the importance of training functional communication systems in language-impaired individuals. Their theoretical biases, however, originate from models based on remedial logic. A normal developmental sequence is not strictly adhered to; rather, the empirically tested performance of numerous children undergoing training determines the final training sequence and the most effective procedures to be employed in remediation.

Nondevelopmental strategies evolved from systems based on a form of logic tied to the functional analysis of behavior, where little emphasis is placed on cognitive or other prelinguistic skills. In this respect, the child's conceptual processes and receptive knowledge are not viewed as being directly programmable. Nevertheless, a basic assumption is that the comprehension of target linguistic components should result as a by-product of the intense production training the child receives.

The focus of the nondevelopmental approach to language intervention is the establishment of a grammatical repertoire that directly reflects the adult linguistic system. Early semantic functions and relations are, therefore, not systematically trained in conjunction with their associated syntactic structures. The child's linguistic responses are built from short simple utterances to progressively longer and more complex sentences. The result is that many target constructions coincide or overlap with those taught by developmental intervention models.

Although the developmental approach was emphasized here as being the more attractive strategy for language programming purposes, our understanding of the normal language acquisition process is being constantly updated by new research and competing theoretical perspectives. Consequently, as part of the communication game, few intervention principles can be taken as absolute standards when we consider how vulnerable they are to being challenged or replaced by rival research.

REFERENCES

Baer, D.M., Peterson, R.F., and Sherman, J.A. 1967. The development of imitation by reinforcing behavioral similarity to a model. J. Exp. Anal. Behav. 10:405–416.

Bates, E. 1976a. Pragmatics and sociolinguistics in child language. In: D.M. Morehead and A.E. Morehead (eds.), Normal and Deficient Child Language. University Park Press, Baltimore.

Bates, E. 1976b. Language and Context: The Acquisition of Pragmatics. Academic Press, New York.

Bates, E. 1979. The Emergence of Symbols. Academic Press, New York.

Bates, E., Camaioni, L.; and Volterra, V. 1975. The acquisition of performatives prior to speech. Merrill-Palmer Q. 21:205–206.

Bereiter, C., and Englemann, S. 1966. Teaching Disadvantaged Children in the Preschool. Prentice-Hall, Englewood Cliffs, NJ.

Bloom, L. 1970. Language Development: Form and Function in Emerging Grammars. MIT Press, Cambridge, MA.

Bloom, L. 1973. One Word at a Time: The Use of Single-Word Utterances Before Syntax. Mouton, The Hague.

Bloom, L., Hood, L., and Lightbown, P. 1974. Imitation in language development: If, when and why. Cog. Psychol. 6:380–420.

Bloom, L., Lightbown, P., and Hood, L. 1975. Structure and variation in child language. Monogr. Soc. Res. Child Dev. 40.

Bloom, L., and Lahey, M. 1978. Language Development and Language Disorders. John Wiley and Sons, New York.

Bowerman, M. 1973a. Early Syntactic Development: A Cross-Linguistic Study with Special Reference to Finnish. Cambridge University Press, London.

Bowerman, M. 1973b. Structural relationships in children's utterances: Syntactic or semantic? In T.M. Moore (ed.), Cognitive Development and the Acquisition of Language. Academic Press, New York.

Bowerman, M. 1975. Cross-linguistic similarities at two stages of syntactic development. In: E.H. Lenneberg and E. Lenneberg (eds.), Foundations of Language Development: A Multidisciplinary Approach, Vol. 1 Academic Press, New York.

Bowerman, M. 1977. Words and sentences: Uniformity, individual variation, and shifts over time in patterns of acquisition. In: F. Minifie and L.L. Lloyd (eds.), Communicative and Cognitive Abilities: Early Behavioral Assessment. University Park Press, Baltimore.

Bowerman, M. 1978. Semantic and syntactic development: A review of what, when and how in language acquisition. In: R.L. Schiefelbusch (ed.), Bases of Language Intervention. University Park Press, Baltimore.

Braine, M.D.S. 1976. Children's first word combinations. Monogr. Soc. Res. Child Dev. 41.

Bricker, D.D. 1972. Imitative sign-training as a facilitator of word-object association with low-functioning children. Am. J. Ment. Defic. 76:509–516.

Bricker, D.D., and Bricker, W.A. 1971. Infant, toddler, and preschool research and intervention project report: Year II, IMRID Behavioral Science Monograph No. 20, Institute of Mental Retardation and Intellectual Development, George Peabody College, Nashville.

Bricker, D.D., and Bricker, W.A. 1972. Infant, toddler and preschool research and intervention project report: Year III, IMRID Behavioral Science Monograph No. 21, Institute of Mental Retardation and Intellectual Development, George Peabody College, Nashville.

Bricker, W.A., and Bricker, D.D. 1974. An early language training strategy. In: R.L. Schiefelbusch and L.L. Lloyd (eds.), Language Perspectives—Acquisition, Retardation, and Intervention. University Park Press, Baltimore.

Bricker, D., Ruder, K., and Vincent-Smith, L. 1976. An intervention strategy for language deficient children In: R.L. Schiefelbusch and N. Haring (eds.), Teaching Special Children. McGraw-Hill, New York.

Brown, R. 1970. The first sentences of child and chimpanzee. In: R. Brown (ed.), Psycholinguistics. The Free Press, New York.

Brown, R. 1973. A First Language: The Early Stages. Harvard University Press, Cambridge.

Bruner, J. 1982. The formats of language acquisition. Am. J. Semiot. 1:1–16.

Carrier, J.K. 1974. Application of functional analysis and a nonspeech response made to teaching language. In: L.V. McReynolds (ed.), Developing systematic procedures for training children's language. ASHA Monogr. 18:47–95.

Carrier, J.K. 1976. Application of a nonspeech language system with the severely language handicapped. In: L.L. Lloyd (ed.), Communication Assessment and Intervention Strategies. University Park Press, Baltimore.

Chafe, W.L. 1970. Meaning and the structure of language. University of Chicago Press, Chicago.

Chomsky, N. 1965. Aspects of the Theory of Syntax. MIT Press, Cambridge, MA.

Courtwright, J.A., and Courtwright, T.C. 1979. Imitation modeling as a language intervention strategy: The effects of two mediating variables. J. Speech Hear. Res. 22:309–402.

Dale, P., and Ingram, D. 1981. Child Language: An International Perspective. University Park Press, Baltimore.

deVilliers, J.G., and deVilliers, P.A. 1973. Development of the use of word order in comprehension. J. Psycholing. Res. 2:331–341.

Dore, J. 1975. Holophrases, speech acts and language universals. J. Child Lang. 2:21–40.

Fillmore, C.J. 1968. The case for case. In: E. Bach and R. Harms (eds.), Universals in Linguistic Theory. Holt, Rinehart & Winston, New York.

Glucksberg, S., Krauss, R.M., and Weisberg, R. 1966. Referential communication in nursery school children: Method and some preliminary findings. J. Exp. Psychol. 3:333–342.

Graham, L.W. 1976. Language programming and intervention. In: L.L. Lloyd (ed.), Communication Assessment and Intervention Strategies. University Park Press, Baltimore.

Gray, B.B., and Ryan, B.P. 1973. A Language Program for the Nonlanguage Child. Research Press, Champaign, IL.

Greenfield, P.M., Nelson, K., and Saltzman, E. 1972. The development of rule-bound strategies for manipulating seriated cups: A parallel between action and grammar. Cog. Psychol. 3:291–310.

Greenfield, P.M., and Smith, J.H. 1976. The Structure of Communication in Early Language Development. Academic Press, New York.

Grice, H.P. 1968. The logic of conversation. Unpublished paper, University of California at Berkeley.

Guess, D., Sailor, W., and Baer, D.M. 1974. To teach language to retarded children. In: R.L. Schiefelbusch and L.L. Lloyd (eds.), Language Perspectives—Acquisition, Retardation, and Intervention. University Park Press, Baltimore.

Guess, D., Sailor, W., and Baer, D.M. 1978. Children with limited language. In: R.L. Schiefelbusch (ed.), Language Intervention Strategies. University Park Press, Baltimore.

Halliday, M. 1975. Learning How to Mean. Edward Arnold, London.

Hollis, J., and Carrier, J.K. 1978. Intervention strategies for non-speech children. In: R.L. Schiefelbusch (ed.), Language Intervention Strategies. University Park Press, Baltimore.

Horstmeier, D., and MacDonald, J. 1978. Environmental Prelanguage Battery. Charles E. Merrill, Columbus, OH.

Huttenlocher, J. 1974. The origins of language comprehension. In: R.L. Solso (ed.), Theories in Cognitive Psychology: The Loyola Symposium. Lawrence Erlbaum Associates, Hillsdale, NJ.

Johnston, J.R., and Schery, T.K. 1976. The use of grammatical morphemes by children with communication disorders. In: D.M. Morehead and A.E. Morehead (eds.), Normal and Deficient Child Language. University Park Press, Baltimore.

Lakoff, G. 1970. Linguistics and natural logic. Studies in Generative Semantics, No. 1, Phonetics Laboratory, University of Michigan, Ann Arbor.

Lee, L.L. 1966. Developmental sentence types: A method for comparing normal and deviant syntactic development. J. Speech and Hear. Disord. 31:311–330.

Lee, L.L. 1974. Developmental Sentence Analysis: A Grammatical Assessment Procedure for Speech and Language Clinicians. Northwestern University Press, Evanston, IL.

Lee, L., and Canter, S.M. 1971. Developmental sentence scoring: A clinical procedure for estimating syntactic development in children's spontaneous speech. J. Speech Hear. Disord. 36:315–340.

Lee, L.L., Koenigsknecht, R.A., and Mulhern, S.T. 1975. Interactive Language Development Teaching: The Clinical Presentation of Grammatical Structure. Northwestern University Press, Evanston, IL.

Lenneberg, E.H. 1967. The Biological Foundations of Language. John Wiley & Sons, New York.

Leonard, L.B., Bolders, J.G., and Miller, J.A. 1976. An examination of the semantic relations reflected in the language use of normal and language-disordered children. J. Speech Hear. Res. 19:371–392.

Longhurst, T.M. 1972. Assessing and increasing descriptive communication skills in retarded children. Ment. Retard. 10:42–45.

Longhurst, T.M. and Reichle, J.E. 1975. The applied communication game: A comment on Muma's "Communication Game: Dump and Play," J. Speech Hear. Disord. 40:315–319.

MacDonald, J. 1975. Environmental language intervention: Program for establishing initial communication in handicapped children. In: F. Withron and C. Nygren (eds.), Language and the Handicapped Learner: Curricula Programs and Media. Charles E. Merrill, Columbus, OH.

MacDonald, J.D., Blott, J.P., Gordon, K., Speigel, G., and Hartmann, M.C. 1974. An experimental parent-assisted treatment program for preschool language delayed children. J. Speech Hear. Disord. 39:395–415.

MacDonald, J.D., and Nickols, M. 1974. Environmental Language Inventory Manual. The Ohio State University, Columbus.

McLean J., and Snyder-McLean, L. 1978. A Transactional Approach to Early Language Training. Charles E. Merrill, Columbus, OH.

McNeill, D. 1966. Developmental psycholinguistics. In: F. Smith and G.A. Miller (eds.), The Genesis of Language: A Psycholinguistic Approach. MIT Press, Cambridge, MA.

Miller, L. 1978. Pragmatics and early childhood language disorders: Communicative interactions in a half-hour sample. J. Speech Hear. Disord. 43:419–436.

Miller, J.F., and Yoder, D.E. 1974. An ontogenic language teaching strategy for retarded children. In: R.L. Schiefelbusch and L.L. Lloyd (eds.), Language Perspectives—Acquisition, Retardation, and Intervention. University Park Press, Baltimore.

Morehead, D.M., and Ingram, D. 1976. The development of base syntax in normal and linguistically deviant children. In: D.M. Morehead and A.E. Morehead (eds.), Normal and Deficient Child Language. University Park Press, Baltimore.

Muma, J.R. 1975. The communication game: Dump and Play. J. Speech Hear. Disord. 40:296–309.

Muma, J.R. 1978. Language Handbook: Concepts, Assessment, Intervention. Prentice-Hall, Englewood Cliffs, NJ.

Muma, J.R. 1981. Language Primer. Natural Child, Lubbock, TX.

Nelson, K. 1973. Structure and strategy in learning to talk. Monogr. Soc. Res. Child Dev. 149:38.

Nelson, K. 1981. Individual differences in language development: Implications for development and language. Dev. Psychol. 17:170–187.

Piaget, J. 1952. The Origins of Intelligence in Children. W.W. Norton, New York.

Premack, D. 1970. A functional analysis of language. J. Exp. Anal. Behav. 14:107–125.

Premack, D. 1971. Language in chimpanzees. Science, 808–822.

Premack, D., and Premack, A.J. 1974. Teaching visual language to apes and language-deficient persons. In: R.L. Schiefelbusch and L.L. Lloyd (eds.), Language Perspectives—Acquisition, Retardation, and Intervention. University Park Press, Baltimore.

Prutting, C.A. 1979. Process \pr'a'/ses\ n: The action of moving forward progressively from one point to another on the way to completion. J. Speech Hear. Disord. 44:3–30.

Prutting, C.A. 1982. Pragmatics as social competence. J. Speech Hear. Disord. 47:123–133.

Ramer, A. 1976. The function of imitation in child language. J. Speech Hear. Res. 19:700–717.

Rees, N.S. 1972. Bases of decision in language training. J. Speech Hear. Disord. 37:283–304.

Ruder, K.F., and Smith, M.D. 1974. Issues in language training. In: R.L. Schiefelbusch and L.L. Lloyd (eds.), Language Perspectives,—Acquisition, Retardation, and Intervention. University Park Press, Baltimore.

Ruder, K.F., Smith, M.D., and Hermann, P. 1974. Effect of verbal imitation and comprehension on verbal production. In: L. McReynolds (ed.), Developing Systematic Procedures for Training Children's Language. American Speech-Language-Hearing Association, DC.

Ruder, K., Bricker, W.A., and Ruder, C. 1975. Language acquisition. In: J. Gallagher (ed.), The Application of Child Development Research to Exceptional Children. CEC Publication, Arlington, VA.

Schlesinger, I. 1971. Production of utterances and language acquisition. In: D. Slobin (ed.), The Ontogenesis of Grammar. Academic Press, New York.

Schewan, C. 1975. The language-disordered child in relation to Muma's Communication Game: "Dump and Play." J. Speech Hear. Disord. 40:310–314.

Sinclair, H. 1971. Sensori-motor action patterns as a condition for the acquisition of syntax. In: R. Huxley and E. Ingram (eds.), Language Acquisition Models and Methods. Academic Press, New York.

Sinclair-deZwart, H. 1973. Language acquisition and cognitive development. In: T.E. Moore (ed.), Cognitive Development and the Acquisition of Language, pp. 9–26. Academic Press, New York.

Slobin, D.I. 1970. Cognitive prerequisites for the development of grammar. In: C.A. Ferguson and D.I. Slobin, Studies of Child Language Development, pp. 175–208. Holt, Rinehart & Winston, New York.

Smith, M.D. 1978. The acquisition of word meaning: A symposium. Child Dev. 4:950–1,008.

Snow, C.E., and Ferguson, C.A. 1977. Talking to Children: Language Input and Acquisition. Cambridge University Press, Cambridge, England.

Stout, J. 1973. Interpersonal communication as a speech and language screening procedure. Unpublished Master's thesis, University of Kansas, Lawrence.

Stremel, K., and Waryas, C. 1974. A behavioral-psycholinguistic approach to language training. In: L.V. McReynolds (ed.), Developing systematic procedures for training children's language. ASHA Monogr. 18:96–125.

Sugarman-Bell, S. 1978. Some organizational aspects of pre-verbal communication. In: I. Markova (ed.), The Social Context of Language. John Wiley and Sons, New York.

Waryas, C.L., and Stremel-Campbell, K. 1978. Grammatical training for the language delayed child: A new perspective. In: R.L. Schiefelbusch (ed.), Language Intervention Strategies. University Park Press, Baltimore.

Waterson, N., and Snow, C.E. 1978. The Development of Communication. John Wiley & Sons, New York.

Afterword

Richard L. Schiefelbusch

Bureau of Child Research
University of Kansas
Lawrence, Kansas

contents

The term "applied psycholinguistics," is often used in this book in place of "language intervention," although the term, language intervention, does occasionally slip into the discussion.

The intent of the authors is not capricious. They intend to say that guidelines for language instruction for children with delays and disorders of language derive primarily from acquisition research. More directly stated, the same conditions that help normal children learn to talk should be used in promoting language in children with various organismic or environmental problems. Furthermore, the sequences involved in learning a language in both cases are approximately the same.

The instructional procedure often used to contrast developmental (applied) psycholinguistics is *remedial* in character. Thus, there is developmental logic and remedial logic. Each of these procedural approaches appear in the same book, *Language Perspectives—Acquisition, Retardation, and Intervention* (Schiefelbusch and Lloyd, 1974). The two procedures evolved from different research designs and different research settings. These differences have been overlooked during the 10 years since the contrastive discussions appeared.

Guess et al. (1974) referred to their work as *remedial*. They designed a language program based upon extensive experiences with severely retarded, nonverbal adolescents. They identified functional tactics for using language as part of a social, interactive design. They selected a set of responses to be taught and used (interpersonally) in contexts simulating daily life. However, through their experimental efforts over a period of several years, they combined functional language responses into a program of steps and arbitrary response classes that were refined into a validated, replicable program.

Miller and Yoder (1974) and Ruder and Smith (1974) had a younger set of language learners in mind for whom a more complete language program was feasible. For them, a facsimile of a developmental sequence could be managed, and the full system of symbol functioning could be expected. An extensive vocabulary, a full grammar, and social effectiveness were reasonable targets.

Smith, Ruder and Waryas (Chapter 1) and Weber-Olsen and Ruder (Chapter 8) make suggestions for integrating these approaches so that the best of each can be available in some combination to the best purpose of each design.

The developmental approaches and remedial approaches can be extrapolated and used with other approaches, whether they are incidental (Hart and Risley, 1975), transactional (McLean and Snyder-McLean, 1979), or environmental (McDonald, 1975), to form the most effective language design for each child.

Because this book cannot be expected to integrate all possible approaches, it explains the developmental approach in detail and, thus, provides the bases for an applied psycholinguistics.

DEVELOPMENTAL ISSUES

Language issues are prominent in studies of child development. The sequences through which a child moves toward a full repertoire of language skills has received increasing attention. Studies of the language of normal children have appeared in the developmental literature for many years. The formulations of Chomsky (1957, 1959) ushered in the "modern era" of child language research.

Theoretical differences range from a nativist view that language competence is innate and emerges readily in childhood, requiring only limited stimulation, to a contrastive, deterministic view that competence emerges from the extensive early experiences of communication. The 1960s were especially important years for cross-cultural studies (Slobin, 1967; Campbell and Wales, 1970; Hymes, 1971) and the 1970s for studies of parent-child communication (Bloom, 1970; Bowerman, 1973; Nelson, 1973; Newport et al., 1977). Although these studies suggested that important modifications should be made in Chomsky's "standard theory" of competence by adding semantic and pragmatic competence to his focus on grammar, they retain the emphasis on psycholinguistic knowledge. This comprehensive, theoretical design for language acquisition includes the earlier emphases of grammatical knowledge and adds the knowledge derived from semantic mapping and contextual usage.

Psycholinguistics, as a current knowledge base, still leaves a number of concerns:

1. There is little agreement about how a child combines language information and uses it differentially and with increasing aptness.
2. There is little understanding of the antecedents of language (Bates et al., 1979)—knowledge that can be used in creating optimal sequential or concomitant designs in teaching a first language or in maximizing the parenting routines.
3. We do not know how to assess the child's developmental deficits or the effectiveness of the instruction.
4. We have incomplete designs for organized language intervention programs. Controversies arise as we attempt to combine theories, strategies, and methods. Our knowledge of language acquisition provides essential information, but this knowledge does not necessarily guide us in planning instruction or intervention. These issues clearly call for an *applied* psycholinguistics.

As this Afterword statement was being prepared, the author realized that the quality of a book may be determined not so much by the questions that are answered neatly and efficiently as by the quality of the unanswered questions that are revealed and the way they highlight the important issues. In this regard, *Developmental Language Intervention* is at the leading edge of intervention planning and analysis. It should stimulate and help to guide a generation of applied psycholinguists in their quest for improved intervention designs.

APPLICATION ISSUES

A useful feature of this book is the combining of *developmental* and *application* issues in each chapter. The value of this practice is apparent in chapter after chapter.

How Does a Child Acquire and Use Language?

Roberts and Schaefer (Chapter 4) examine possible relationships between cognitive structures and language. Although the relationship is generally assumed to exist, there are few data to support this assumption. Some positive correlations do not support the assumption that cognitive features, i.e., symbolic play and means-ends abilities, are prerequisite to language responses. There is even less consensus regarding the relationship between cognitive concepts and language development. Problems of measurement form the primary obstacle to better documentation. Research on early language intervention may provide an opportunity for further understanding of the contributions of cognitive structures and concepts on language development.

Leonard (Chapter 5) examines the research on semantic notions as they relate to the emergence of speech and to cognitive development. Language-deficient children seem to be deficient in semantic notions. Leonard finds semantic notions central to early language acquisition; however, the data do not show that they are prerequisites of language responses. Leonard also analyzes the development of language-handicapped children, and, like Roberts and Schaefer, he extends his research into intervention procedures.

In Chapter 6, Smith, Ruder, and Stremel-Campbell consider the acquisition of morphological forms in cognitive and linguistic development. They are more concerned with integration of theory than with how a child acquires language, but they find important evidence that morphology is linked with other linguistic forms in the emerging language of children.

Perhaps the important feature of each of these chapters (4, 5, 6) is that the authors turn to intervention research to develop supportive data about developmental strategies after finding that the descriptive data base provides only limited information about how language emerges. A combination of descriptive and intervention research data will eventually give us a more complete picture of how language is acquired.

Language Prerequisites and Strategies for Training

Bates et al. (1979) suggested that language specialists often confound prerequisite, antecedent, and concomitant events. We may naively assume that if a child's motor development tends to parallel linguistic development or if cognitive stage development (Stage 6) happens during the same chronological frame as speech (new words), then the motor or the cognitive stage is prerequisite or antecedent to language. More realistically, what is shown is that the two are somehow correlated; they both may emerge because of other factors. Consequently, the intervention scientist may use strategies that link linguistic emerging language forms to other emerging indicators, such as cognitive structures and concepts (as Roberts and Schaefer do) or to semantic notions (as Leonard does), or to levels of interdependence (as Smith, Ruder, and Stremel-Campbell do), even though none of them have assurance that these indicators are prerequisites or antecedents of language. What is really gained by using a combination of developmental indicators is the best determinable entry point and the best available guidelines for training sequences. The full knowledge about how a child acquires, combines, and processes language must emerge from continuing research. Before that is accomplished, Smith, Ruder, and Stremel-Campbell suggest that we combine the knowledge we have and use the indicators to expedite a developmental design for language instruction. As applied psycholinguistics advances, so can the application strategies.

ASSESSING DEVELOPMENTAL DEFICITS AND THE EFFECTIVENESS OF INTERVENTIONS

Longhurst (Chapter 2) and Muma (Chapter 3) discuss language assessment. Longhurst examines and reports on formal tests and assessment strategies that are limited to the assessment of the child's language at the beginning and, possibly, the end of a period of training. Muma explains that standardized tests have limited value for a range of purposes that assessments should serve. Muma discusses descriptive assessments. Although he cites a number of research studies and identifies descriptive methods with a number of prominent language researchers, he recommends only one descriptive procedure: the Muma

Assessment Program. Neither chapter covers the entire range of strategies or procedures for developmental assessment. Each chapter provides important issues competently and well. They simply have undertaken to cover only a part of the assessment picture. (To further extend the discussion of the development of psycholinguistic perspective to assessment strategies, consult Miller, 1978, 1981 and Shane, 1981.) There are certain advantages in using various developmental testing strategies, including developmental scales, nonstandardized tests, and direct observations. Longhurst discusses the range of possibilities for formal tests.

DESIGNS OF LANGUAGE INTERVENTION PROGRAMS

Each chapter contributes to a perspective on developmental intervention. Chapter 8 provides a comprehensive discussion of current approaches, including possibilities for integrating all prominent psycholinguistic domains (structure, content, and pragmatic function) and combining application of psycholinguistic and behavioral models. In the developmental design, Weber-Olsen and Ruder feature content, assessment, and teaching strategy, leaving a place for nondevelopmentally based, developmentally based, behavioral, and remedial logic.

Their analysis of developmental interventions features language structure and content as well as pragmatics and the communicative environment.

An unexpected bonus for developmental intervention planning is provided by Kretschmer (Chapter 7). The metacognitive and metalinguistic issues are analyzed for inclusion in formal, semiformal, and situational training programs. Metalinguistics refers to a person's knowledge about language and language operations and about the planning, monitoring, and checking activities that an individual might undergo during language comprehension and production. The metaabilities may enhance the organization of language use or the child's implicit knowledge of it. There is also the possibility that metafunctions can be introduced into training sequences so that they become a practical, enhancing part of the learning process and subsequent generalized language usage.

A FORWARD LOOK AND AN AFTERTHOUGHT

Several forward-reaching ideas emerge from this book. For instance, Roberts and Schaefer suggested that intervention studies may provide additional information about the relationship of cognitive and language abilities. Of course, they have certain specific targets of research in mind. In Chapter 4, they advocate the training of selected cognitive abilities (categories and concepts) as a way to advance language competencies of children and as a way to explore cognition and language.

Several problems are inherent in their undertaking:

1. They attempt to assess and train categories during infancy before the emergence of words. The linkage between categories as a basis for subsequent words assumed to be involved in the mapping of language is difficult to establish.
2. They attempt to assess cognitive events for which precise operational definitions have not been established.
3. As related to research method, specifically to experimental methods for researching cognitive events—the question is posed, "Can cognitive abilities be trained?" Such an effort calls for a general training framework—experimental analysis of behavior. The framework provides precise operational definitions of behaviors and the component tasks and sequence that lead to attainment of specific behaviors.

The approach of Roberts and Schaefer does contribute to our understanding of how to train cognitive abilities of infants and small children and how to provide the possible evidence of the relationships between cognitive abilities and language.

A second forward-reaching idea emerges from Kretschmer's discussion of metacognition, metalinguistics, and a compelling concept used incidentally by the author—meta-performance. In Chapter 7, he suggests that training might be keyed to the child's awareness or level of understanding of the task/s being taught. Kretschmer discusses three levels of formality for possible instructional systems: formal, semiformal, and natural (informal). The ability to accommodate to formal meta-performance instruction apparently increases as the child develops. Older children can demonstrate understanding of performance functions better than younger children. Thus, the child learns from language performance experiences and is able to understand formal explanations. Interesting questions might be raised about meta-performances. For instance, "Do increasing meta-abilities arise as an effect or as a means?" In other words, "Do children learn meta-skills from experience; and do meta-skills, in turn, accelerate cognitive or linguistic skills?"

Similar questions might lead to other interesting research questions if we can establish a means to research them. Also, such experimental approaches could help to establish effective intervention procedures. Further operational research should open up the meta-issue and increase both the interest and the practical value of the concept.

That might cut directly into the controversy created by the formal versus informal approaches to language intervention.

Another forward-reaching possibility emerges from the discussion of applied psycholinguistics by Smith, Ruder, and Waryas (Chapter 1). The predominant use of the term "applied" relates to the basic applied research concept. In this sense, the term means to extend the data or the "findings" of basic researchers so as to verify them further or to test their practical value or even to determine their commercial value.

However, the authors here mean something different by the term "applied." Their meaning might entail studies of psycholinguistic frames of reference to the instruction of (usually a first) language. Psycholinguistics is a descriptive discipline that derives its data primarily from observational studies. Developing a means for instruction requires analysis of task variables and designing operational tactics. A clinician could avoid such experimental procedures and proceed directly to undescribed or perhaps untestable conditions from which he or she could not readily determine either outcomes or functional conditions. In other words, the clinician could only guess at what works.

Perhaps we should acknowledge that there is a descriptive science and an instructional science in psycholinguistics. We may have some difficulty deciding which is basic and which is applied. A case in point are the studies of miniature linguistic systems (MLS), discussed by Wetherby (1978). The focus of the early studies using the MLS were directed toward explicating the procedures and/or strategies by which normal children might acquire the syntactic rules of a language. At the same time, this primary basic work has provided the interventionist with an instructional strategy that maximizes teaching efficiency and generalization potential. The data from these MLS studies can thus be construed as being either basic or applied, depending upon the perspective and/or the personal needs of the researcher and/or reader. Perhaps we should not require that either be so designated. We should examine them both and encourage that they be combined. They are highly relevant to each other, and they can be fully expedited in graduate programs of training and in language research laboratories. Thus, language acquisition and language intervention in combination can be called *applied psycholinguistics*, *child language*, or, perhaps, *psycholinguistics*. In any event, they all allude to the application of science to the study of human language. In this book, the human language users most often are assumed to be children with language deficits or disabilities.

A fourth forward reaching issue arises from the role assigned to *developmental* logic. Without ever fully explaining the functional importance of developmental planning or developmentally related data in planning and conducting language interventions, the authors have endorsed the developmental frame of reference. Perhaps, as a final Afterword issue, we should discuss *development*.

One obvious value of development is to establish a sequence of events or stages through which the learner moves in acquiring a mature language system. If a child engages in developmental acquisition, the teacher should promote events and stages observed to be *developmentally* realistic for normal children. Right? Perhaps *yes* or perhaps *no*. Important differentials may be found in the contexts, contingencies, and in the risks that we identify for children who do not keep pace with normal peers.

Bates et al. (1979) discussed prerequisites to language as a developmentally linked concept unfortunately without describing a way to verify or disprove its importance. Nevertheless, it is an exciting formulation:

> We are referring to some sort of software package, a "program" that an individual child or adult "has" which permits generation of behaviors that are externally identifiable as "linguistic," "cognitive," or "social" (p. 6).

Bates further suggested that these behavioral domains are developmentally dependent, each on the other:

> We are talking about a developmental interdependence such that one system requires input from another in order to derive or build its structure. We are suggesting that there is a Great Borrowing going on, in which language is viewed as a parasitic system that builds its structure by raiding the software packages of prior or parallel cognitive capacities (p.6).

If the clinician should attempt to verify or test the applicability of this magnificient set of assumptions, he or she would be into a greatly different research arena than if testing the assumptions that turn-taking, rhythmic patterning in early mother-infant interaction or object permanence is prerequisite to some developmental language ability. The experimental task in both instances, however, is to specify units of behavior that can be observed, assessed, and compared or correlated within an experimental frame. "Software packages" could either be designed and tried out in training or they could be inferred from contextual events, but in either case, the verification must be expressed as explicit behavioral events. Consequently, if the clinician were to key in on developmental *interdependence*, he or she would be inclined to increase the scope of the intervention design and would be likely to agree to an extension of plans for researching the prerequisites for developmental language intervention. The amount of time and effort that would be required to analyze and instrument the essential studies would be enormous, but we may ultimately find there is no better way.

REFERENCES

Bates, E., Benigni, L., Bretherton, I., Camaioni, L., and Volterra, V. 1979. The Emergence of Symbols: Cognition and Communication in Infancy. Academic Press, New York.

Bloom, L. 1970. Language Development: Form and Function in Emerging Grammars. MIT Press, Cambridge, MA.

Bowerman, M. 1973. Early Syntactic Development: A Cross Linguistic Study with Special Reference to Finnish. Cambridge University Press, Cambridge, England.

Campbell, R., and Wales, R. 1970. The study of language acquisition. In: J. Lyons (ed.), New Horizons in Linguistics. Penguin Books, Harmondsworth, England.

Chomsky, N. 1957. Syntactic Structures. Mouton, The Hague.

Chomsky, N. 1959. Review of Skinner (1957). Language 35:26–58.

Guess, D., Sailor, W., and Baer, D. 1974. To teach language to retarded children. In: R.L. Schiefelbusch and L.L. Lloyd (eds.), Language Perspectives—Acquisition, Retardation, and Intervention. University Park Press, Baltimore.

Hart, B., and T. Risley. 1975. Incidental teaching of language in the preschool. J. Appl. Behav. Anal. 8:411–420.

Hymes, D. 1971. Competence and performance in linguistic theory. In: R. Huxley and E. Ingram (eds.), Language Acquisition: Models and Methods. Academic Press, London.

MacDonald, J. 1975. Environmental language intervention: Program for establishing initial communication in handicapped children. In: F. Withron and C. Nygren (eds.), Language and the Handicapped Learner: Curricula Programs and Media. Charles E. Merrill, Columbus, OH.

McLean, J. and Snyder-McLean, L. 1978. A Transactional Approach to Early Language Training. Charles E. Merrill, Columbus, OH.

Miller, J. 1978. Assessing children's language behavior: A developmental process approach. In: R.L. Schiefelbusch (ed.), Bases of Language Intervention. University Park Press, Baltimore.

Miller, J. 1981. Assessing Language Production in Children. University Park Press, Baltimore.

Miller, J., and Yoder, D. 1974. An ontogenetic teaching strategy for retarded children. In: R.L. Schiefelbusch and L.L. Lloyd (eds.), Language Perspectives—Acquisition, Retardation, and Intervention. University Park Press, Baltimore.

Nelson, K. 1973. Structure and strategy in learning to talk. Monogr. Soc. Res. Child Dev. 38:1–2 (Serial No. 149).

Newport, E., Gleitman, H., and Gleitman, L. 1977. Mother, I'd rather do it myself: Some effects and noneffects of maternal speech style. In: C.E. Snow and C.A. Ferguson (eds.), Talking to Children: Language Input and Acquisition. Cambridge University Press, Cambridge, MA.

Ruder, K., and Smith, M. 1974. Issues in language training. In: R.L. Schiefelbusch and L.L. Lloyd (eds.), Language Perspectives—Acquisition, Retardation and Intervention. University Park Press, Baltimore.

Schiefelbusch, R.L., and Lloyd, L.L. 1974. Language Perspectives—Acquisition, Retardation, and Intervention. University Park Press, Baltimore.

Shane, H. 1981. Decision making in early augmentative communication system use. In: R.L. Schiefelbusch and D. Bricker, Early Language: Acquisition and Intervention. University Park Press, Baltimore.

Slobin, D. (ed.). 1967. A Field Manual for Cross-Cultural Study of the Acquisition of Communicative Competence. A.S.U.C. Bookstore, Berkeley, CA.

Wetherby, B. 1978. Miniature linguistic systems and the functional analysis of verbal behavior. In: R.L. Schiefelbusch (ed.), Bases of Language Intervention. University Park Press, Baltimore.